an autobiography
by
MERV GRIFFIN
with
Peter Barsocchini

MERV

SIMON AND SCHUSTER
NEW YORK

1 2 3 4 5 6 7 8 9 10

Library of Congress Cataloging in Publication Data

Griffin, Merv.
  Merv : an autobiography.

  Includes index.
  1. Griffin, Merv. 2. Television personalities—
United States—Biography. I. Barsocchini, Peter,
1952– joint author. II. Title.
PN1992.4.G77A36   791.45'092'4   [B]   79-26727
ISBN 0-671-22764-5

As in the production of a television show, the creation of a book involves the efforts of many talented "off-camera" people. We would like to offer a general Thank You to everyone involved with this book. But in particular we wish to give special thanks to our friend and editor, John Dodds, for his enthusiasm and patient creative guidance. We are also particularly appreciative of the efforts of Murray Schwartz, Roberta Pryor and Virginia Barber; and also for the contributions of Barbara Goldfus, Nancy Nottingham, Jim Ramsay and Vincent Virga.

To all . . . Thank you.

—MERV GRIFFIN

PETER BARSOCCHINI

Manhattan, November, 1979

To my mother, the most unselfish person I've ever known, who inspired in me a love of family and friends

and to my son, Tony, whose natural joy and curiosity about life and people have constantly renewed mine.

Contents

PART ONE

The Host's Chair

1969-1980

1

IN EARLY SPRING of 1969 my life was what my viewers envisioned it to be. I was happily married, father of a son my wife and I adored. We lived during the week in a roomy Manhattan apartment overlooking Central Park, and spent weekends at our peaceful New Jersey farm. My late-afternoon talk show was in its fourth year with Westinghouse Broadcasting; ratings indicated we could easily roll on for another four years of afternoon television.

The network talk shows remained in the familiar late-night time slot. NBC sailed along with Johnny Carson and "The Tonight Show," chased by ABC's "The Joey Bishop Show." CBS didn't have a network after 11 P.M.; instead, their affiliate stations ran old movies on a local basis.

So when CBS secretly decided late in 1968 to jump into the late-night talk show wars, I had no idea I'd be thrown into the middle of the battle, and that my personal and professional lives would change drastically because of it.

That spring my contract with Westinghouse was coming up for renewal, and both Westinghouse and my representatives assumed we'd have a simple renegotiation. However, when a show is pulling strong ratings over several years, and the star's contract is up for renewal, word leaks; CBS had its ear to the ground.

Royal Blakeman, my attorney and business manager, called one morning and asked if I could meet immediately with him and Sol Leon, who was my representative from the William Morris Agency. They rushed to my dressing 13 room and Sol got right to the point: "CBS is thinking about a show to go against Carson, and they're interested in you."

I didn't jump for joy at the thought. "Sol, 'Tonight' is a national habit. It's too tough to break."

"Maybe not," Roy said, laying out sheets of rating reports indicating a slide in "Tonight Show" strength. "CBS evidently feels they can go to their affiliates and show them a property that could compete as a network in the eleven-thirty slot. They want a talk show. Would you be interested?"

"If I was interested, Roy, it would only be for money. We're doing fine right where we are. What makes you think CBS is interested in me?"

"Mike Dann asked to meet with us." Mike was a powerful senior Vice-President of CBS programming.

"Then why don't you just go listen to what he has to say?"

Sol Leon said, "Knowing Mike Dann, he might want a strong show of interest from us on the spot."

"Meaning what?"

"Your price."

"Well if they want a show of interest, find out what Johnny is making per week, double it, and tell them that's my price."

Roy and Sol stared at me. "We can't do that, Merv. It would end the talks right there."

"If they're serious, they'll pay it. If they're not, we'll know it."

"We can't walk into a preliminary negotiation with that attitude."

"What do you think Johnny makes?"

"Probably about forty thousand a week."

"Tell them I want eighty thousand."

Both men started arguing at once.

"Guys, look, *I'm* the client, *you're* the lawyer and *you're* the agent. I'm telling what it would take to get me interested. And that's about the size of it."

14   I knew I was being unreasonable, but I was happy at

Westinghouse and I was sure CBS would look at my deal, laugh, and I'd go right on where I was.

Two hours later Roy and Sol returned from their meeting at CBS with Mike Dann, elated but confused.

Roy said quietly, "They accepted your terms."

I leaned forward as if I hadn't heard. "What?"

"Eighty thousand dollars a week. That is acceptable to CBS."

"They're out of their minds."

Sol said, "Call and tell them that. Merv, they accepted your price. Mike Dann walked out of the office for a couple of minutes after we named your price, then he came back and said, 'We'll take it.' Now, what are you going to do?"

"How long would the contract be?"

"Two years firm, renewable at six-month options."

"They are absolutely *out* of their minds." Sweat poured down my sides.

Roy ticked off a few of the finer points of the offer and I listened in a daze. He said, "They'd like an indication from us today."

"O.K.," I said, "let's go ahead with it."

Sol and Roy left.

Suddenly I felt sick. It was such an enormous amount of money, particularly to someone like me, who knew what it was like to lose the family house in the depression; already I felt the weight of the deal pushing down on me. I went home to tell my wife, Julann.

I should say right here that I've never been a person who runs around discussing career decisions with family and friends. From the time I started entertaining people for a living, at age nineteen, I've followed my instincts more than anyone's advice. Julann always said that if I were a bank teller she would not be down at the bank telling me how to count the money, so she didn't come down to the studio just to see what was going on. Certainly we shared success and failures together, highs and lows, but when it comes to decisions I've been a loner all my life.

When I sat down in the living room of our apartment, 15

Julann knew it was a big moment. "I don't know what the hell I've just committed myself to, Julann . . ." and I explained the events of the day, ending with "I think I sold out and did it just for the money."

We also agreed that I was disappointed that Westinghouse hadn't approached me yet for renegotiation. We were a few months away from the contract date, but any entertainer, and I'm no exception, likes to hear a vote of confidence whenever possible. If Westinghouse had started negotiations a week earlier, I might not have listened to the CBS offer; at least, I told myself that.

Julann was thrilled with the size and importance of the CBS offer, but wondered if in leaving Westinghouse and moving back into network TV I was leaving my television "home."

I called Roy Blakeman next morning and started listing additions to my contract which I thought CBS would turn down.

"Roy, I want control of the show, just like at Westinghouse. I don't want executives telling us how to produce the show."

"Merv, we are dealing with a large corporation. Only a large corporation could pay this kind of money. You can't ask them to have no voice whatsoever in the show."

"Then secure *creative* control. I just don't want to hear from them about the bookings."

"You'll have creative control."

I threw in more demands about vacation privileges, cancellation clauses, budget limits.

CBS agreed to everything, with one point under contention—the studio.

We signed the CBS contract without a definite agreement as to where the show would tape.

The story hit newspapers all over the country, and predictably my phone started ringing with reporters wanting to do "Can you really take on Carson?" interviews, but I wasn't ready for them; I wanted to settle the issue of the studio first. CBS network President Robert Wood called me to discuss the subject. He suggested CBS Studio 52, and I quickly disagreed. Not everyone understands the importance of a studio audience to a talk show, or any improvised show. When I'm in the middle of an un-rehearsed interview I rely on audience response to decide whether to keep the guest talking, or change the subject or, when things are really going badly, bring out another guest right away. I'd worked in CBS Studio 52 and knew it was around the corner from the unemployment office. All a talk show needs to bomb is an unemployed, depressed audience. "Bob, one of the reasons my show is working on Westinghouse is we're in the heart of the theater district, and we draw an enthusiastic studio audience there."

"But a theater will be too costly, Merv."

"So would a cancellation. I'll be taking on a show that is en*trenched,* Bob. I'll be on the hot seat."

I told him I'd find a good deal for the network, and called Lawrence Shubert, whose family owned several New York theaters. He gave me a list of available leases and I walked through them all. I liked the Cort Theater on Forty-eighth Street.

"It's available," Larry told me.

"In what price range could I get it?"

"Well, how does a hundred thousand a year sound?"

"O.K. Fine."

When I informed CBS of my investigation they weren't happy at all. "Merv, we have an entire real-estate depart-ment that handles negotiations. You've got to stay out of the business end of things. Let us handle the Shuberts."

CBS sent their negotiating team into battle, and they captured the Cort Theater for two hundred fifty thousand dollars a year.

Before the lease could be signed, we had to come up with a cost figure for converting it for television.

I called the same people I had used to redo "The Little Theater" for our Westinghouse show, and they gave me a price of three hundred thousand. CBS didn't like that either. "Merv, *we'll* handle the business if you don't mind. 17

We've already determined it will cost a million, six hundred thousand to convert the theater.

"You don't understand something. The company has designated how each detail of our facilities in this network will look. The CBS 'eye' out front of the theater must be an exact size. The control room must be uniform with our other control rooms. And all this will cost, along with the two-year lease, two million dollars. Already we're giving you the largest contract in television history. I don't see how we can do the theater, too."

Maybe I should have pulled out of the deal right there. I kept telling them my show would not have a chance of working if I wasn't in a theater, and they weren't listening to me. I *did* go home and write a letter of resignation which would have allowed CBS and me to part amicably, but Bob Wood knew both the network and I were too far into the deal to walk away. He tore up the letter and CBS went to work on the Cort Theater.

I thrive on activity and change, and the thought of starting a new show on CBS in two months' time turned me into a whirling dervish.

I bought a dilapidated office building near the Cort to house my production staff, and decided to open a restaurant on the bottom floor. Everyone in charge of looking after my finances warned me that the fastest way to lose money is owning a restaurant, but I was on a roll and wanted to take a chance. We named the restaurant "Pip's," Arthur Treacher's nickname being "Pip." Instead of using an overpriced Manhattan remodeling crew to do our office and restaurant, I brought in the workmen from New Jersey who had remodeled my farm. Every day of June and July 1969 I was in my Levi's and sweatshirt, directing the work on my building and the renovation of the Cort Theater, while my producer, Bob Shanks, was frantically trying to pull together an opening show for August 16.

The reason for starting in August was to give us a chance to work out the kinks by fall, when the important rating 18 period began. But starting the show in August caused a big booking problem: it seemed everyone we wanted for our show was either on the road in summer stock, taping fall TV shows in Hollywood, shooting a movie or hiding out in the country from the humid heat of Manhattan.

A week before our opening, two CBS executives visited my offices and found me in the basement knee-deep in water, trying to repair a broken sump pump. I don't think their eighty thousand a week looked too hot right then. But I assured them we were spinning our wheels in search of ideas for the show.

Naturally we wanted to open with Charles Lindbergh, Howard Hughes and Frank Sinatra, but we settled for Joe Namath (who never showed), Woody Allen, Moms Mabley, Hedy Lamarr and Presidential speechwriter Ted Sorensen.

NBC pulled out its big gun, Bob Hope, to guest on Johnny Carson opposite us opening night. Joey Bishop on ABC offered the return to television of the Smothers Brothers, following their much publicized cancellation at CBS. All three networks bought lavish ads in major newspapers to announce their lineup, and reporters wrote up the opening like a showdown: at stake was a total of eighteen million viewers. "The Tonight Show" charged seventeen thousand five hundred dollars per commercial minute, "The Merv Griffin Show" charged ten thousand five hundred dollars per commercial minute, and Joey Bishop seven thousand five hundred dollars; together we were battling for fifty million dollars in yearly advertising revenues.

It was unusually quiet in my dressing room before the show. Everyone, from Bob Shanks to the writers to the makeup man, all felt the tension. I read and reread the opening monologue, chewing away what remained of my fingernails. Half an hour before showtime I said to Bob Shanks, "This isn't the strongest monologue we've ever done, is it?"

He looked at it again and agreed. We started rewriting it. The original monologue probably was fine, but I had to do something to divert myself as the seconds ticked away. 19

By this August night in 1969 I had done nearly fifteen hundred Merv Griffin Shows, but when the stage manager arrived to bring me to the curtain for the start of *this* one, my nerves were as shaky as they had been seven years earlier, the first time I hosted a talk show, substituting for Jack Paar on "The Tonight Show." The difference was this time I had my entire professional family around me. Bob Shanks was there; Bob Murphy, a lifelong friend from my hometown and now my associate producer, my attorney and business manager Roy Blakeman, the writers and talent coordinators were all standing by; I was surrounded by familiar and trusted faces.

Mort Lindsey started the theme music and Arthur Treacher began his announcement, "From the Cort Theater it's 'The Merv Griffin Show' with tonight's guests Joe Namath, Woody Allen, Hedy Lamarr, Moms Mabley and Theodore Sorensen. . . . Look sharp now, here's the dear boy himself, *M . . . E . . . R . . . V . . . Y . . . N.*

I sucked in my breath, trotted out to center stage, took a look at the first few rows of people and my heart stopped. They were applauding politely, but nothing like the cheers from the balcony. I started recognizing faces, and realized these were the people who had been interviewing me the past few months. As a surprise, CBS had flown in television critics from all over America and placed them in the front rows, and now they were looking at me like *"another* late night talk show, whoopee . . . " I couldn't believe the network would do this without telling me. How do you crack jokes in a monologue when your front rows are stacked with critics? I don't even like to do a show when friends are in the front rows. The monologue got a few laughs, but I'd done enough shows to know we weren't off to the races.

Woody Allen was my first guest. He'd just released *Take the Money and Run* but was still a few years away from major stardom. Our brightest moment came when I told him of an article that referred to him as a sex symbol. "Yes," he said, "but which sex?"

20   Hedy Lamarr didn't have much to say, Moms Mabley

grabbed a few laughs, Ted Sorensen evaded most of my questions and Joe Namath never showed.

A pleasant, average show. In 1962, when I was a discovery as guest host for Jack Paar, a pleasant show would be enough to satisfy the audience and critics. But this is seven years later and I'm holding one of the largest, most publicized contracts in the history of television. Everyone, especially me, expected more than we got out of the opening show.

CBS threw a huge opening night party at the Americana Hotel, where I received a lot of backslapping and "great show, Merv," "Wonderful job, Merv, it's a great start," "Super show," and I nodded and smiled while in my mind I said Baloney to the compliments. I lasted about twenty minutes at the party, then went with Julann to a suite at the Hilton across the street. We were joined by a few friends for a quiet supper in the room.

After eating, I flopped down on a couch, closed my eyes and let my mind clear itself out. I thought about the night seven years earlier when I'd taken over for Paar on "Tonight," and the excitement of the next morning when I walked out of my apartment and cab drivers slammed down their brakes, shouted approval of last night's show and asked if they could give me a ride. Now it's seven years later, I'm on the cover of *Newsweek* magazine, I've one of the largest contracts ever handed out in television, and a hundred congratulatory telegrams are stacked on the coffee table. But all I can think about is how those cabbies are going to react when I walk out on the street tomorrow morning.

2

I KNEW, that August night in 1969, that my CBS debut was less than the network and I had hoped for. By then I knew enough about talk shows to sense when one works and when one doesn't. But even today I remain fascinated with the format because each show, often each guest, requires a different, special treatment to work. After twenty years of doing talk shows, however, I've developed definite ideas about what elements *have* to be present to make my show hum with professionalism and entertain the viewer.

Let's start with the physical setup. The first thing you see tuning in our show is the set, but if we have done our job well nothing about it jars the eye; the set needs to be a comfortable background for conversation and performance; it should blend both with people in front of it and with your living room, kitchen, bedroom or whatever room you are watching the show in. The texture of the set must not divert your eye from the face of my guest; it should flatter skin tones, and should not make slim women look wide, or wide women enormous; it should not make leading men look small or tall men look like mutants. The regular set must be movable, to accommodate "theme" backgrounds for singers or special shows. And it must be able to absorb an infinite variety of lighting effects.

Each day, set designer Henry Lickel comes to the studio to add props to the set for a singer, or to bring a special look for a fashion show. A plastic tree in the studio surrounded by Styrofoam rocks, when lit against a good set, should seem like an idyllic mountain setting on your own TV. Anything on our show that appears on camera, in front, back or to the side of a guest, is there for a reason, positioned, lit and prepared by the set director, the lighting director and the director.

The lighting is an art within itself. Our Emmy-winning lighting director, Vince Cilurzo, must flatter the facial features of my guests or they won't be in a hurry to return. The panel where I sit—we call it "home base"—is bathed in light, while the light on the audience is kept fairly dim, which helps keep all eyes in the theater on the interview. Because of the hot spot lights, the studio is kept cool. Air-conditioners keep the temperature at sixty-seven degrees. Does that sound inhospitable? Well, it keeps the studio audience from taking a nap (hopefully *I'm* doing something to prevent that, too) and it won't surprise you to know applause comes more enthusiastically when it also brings warmth.

Home base is a small island on wheels; we can roll it out of the way when a musical group needs lots of room to work. It is carpeted in red, a warm, exciting color to the eye, which lends a touch of formality for our evening markets. "The Merv Griffin Show" plays in prime time in both major revenue markets, New York and Los Angeles; we want the panel's colors to be appropriate for both the late-afternoon markets, where the majority of the country sees us, and for the evening stations. The chairs are upholstered in neutral tones and are comfortable without being *too* comfortable; I don't want guests so relaxed that their attention wanders. You'll notice the chairs are angled so the guests face me more than they face the audience. This is done so I can keep eye contact. I want my guests aware of the audience without being intimidated by it. The angle of the chairs also allows cameras on either side of home base to get closeups of all of us on the panel at the same time.

We use four cameras. Here again, nothing about the technical structure of the show is done by chance. First, the 23 stage is raised four feet above the front row, and I sit only ten feet from the audience. I never felt comfortable working with the panel off to the side of the stage, with the audience fifteen yards from the guests and cameras and sound equipment obstructing everyone's view. I worked that way on NBC, Westinghouse, and my first year at CBS; "The Tonight Show" is still set up that way. In 1970 I got rid of my desk and couch and switched to chairs on a panel that moves close to the audience. The studio audience is my barometer; interview shows without a studio audience, I find, often become too "inside," and the hosts allow answers to slip by that the general public might want a further explanation of. To make sure the studio audience isn't cut off from the show, we are careful about placing cameras. I don't want a camera between the audience and me, so here's what we do. In the back of the studio, behind the audience, we have two long-shot cameras atop a platform; this position allows cameramen to work unnoticed. On stage we use two close-up cameras, one on either side of home base. Because of the angle of the chairs, the stage cameramen can shoot closeups without obstructing the audience's view.

To pick up sound we use two booms, which are simply microphones attached to telescoping tubes, operated from the corners of the stage. The microphones are covered in black and remain above the light flooding the panel; that way the guest is not confronted with the intimidating sight of a microphone.

The result of this carefully planned technical setup is that "The Merv Griffin Show" is shot like a live drama, a "Playhouse 90" for conversation. Our director watches his monitors and listens to my interview, waiting to pick out a poignant expression or strong reaction. He may choose to ignore the person talking because someone else's reaction on the panel is more expressive. For example, a few years ago we did a show about rape; with the assistance of psychiatrist William Rader, we presented three rape victims, 24 the husband of a rape victim, and a convicted rapist. The victims came out first and gave moving, dramatic interviews. When I interviewed the rapist, we kept a camera on the faces of the victims. At home, you heard the rapist discussing his problem, and on your screen you saw the rage and hate in a victim's trembling face. The show had tremendous impact on viewers, bringing us praise from law-enforcement and psychiatric professionals all over America. On another show I asked veteran Washington, D.C., journalist Sarah McClendon if she could name one politician she completely trusted; the camera stayed on her in close-up for thirty seconds as she sat in silence, racking her brain to come up with a name. It was a marvelous moment of television, and I like to think the time we've taken in constructing our technical setup makes such moments possible.

The director sits sequestered from the studio in a glass booth, accompanied by an assistant director, who is in charge of keeping the show on time, cueing film clips, commercials and songs, and editing the show; a technical director sits in front of a board of buttons which he punches to feed the various camera shots into the actual videotape of the show; the lighting director watches monitors for unflattering shadows and cues his crew when special effects are needed; finally, a production assistant, who times each segment of the show. In another booth a sound man is watching voice levels and mixing singers with the music behind them; a video engineer in a nearby room is making sure the colors coming through are correct. A few doors away still another engineer is insuring that all the electronic signals coming from these various booths are being translated correctly on videotape. All those people, along with cameramen, sound men and stage managers, are connected by headsets and stay in constant contact with each other.

Here's how the director gets the pictures he wants. Each of the four cameramen feeds pictures into a bank of monitors in the director's booth. Above the four black-and-white monitors are two full-screen color monitors, one to 25 "preview" the next shot the director is going to call upon, and the second showing the "line" picture, which is the picture actually going to videotape (the one you see at home). While the director is watching these six monitors, he listens intently to the content of the show to know the precise moment appropriate to cut from one face to another, or when to instruct a close-up cameraman to zoom in on a dramatic hand gesture or an expressive audience reaction. Next to him, the technical director is waiting to "punch up"—that is, hit the proper button—for whichever shot the director calls to the "line." Sounds complicated? It is.

But once tape is rolling and I'm on the air, I am unaware of the technical crew; I wouldn't be if I didn't know I had some of the best people in the business wearing those headsets.

While I'm hosting the show I'm in touch with only three people. The stage manager, Ray Sneath, lets me know by cards and hand signals how much time remains for an interview, when it is time to cut to a commercial, or if a film clip or song is due. All of that information is being fed to the stage manager over wireless headset from the director's booth. My producer is sitting offstage, to the side of the theater, where he watches the show both from a line monitor and from the studio audience's perspective. He decides when it is time to bring out another guest, call for a film clip, or maybe let a particularly good interview run past its alloted time. This information is communicated through the stage manager. During commercials one of the show's writers, who studies the pre-interviews we do with all guests, comes up to the panel to remind me of a few high points in the research I've read before the show.

That's what's going on around me when we're taping. Now let me talk about what goes on before we ever walk into the studio.

"The Merv Griffin Show" day begins officially at 11 A.M. with a meeting in the producer's office, attended by bookers, interviewers, production assistant, head writer, and contract person. Each has his special area of responsibility. The bookers bring in the talent. They attend screenings, watch TV, read reviews and answer a ceaseless stream of calls from agents, managers, publicists, publishers and the members of the general public who have nieces who "sing like Streisand." Potential guests and theme-show ideas are written on three-by-five cards and pinned on a wall in the producer's office. Once a guest is booked, the research department assembles a file of information and turns it over to an interviewer, who calls the guest to talk over areas of conversation for the show. If the guest is a singer or has a film clip, the production assistant steps in to make sure the technical details of the appearance are taken care of. The contract person keeps track of payment to guests; everyone who appears on the show receives the same money, whether he's an unknown actor or Marlon Brando. Four hundred twenty-seven dollars and fifty cents. That's the amount set by the American Federation of Television and Radio Artists for an appearance on a talk show.

The meeting each morning insures that the staff is communicating with the people necessary to make a guest's appearance run smoothly; wires do get crossed, but from the feedback I hear from guests, we run a pretty tight ship.

Once the nuts and bolts of a show are discussed, the meeting is opened up for creative suggestions aimed at making the show more interesting. For instance, if Orson Welles is booked, we kick around the ideas that might add spice to his appearance. In this situation a few years ago, someone suggested we book Gore Vidal with Orson, because Gore had written a magazine piece critical of Orson. In the pre-interview both men fired potshots at each other. But what looks good on paper doesn't always play itself out on air. Orson was out first and, as usual, did an interview rich with interesting opinions. Then came Gore, and I rubbed my hands together in anticipation of a first-rate intellectual tussle. Just as I started to introduce Gore, however, Orson stopped me and said, "Before you bring him out, let me just say I'm delighted he's here today. He is one 27 of America's finest writers and truly has a first-rate mind. I'm anxious to talk to him." *That* fight fizzled before the opening bell. But that's what I love about a talk show; we might just as easily have had a real verbal battle.

We tape five shows a week, Monday through Thursday. One on Monday, two Tuesday, one Wednesday and one Thursday, all in the evening. I will attend a couple of production meetings a week, then spend the morning and early afternoon attending to the business of my company. About three o'clock I head downstairs to the studio for rehearsal. An hour before the show I meet with the interviewers and producer to discuss each guest, and then my construction crew arrives (makeup and wardrobe) and I'm ready to go.

That's the basic setup—planned chaos.

My own day goes something like this. I'm up at eight every morning, regardless of what time I went to bed. I read the *Los Angeles Times,* front to back, and on Sundays *The New York Times;* then I tackle the crossword puzzle for my morning mental exercise. If an article in the paper or a magazine strikes me as interesting, I jot down notes and turn them over to my producer. Two or three mornings a week I play tennis, then it's off to the office.

I usually stick my head into the producer's office to see what shows are on the board, and I offer a few suggestions. I have learned exactly how many serious shows and how many variety shows I can do a week, and I need a balance of each to stay fresh. What I like best is seeing a good theme show taking shape. We've done ninety minutes on literally hundreds of different themes, including: "Rape," "Self-made Millionaires," "Couples," "Adventurers," "Life After Death," "Astrology," "Housewife Alcoholics," "Stars' Secretaries," "Futurists," "Fantasy Real Estate," "Fame," "Transsexuals," "Models," "The Kennedys," "Reincarnation"—and the list goes on. . . .

Ideas for themes come from articles, books or the availability of certain compatible people at a given time. Some shows, like "Children of Stars," we can put together in a day or two; others, like "Life After Death," take six months in order to bring together a proper panel of entertaining experts.

One of our first attempts at a theme was "A Salute to the Stars of the Silent Screen." Nineteen seventy-one was a time when the media were putting down anything connected with Hollywood as plastic and pointless, so we decided, after moving there in 1970, to put something back into Hollywood. We chose to honor the people who pioneered the first films. Our guest list included Betty Blythe, star of *Queen of Sheba;* Buddy Rogers, best known for *Wings* and for being Mary Pickford's husband; Betty Bronson, the Peter Pan of 1924; Richard Arlen, who costarred with Rogers in *Wings;* Beverly Bayne, Francis X. Bushman's leading lady; Viola Dana, a comedy star; Minta Durfee, Fatty Arbuckle's first wife and Charlie Chaplin's leading lady; Eddie Quillan; Jackie Coogan; Carter De-Haven, the vaudevillian; Neil Hamilton; Chester Conklin of the Keystone Kops; Babe London, a comedienne; Lillian Gish, Vivian Duncan and the great cowboy star Ken Maynard.

We built a special set that—remember this—required eight stagehands to push into place. In the Green Room, where guests relaxed before going on the air, we catered a buffet. Out front of the theater Army Archerd from *Daily Variety* announced the stars' arrivals like it was Academy Award night.

As a surprise feature, Buddy Rogers arranged for me to do a telephone interview with Mary Pickford, the greatest silent star of them all; she wasn't well enough to come to the studio. We decided to tape the interview in the afternoon and roll it into the show when Buddy was on the air. I made the call from the control booth, with Ray Sneath and director Dick Carson standing by. Buddy answered the phone and put Mary on the line.

"Hello, Merv?" came the distant, high-pitched voice.

"Mary, how lovely to talk to you. We're proud to include you in the show this way."

"Thank you, Merv." Her voice sounded very vague.   29

"Now, Mary, tell me about your first meeting with Buddy. Was it a romantic meeting?"

"Whoop night."

"I beg your pardon, Miss Pickford?"

"Whoop night."

". . . I'm wondering about the first time you met Buddy."

"Whoop night, whoop night."

Mary must have been having an afternoon nip of sherry because the interview got stranger and more incoherent by the second.

We tried to splice the tape together as best we could.

Came showtime and the audience was filled with people from the film community. When Lillian Gish and Buddy Rogers were on the panel with me I announced we had tape from the legendary Mary Pickford. As it started playing, "whoop night" drained the color from Buddy's face and Lillian Gish looked like she was going to have a coronary. The audience covered their faces. Immediately after the show, Buddy asked us to strike the tape, and of course we did.

Next out was the legendary Western star Ken Maynard. He arrived wearing a ten-gallon hat and in the company of a girlfriend who wore a wild red feather boa. They looked like they had just walked out of a Western saloon. Ken lumbered out on stage with his bowlegged gait, and with a huge sigh eased into the chair.

He answered questions for three minutes then stood up abruptly.

"Ken, are you leaving?"

"Just for a minute. I gotta piss!"

He started walking back toward the set.

"Not that way, Ken, that won't open . . ."

He never heard me. He reached up toward the separation in the set, which had required eight stagehands to push together, and this seventy-year-old cowboy let out a great grunt, pushed the set apart and walked right out through the back of the stage to the bathroom.

30   If all this wasn't enough, out walked Betty Blythe, the

"Queen of Sheba." Her nurse had told us earlier that Betty had good days and bad days; we were hoping for one of the good ones. We had obtained a scene from a film in which she fends off a pack of wolves. I described it to her on the air and asked if she recalled making the movie.

"*Noooooooo.*"

"Oh, don't you remember all those wolves? It's quite realistic . . ."

"*Noooooooo.*"

"Ah. *Well,* you remember making movies, don't you? So many wonderful movies . . ."

"*Noooooooo.*"

Of all our recurring themes, one of the most famous is "Hollywood Couples," which we do about three times a year. I've got some sort of jinx going, because more than a dozen couples who've been on the show have split up shortly after their appearance. Buddy Greco and his wife Dani were the first victims, Sonny and Cher were next, along with Lucie Arnaz and Phil Vandervort. Don and Dorothy Adams I introduced as "Hollywood's happiest marriage"; then Dorothy filed for divorce between the time the show was taped and the day it aired; Dean Martin and his wife Cathy also make the list.

I will never be known as Hollywood's marriage counselor.

My preparation for an interview begins the moment a guest is booked; once I see a name with a red check on the producer's board my curiosity goes to work: What do I want to know about that person?

An hour before showtime I sit in my dressing room studying the pre-interviews my talent coordinators have prepared. These informal notes contain five or six general areas to use as a basis to construct my own interview. While I'm doing my homework, the guests are arriving downstairs. They are assigned dressing rooms, then brought to the Green Room, where they can relax and gather their 31 thoughts prior to the show. We try to keep guests from talking too much to each other backstage.

My technique of interviewing relies on a guest's slowly unraveling in conversation. This is a point Walter Cronkite envies about talk shows,—we can get newsworthy, important revelations by taking a side route with the guest, instead of having to grab at answers in a three-minute news interview.

The best example I can think of to illustrate this point is an interview I did with Spiro Agnew. After resigning from the office of Vice President, he wrote a novel entitled *The Canfield Decision*, and his publishers urged him to make some public appearances to promote the book. He chose to appear first on my show. The press started sounding off the minute we made the booking: Agnew was down on the media and the media were down on him. The complaint was we were providing national air time to a "crook." But what critics sometimes forget is I'm in the business of doing interesting television shows, not keeping people off the air because I don't agree with their politics.

Obviously we draw the line about certain interviews because of matters of taste,— such as a suggested interview involving Elvis Presley. In August of 1977 I was sitting in on a production meeting when someone suggested using two former bodyguards to Elvis who'd written a book about him. A few months previously I'd seen Elvis at the Hilton in Las Vegas; he was overweight, obviously distraught and incoherent. It saddened me, knowing what a great performer he was. I turned down the authors, saying, "I think we should let Elvis alone now, this kind of thing would hurt him." I left the meeting and checked with my secretary, Madalyn Shrier, for messages. I returned the call of a friend who had phoned to tell me Elvis had just died of heart failure.

But the Agnew case was different. I thought my audience wanted to hear what he had to say in the wake of Watergate. We decided to do ninety minutes with him; I buried myself in research. As the date of the interview approached, we began receiving messages from Agnew through his publishers, indicating he didn't want to discuss Nixon, Watergate or his personal life. By the day of the show I was ready to cancel because all I had left to ask him was "How did you like writing a novel?" I wasn't about to go on national television and make a fool out of myself by avoiding topics every viewer expected me to cover.

My only hope of getting a good interview was taking Agnew to the issues I wanted through the only route available to me, —his novel.

I started the interview with pleasantries about his family and their recent travels. Right there I lost a number of critics because they felt I had no business being cordial to a man who, they felt, had betrayed his country. But I knew I would get *no* interview if I was hostile and arrogant.

I moved to the book. "I would have to ask you, Mr. Agnew, if any part of it is autobiographical, because you've written about an office you certainly know, the Vice Presidency."

"Merv, it isn't. Because Porter Canfield is a different kind of Vice President than I was. First of all, he's on the other side of the political spectrum; he would be classified as a moderate-liberal Vice President."

"And your label, Mr. Agnew?"

"I would say I'm a conservative."

No big revelation there, but I had established a beachhead, and I tried moving in to a discussion of politicians in general. The politicians portrayed in the book were involved in all sorts of scandals, and struck me as notably lacking in morals. I commented on them: "I must say, I didn't care about either of those men . . . I didn't care about President Hurly and I didn't care about Vice President Canfield. I thought they were not humane people."

"Normal people."

"For politics, you mean?"

"They suffered the infirmities of real people."

He danced away from that lead, but I pursued him, deliberately confusing Agnew's identity with that of Vice 33

President Canfield in an attempt to force him into differentiating between his own policies and actions as Vice President and those of Canfield in the novel. There is a crucial scene in the book where Canfield meets the Prime Minister of an Indochinese country, and the Prime Minister, Ling, accuses America of being impotent. (I'll italicize my use of the word "you" to show how I tried drawing Agnew out by making him forget he was talking about the novel.)

"You had a meeting with Ling in Singapore . . . and he accused the United States of being impotent . . ."

"Yes."

"And *you* started to argue with him as *our* Vice President. And he said to *you*, 'I'm afraid the Communists understand you better than your World War II adversaries. They're far too wise to give you such clearcut provocation. Their technique is to attack your credibility. First, they get your attention with an outrageous act of aggression by one of their small surrogates, such as North Korea or North Vietnam, then, when you're forced to respond, they run to the rest of the world and complain that the big bully is at it again, aided and abetted by your masochistic news media, and use the United Nations to chastise your government for warmongering and imperialism. Then the hacks of both your political parties rush to show compassion by emasculating your military effort. The end sees you withdraw in disgrace, apologizing for all the crimes others committed and laid at your doorstep. That's why you're impotent. If you were not impotent, North Vietnam would today be the only Communist nation in Indochina.' " Then I looked Agnew straight in the eye and said, "That's *your* philosophy, really, isn't it?"

"That's my philosophy and it's as current as yesterday's newspaper if you read what's happening in Cambodia and Indochina where they claim half a million people have been executed by the Communists . . . and, of course, there are no investigative reporters there to complain about. . . ."

34   I knew I had turned a corner, and I pursued my advan-

tage. "Is our withdrawal from Vietnam still, to you, Mr. Agnew, a disgrace?"

"I think it's the greatest tragedy that ever happened to us as a great nation. That we left the battlefield at a time when we could have accomplished a victory. I don't think that we should congratulate ourselves. I don't think there was a peace. To award a Nobel Prize for what happened in Vietnam is a charade, because we all know that's a Communist Indochina now, and we all know also that it was not a war of national liberation, it was an aggression by the North Vietnamese, who came down and took over South Vietnam just as the Khmer Rouge took over Cambodia. . . ."

"Should we have kept on fighting, then?"

"I think we should have won it long before the Nixon Administration ever came to power."

I played my ace: "Was Mr. Nixon wrong in how he ended it?"

"I think so."

We'd gone from a refusal to discuss his foreign policies as Vice President and his stand on Vietnam or anything to do with Nixon to a fairly complete picture of how he stood on all three issues.

3

IF I CAN BE immodest and consider the question of what, if any, particular asset I have as an interviewer, my own answer would be curiosity, or what Orson Welles called my "evergreen enthusiasm." Without a doubt I have always been enormously curious about people, and the day I stop being curious is the day my show goes off the air.

Which is why I don't talk to guests before a show, even if they are friends of mine. The show suffers if my reactions aren't genuine, and I'm no good at feigning curiosity. That's why, the moment we finish taping our last show of the week on Thursday evening, I'm out the door in ten minutes and on the way to my plane at Burbank airport. An hour and a half later I'm sitting in my mountaintop Carmel Valley ranch, four hundred miles from Hollywood. The ranch gives me the distance from show business necessary to stay attuned to the interests of my audience. By putting those four hundred miles between me and my guests I am able to ask questions a friend might take for granted; I don't want guests on my show responding with 'you know me better than that, Merv.' I want to be surprised by my guests and learn about them during the interview. And I don't want to be in the middle of an interview thinking, "I'll be playing tennis with him tomorrow, so I'd better not ask him about that *Los Angeles Times* review of his film. . . ."

I'll give you an example of what can happen when I
36 socialize with someone who appears on the show. In Octo-

ber of 1978 we took the show back to New York for the first time since 1969. One of the guests we booked was the Speaker of the House, Thomas "Tip" O'Neill, the man second in line of succession to the Presidency. Next to President Carter, Tip was probably the most powerful man in Washington; he controlled which legislation ended up on the floor of the House and could bury a bill in committee faster than you could sneeze. When you combine the power of his position with his witty, colorful Irish personality, you've got the kind of man talk shows live for. I first met him the previous summer in Washington when I was in town for a White House tribute to jazz. My son and my Uncle Elmer were with me, and we spent an afternoon at the House of Representatives. Tip excused himself from the floor to say hello, which not only shocked us but stunned his secretary, who said, after Tip spent forty-five minutes with us, "He doesn't even give the President that much time."

When he agreed to do my show in New York I was thrilled. We booked journalist Jimmy Breslin for the same show, because Breslin had written extensively about Tip in *How the Good Guys Finally Won.*

And I arranged a dinner party in honor of the Speaker following the taping.

So the show started, and my interview with Tip began with a discussion of the 95th Congress and Tip's role as Speaker of the House. He subtly nudged the interview toward funny stories about Irish characters, of which he knows many. Each time I slipped in a serious question about the Hill or about his alleged power struggles with President Carter, he would answer, but slowly and without color, knowing I'd go to one of the funny notes to pick up the slack. The pattern persisted, with Tip being lively and witty when telling his time-tested anecdotes, then deliberately tedious when I tried zeroing in on newsworthy issues. Normally I would have pinned him down, but knowing I was joining him for dinner afterward ruined that strategy. At dinner, after the whiskey, wine and food, out came the 37 behind-the-scenes Washington stories I didn't get on the show.

I didn't sleep well that night, thinking about the interview I *might* have done. And I decided once again that I can't be a popular guy among all the people who appear on my show and still be a respected, probing interviewer.

The only "star" and guest I socialize with regularly is Clint Eastwood, who lives in my neck of the woods in northern California. Clint is about as un-Hollywood a star as you can imagine; he dislikes crowds, parties, interviews and getting dressed up. That doesn't mean he is the cold-blooded, fist-swinging person represented by some of his famous film characters; Clint is a quiet, thoughtful, sensitive man who wouldn't hurt a living thing unless he absolutely had to. The best example of what he's really like is demonstrated by a stunt he pulled on my show. He joined Mary Tyler Moore in making an appearance on a show I did about transcendental meditation with Maharishi Mahesh Yogi. Clint and Mary are meditators, and Clint is responsible for interesting both Burt Reynolds and me in meditation.

This was in 1973, after my divorce, and my life at the time was in disorder. I couldn't relax, wasn't sleeping well and didn't like the way I was handling my show. Clint explained to me that TM is a technique for gaining deep rest at will, for ordering the mind and easing stress without any complicated procedure. So I gave it a try and it worked wonders. TM helped me put my life back in order; I became more productive and once again felt great enthusiasm for living. I'd never endorsed a "cause" or a self-help movement on my show. But I decided to invite Maharishi, the Indian guru responsible for popularizing TM, to my show. The day after our program with Maharishi aired, TM centers around the country reported forty thousand initiations into the technique, and hundreds of thousands of calls of interest.

We decided to tape another show with Maharishi in September of 1975, and Clint accepted our invitation to appear on the panel. When Clint walked onstage to meet

Maharishi, he reached inside his coat pocket as if to pull out his famous .44 magnum pistol; instead, he produced a red rose, which he handed to Maharishi. It caused one of the longest laughs I've ever heard on my show. That's the "Dirty Harry" I know.

I've been talking about what we do to make the show work, but I'm the first to admit that all our planning and preparation do not always pay off. Our batting average is good, but there have been plenty of nights when I've gone home wishing I could erase the show we've just taped. We play the bad ones along with the good, and only a couple of times in my memory have we "doctored" a show. I'll tell you about one of those times.

During the end of my association with CBS we did a salute to Burt Bacharach, and to open it, I sang a ten-minute Bacharach/David medley. However, the show came during that rough period in my life when I was battling CBS at the same time that my marriage was falling apart. I felt constantly run-down and tired. I went out to eat before the Bacharach show and had a few drinks to get a quick jolt of energy. Well, for the first time of my life I went out bombed to do a show. I slurred through the Bacharach medley, and on the closing note I dramatically flung my arms open, forgetting that I was taking the microphone away from my mouth. Next day I viewed the tape of the show and immediately redid the song. I've never had a drink before a show since. In fact, I hardly drink, period.

The only other time I did an interview half in the bag was a "remote" in Mexico with John Wayne. The Duke was shooting *War Wagon* in the intense Mexican heat, and we all had a few beers to cool off in the afternoon. Then we had a few daiquiris, and by the time John and I went outside to tape the interview we were both three sheets to the wind. There is nothing sillier than two drunks trying to pretend they're sober, and any time I run that film clip the audience goes into hysterics and I just sink down in my chair.

39

It's an odd feeling to have your bad moments as well as good become part of prime-time television. We do so many shows, working such long hours, that sometimes I forget that several million people a day are looking over my shoulder. The power of the show hits home when I get a letter like one I received from the president of a major chain of bookstores, who wrote to tell me that every time an author appears on our show the book sells right out of his stores. Once, I mentioned that the best ice cream I'd ever tasted was made by a tiny farm in New Jersey called Welsh's. Next thing I knew, lines of cars jammed the streets outside the farm. An adventurer we often have on the show, Jack Wheeler, introduced us to a young scientist named Durk Pearson. Durk is an honored graduate of the Massachusetts Institute of Technology, who specializes in studying the human aging process. Durk had never given a thought to coming out of his laboratory and appearing on television, but we convinced him to do so. From Durk's first appearance onward he became the largest mail pull in the history of "The Merv Griffin Show," and as a direct result of his numerous subsequent visits he has received book contracts, lecture invitations, inquiries into his work from Senators and Congressmen, and several consultant contracts with major American corporations.

This daily national exposure makes me a target for any-one with a niece who's the next Garland. I'll be sitting in Musso and Frank's Grill in Hollywood and the waiter will bring a message from another table: "May I sing 'Feelings' for you?" One night in New York I walked out the stage door to find a pickup truck blocking my way. As soon as the driver saw me he pulled a rope, dropping down the canvas frame on the bed of the truck, to reveal a man at a piano with a girl singer fronting him. Instant audition.

The plus side of being this well known is the opportunity to travel the world and be received by heads of state, to have unusual access to historically rich institutions like the Vatican and the shrines of Israel. Behind this occasional hobnobbing with the celebrated, I'm still the wide-eyed boy from Eldorado Street in San Mateo, California, and I've stuck my foot in my mouth on more than one of these exalted occasions. The worst incident occurred at the one place my mother always wanted me to be prepared to visit —the White House.

In 1975 I was invited to a state dinner at the White House honoring the Shah of Iran—remember him? No matter how many elegant places you've visited or how many celebrated people you've met, it's still a thrill to get an invitation to have dinner with the President of the United States; besides, with all the taxes I've paid over the years, the Government owes me a few dinners, at least. When the big night arrived, Barbara McFarland, my date, and I dressed in our formal clothes and met the limousine for the short ride to the White House. I had butterflies like it was my first time in front of a camera.

I told our driver the invitation instructed us to enter through the east gate.

"Don't pay attention to that, Mr. Griffin. Is this your first visit to the White House?"

"Yes."

"Then you belong in the *main* gate; no east gate for Mr. Merv Griffin, no sir."

"This invitation is kind of specific . . ."

"Don't you worry about a thing."

I figured the driver knew what he was doing. He pulled up to the front gate and told the guard, "Mr. Merv Griffin."

The guard took a look at me and signaled the car through. There weren't any other cars entering before or after; I started getting nervous. Our car wound around the circular driveway leading to the front door and suddenly I *knew* something was very wrong; The Marine orchestra was at attention on the front steps of the White House, and a color guard with the American and Iranian flags stood at the foot of a red carpet. As we pulled up to the steps, the soldiers started saluting, the band struck up the Iranian national anthem, and President Ford and Secretary Kissin- 41 ger came walking down the steps to my car. I yelled at the driver, "What do we do now? This isn't for us!"

"Well, I *can't* make a U-turn. You just walk out and go in the front door, Mr. Griffin."

Barbara and I slinked out of the car. The President looked at his aides and the aides looked at each other and all shook their heads. Kissinger was chuckling.

"Mr. President," I said. "I think I've got the wrong door."

"Hello, Merv—you're not the Shah of Iran, are you?"

"A . . . no . . . we'll just duck out and go in at the other gate."

Then an aide said to me, "Please don't step on the red carpet, Mr. Griffin."

Well, you don't say *that* to a heavy taxpayer like me. I've paid for that red carpet a million times over.

The hell with the Shah. We went in the front door.

President Ford had a rough night, too. When it came time to introduce the Shah, the President said, "It is a pleasure for me to welcome our honored guests this evening, the Shah of Iran and the Shabe . . . Shebaba . . . Shebarea . . . Shababa . . . the Shobo . . . the Shah's wife. . . ." Evidently the Shah's wife was to be referred to as the Shabanu, but Mr. Ford had forgotten his briefing—forgotten all sorts of briefings. Next he introduced the headline entertainer for the evening, Ann-Margret. "It's certainly my pleasure to introduce a performer of the caliber of the young lady who is going to sing for us tonight. It is a pleasure not only because she is such a talent, but also because she is a friend of ours . . . will you welcome Miss Margaret Ann . . . ?" But that's why you can't help liking Mr. Ford. He is too real a person to take on the glibness and slickness of so many punched-out politicians.

If you liked my entrance at the White House, listen to what went on during my 1976 trip to Israel. I had no idea what to expect upon my arrival in Jerusalem, but I found myself filled with wonder and awe from the first moment 42 I stepped into that ancient city of landmarks and shrines.

We were taping three shows in Israel, but I spent the first day without the cameras, walking the streets to experience the city of Jerusalem as any tourist would. The Church of the Holy Sepulchre, Christ's burial place, impressed me most; the silence and quiet dignity of the church were deeply moving, almost palpable. On my way out I was stopped by a flock of tourists from Miami, who suddenly forgot where they were and why they were there. *"Merv Griffin!* Is that really you, Merv? I'm Gladys from Miami. What are you doing here? Alice! Look who's here —*Merv Griffin!"* I was surrounded by people with Instamatics flashing full blast, shoving airline tickets, newspapers and postcards in my face for autographs. Here we are in one of the holiest shrines in Christendom and I'm handed a Bible—to autograph. Pilgrims from other countries look horrified, and when the priests saw what was going on I pushed through the crowd and bolted.

God took His revenge the next day. Jerusalem's Mayor, Teddy Kollek, accompanied me on a walking tour of the city, this time recorded by "mini-cams," a sophisticated version of the home videotape cameras available in your local department store; the mini-cam consists of a portable recording unit, carried on the back and powered by batteries, and a small camera much like the ones you see on the sidelines of sporting events. Tape cassettes are used, rather than the large reels we use in the studio. To record the walking interview with Mayor Kollek we used wireless range-finder microphones that clip unobtrusively to a shirt collar. With the combination of inconspicuous mini-cams and range-finder sound equipment, people were unaware that Teddy Kollek and I were taping a television show as we walked the streets. Everything went smoothly until we stopped in a crowded courtyard in the Arab section of the city. The camera was shooting us from a stairway fifteen yards away, but still I noticed a few Arabs pointing in our direction. They were talking to someone who was too small for me to see, but I did see money changing hands. I went ahead with the interview, talking with Teddy about the relationship between Jews and Arabs in the city. Suddenly 43 a midget popped up in front of me, gave me a quick punch in the you-know-whats, and just as quickly lost himself back in the crowd. As I was doubling over in pain, I heard hysterical laughter from the group of Arabs who had been pointing at us; they ran off, yelling "American TV Star . . . *haaaaaaaaaaaa.*" I took it as Divine revenge for the scene I'd inadvertently caused in the Church of the Holy Sepulchre.

I recovered sufficiently to go in the afternoon to Bethlehem and the Church of the Nativity, on the site of Christ's birthplace. I was deeply impressed, thinking of all the hours I'd spent in the choir loft of St. Matthew's Church in San Mateo, watching the mysterious pagentry of the mass unfold—and there I was standing in the place where it all began—and began so simply—with a child born in a straw-covered manger.

One of our three shows in Israel was to be a Christmas special tracing the life of Christ. Here at the Church of the Nativity I was to do a brief historical monologue in the courtyard in front of the church, then go inside to sing a hymn in the cave of Christ's birth. It was hard to feel the spirit of Christmas, however, when I took a look around the courtyard.

The Israeli government was quietly nervous about my safety during the trip, and wherever I went a bodyguard accompanied me, as well as dozens of soldiers who happened to be scattered around the stops I made. In Bethlehem, which is populated heavily by Arabs, the rooftops surrounding the church's square were lined with machine-gun-toting soldiers; there must have been one hundred and fifty soldiers looking on. "Behind me is the church built to commemorate the birthplace of Jesus Christ," my monologue began "It is a symbol of hope and peace and love to millions of Christians through the world. . . ." As I was saying this, all I saw were soldiers with guns resting on their hips.

The church is built over the cave. Pilgrims file one by one through a stone arch in back of the sanctuary, down twenty stone steps to the small cave. They are allowed only a few moments there, then must move up the stairs to allow the next group to enter. Thousands of people a week come from the far corners of the earth to say a brief prayer in this cave. The shrine is governed by three religious groups —Catholic, Armenian and Greek Orthodox; we had to receive special permission from all three to tape the hymn in the manger, because it was necessary to block the cave off to the pilgrims for at least fifteen minutes. Obviously we weren't going to bring an orchestra into the cave, so I prerecorded the hymn in Los Angeles and brought the tape so I could do a lip-synch. The audio crew concealed two speakers in the cave and ran wire through the church to our trucks out front. We did our best to keep the equipment as inconspicuous as possible. Evidently we succeeded —too well.

To absorb the feeling of the cave, I walked in the exit door with Dick Carson as a group of pilgrims knelt in silent prayer. While we were standing there, Kevin McCarthy, the assistant director in the truck, hit the switch accidently that started the prerecorded hymn playing in the cave. A shimmering sound of violins emerged from behind the manger. Then my voice sang, "Sleep, my child, my first-born son. . . ."

A shock wave went through the cave. Color drained from faces, lips moved without sound. The pilgrims seemed to crouch in fear, as if this might be the second coming of Christ. We rushed word to the truck to stop the tape, but not soon enough to prevent three dozen people from believing they'd witnessed a miracle.

Location tapings frequently go awry with technical problems, and the actual taping in the cave started running past the allotted fifteen minutes. The various priests watching over us became upset, pointing at their watches and grumbling. I'm in the cave of Christ's birth lip-synching a Christmas hymn, and from the corner of my eye I see our unit manager, Ross Easty, pulling out wads of money and pushing it at the Armenian priest and arguing about how much 45 longer I'd need to finish the segment. When I watched the show at home, the scene in the manger looked like the holiest moment of my life—nothing like the pandemonium going on outside the camera's reach.

While in Israel I was the guest of a Bedouin sheikh in the Negev desert. The event was to be a fantasia for my cameras; first there would be a special meal of rice, chicken and lamb, and then a series of camel races. To arrange all this, the Israelis had told the sheikh I was "a great light from America," somebody's translation of television star. The Bedouins are a nomadic people who live off their herds of sheep, so the sheikh would not know a television star from a used-car salesman; he understood "great light from America" to mean I was a revered holy man. He had decided one sheikh was not enough to honor such a great holy man, and he had invited twenty neighboring sheikhs to join the feast and add to its importance.

We drove for hours in the Negev desert, beyond Barasheba, to find the sheikh's tent. I kept asking my driver how we'd ever find it among all the sand dunes.

"We'll know," was his only answer.

Finally we came to a hand-painted sign reading "Merv" with an arrow pointing over a sand dune. And there was the enormous tent in a place that might have inspired the phrase "the middle of nowhere." The sheikhs and their warriors were waiting to welcome me. The scene looked like lunch break on the set of *Lawrence of Arabia*. There were no women in sight; they were behind another dune cooking our food, and were not considered by the sheikhs worthy of being in our presence.

It was a blistering hundred and ten degrees outside. We retreated immediately to the shade of the tent, where we were seated on silk pillows and given tea to drink. The smell of hashish was heavy in the air. Our translator was a young man who'd left his Bedouin tribe to go to Barasheba to become a doctor. He explained to me the tradition behind the meal we were going to be served. But he said 46 nothing to prepare me for the sanitary habits of the Bedouins: for instance, whenever one of the camels started acting up, its owner went outside and adjusted the saddle or mouth bit, then used his robe to wipe his hands. The food arrived on large platters and, you guessed it, our hands were the only utensils. I had a vision of a headline in the *Hollywood Reporter*: MERV GRIFFIN SUCCUMBS TO RARE AMOEBIC POISONING IN SHEIKH'S TENT. Film at eleven.

It would have been an insult to refuse the meal. As soon as the food arrived, the doctor said, "I must return to the hospital now."

And I answered, "I'll probably see you there."

After the meal, pipes of hash were passed around, which we declined. There was dancing and camel racing and an exchange of gifts. I told the sheikh, "You are a great and mighty leader and I will tell all America of your greatness, but now I must leave and return to Tel Aviv."

Back at the hotel I soaked for two hours in the bathtub to get the dust out of my pores, and for the next twelve hours I did not dare go farther than twenty steps from a toilet.

"The Great Light from America" decided that interviewing Spiro Agnew was a song in comparison to visiting a Bedouin sheikh.

4

1962–1965

My FIRST-HAND KNOWLEDGE of talk shows began on the first
Monday night in April 1962 when I stood backstage at
studio 6B at NBC in New York, my knees knocking while
I listened to the stage manager counting down in a dull,
flat tone: "Ten seconds to show, nine, eight, seven . . ."
Each of my thirty-six years had gone into preparing for
what in seconds would begin, my life's dream about to
come true.

I was guest host on "The Tonight Show," substituting
for the man who had become an American institution—
Jack Paar.

"What the heck is he shaking about," one of the jaded
stagehands whispered behind me.

"Five seconds to theme," the stage manager's monotone
continued, "four, three, two . . ."

Sweat poured down my sides.

"CUE THEME."

The music started; then another American institution,
Hugh Downs, made his announcement; "Welcome to-
night's guest host, Mr. *Merv Griffin*. . . ." And I went charging out to a studio audience of two hundred and fifty
people and a home viewing audience of ten million.

As the applause washed over me I looked out at the
crowd and wondered if I could ever satisfy Jack Paar's loyal
fans; I couldn't count all the Monday nights I'd watched a
guest host wilt trying to fill in for the master.

"Thank you very much for your applause," I began,

"and I'm thrilled to be filling in for Jack Paar tonight. But I realize people in the audience here and at home have no idea who I am. It's eleven-thirty at night and I happen to be a daytime person. If your wives are sleeping, men, wake 'em up and they'll explain who I am, because I spend mornings with them while you're at work, on a game show called 'Play Your Hunch.' So let me tell you a little about my career and then we'll get on with the show. I started out as a radio singer in San Francisco just as television was invented, so I joined Freddy Martin's Orchestra to learn how to be a stage performer. But big bands were fading, so I signed a contract in Hollywood with Warner Brothers to make movies. My first leading role came in a movie released just as CinemaScope was introduced, and our picture looked like a postage stamp on the screen. Then RCA Victor signed me for records, but released my new single at the same time as another of their new records called 'Hound Dog' by a guy named Elvis Presley. Somehow my record got lost in the shuffle. After that I tried hosting a quiz show, and in two weeks everyone connected with quiz shows was called to Washington to testify about cheating scandals. But I moved on and tonight I'm here to see if I can do for 'The Tonight Show' what I've done for all my other careers.

"I should mention one person, though, who has stuck by me through all the disasters and thinks I'm going to be a star. He is an agent. You probably think agents are sleazy little men with cigars, so I'd like you to meet *my* agent, who will come out here and give you a better idea of who I am. Will you welcome Mr. Marty Kummer . . ."

Out walked Al Kelly, a comedian who specialized in double-talk.

The audience applauded politely, wondering if this was "The Tonight Show" or a testimonial dinner for Merv Griffin.

Al shook my hand, then with a grave expression addressed the audience: "Let me tell you about this fine young entertainer, Merv Griffin. He is an excellent game- 49 show host and his ducks car into equal acclaim. In all my years of show business never has the frimmel of ability trolled my eyes as much as in this case. . . ."

Weaving facts from my career into double-talk, Al's voice went from a whisper to sudden Shakespearean eloquence; the studio audience inched forward in their chairs, nudging each other and shrugging. Pretty soon they were roaring, though I was concentrating too hard to know it.

When Al finished, I asked, "Now can you see what a nice guy I really am?"

We cut to commercial and I rushed offstage without looking back at the audience.

I thought the entire routine had bombed.

Bob Shanks, the young man on the Paar staff acting as producer for me, was waiting in the wings. He caught up to me heading for the dressing room.

"I have to leave, Bob," I babbled. "I don't know how to do this show, you'll have to get someone else. Paar can *have* it. This isn't going to work."

Shanks stared at me in shock. Eighty minutes of show remained.

"Bob, this just isn't working. Get me out of here and back to my game show. The opening didn't work at all."

He grabbed me by the shoulders, "Are you crazy?" Can't you hear them out there? They're still laughing. It worked like magic, Merv. That was the best opening we've ever done on the show. The commercial is almost over. Now get back out there." He shoved me out of the wings and onto the stage.

I stumbled out looking, I'm sure, amazed, causing the studio audience to laugh even more than before. I glanced back at Shanks, who frantically pointed to the camera.

"Three . . . two . . . one. . . ."

My agent, the real Marty Kummer, had been pushing Jack Paar for months to let me host "The Tonight Show." As a moderately famous singer and game-show host, I had
50 appeared with Julann twice on Jack's show, but I don't

think he had any idea of who I was until one morning in March 1962, when he decided to come to work early, and by making this decision he changed the direction of my life.

"The Tonight Show" taped in studio 6B. "Play Your Hunch" taped in studio 6B also. We did our show at ten-thirty in the morning and were packed and gone long before Jack Paar arrived for work at four.

A creature of habit, Paar always took the same route through the building to his office. The path involved a complex series of stairways and back doors, chosen by Jack to avoid riding in elevators. The route took him across the stage of studio 6B, up through the audience seats to the seventh floor and finally to "The Tonight Show" offices.

One morning he stopped unexpectedly at NBC and followed his usual labyrinth of stairways and side doors; during a quiet moment of "Play Your Hunch" Jack walked right past the curtain and into our set. The audience's attention shifted suddenly; I turned and saw America's hottest television personality looking confused in a way only he can. Our director had the presence of mind to zoom in on Jack, and I seized the moment.

"Why, Mr. Paar, what are you doing?"

"What am *I* doing? What are *you* doing?"

"We're taping a show."

"This is *my* studio."

"Only after four o'clock. It's my studio in the morning."

"Well, NBC never told me that."

The audience realized our conversation was not a setup, and they were loving it.

Jack said, "What are those people doing?" He pointed to the contestants.

" 'Play Your Hunch.' "

"Play your what?"

" 'Your Hunch,' Mr. Paar, it's our show.

"So *this* is what you do during the day."

"Yes."

"Well, sorry to bother you, Merv. I'll be on my way."   51

He waved and left to enormous applause.

The next time Marty Kummer presented my name as a guest host to "The Tonight Show," Jack remembered our exchange and decided to let the kid on 'Play Your Hunch' have a crack at it."

Even before Marty started offering me to "The Tonight Show" I glibly told friends that someday I'd get a chance to host the show. I tuned in Paar every night and it was a major education; I watched him interrupt a guest when a story went on too long, and I noticed his use of dramatic silences to underscore emotional moments. I just had a feeling I'd get a chance to sit in that host's chair, and when I did, everything I learned from watching all those nights paid off.

The first time Julann and I appeared as guests on "The Tonight Show," a young, bespectacled talent coordinator named Bob Shanks handled our pre-interview; he sat us down in his tiny cubicle at NBC and patiently pulled stories out of us for Paar to prompt us with. Almost every first-time guest is brought in, as we were, for a talent coordinator to make a decision about his or her suitability as a guest, and one thing I remember about Bob Shanks is, the stories he passed on to Paar to use on the show brought big laughs; I knew that was Bob's doing.

Once the date was set for my appearance as guest-host, Marty Kummer warned me that the staff of "The Tonight Show" liked to take Monday nights off; no one wanted his name connected with the Monday night bomb, not even the show's producer, Paul Orr. To everyone's surprise I didn't want Paul Orr to produce my appearance; I wanted the tried-and-true Bob Shanks.

That problem solved, Bob and I had then to try to find someone willing to go on the show with me. All the big stars wanted to appear with Paar, and you couldn't blame them for being unwilling to trust a national television appearance to the hands of a rookie.

I met with Bob a few days prior to the show. "Do you think we can get *any* names?" was my first question.

"They won't do it, Merv. But I've got some people I've pre-interviewed who Jack won't take a chance with, and I know they'll be funny with you."

So, on that Monday night after my opening monologue Shanks pushed me back out onstage, the stage manager cued me and I pressed on: "I know we don't have a normal 'Tonight Show' lineup tonight, but I think you'll find this a fascinating group. Let me introduce my first guest, psychologist Dr. Cleo Dawson." Cleo was a Shanks discovery; a Southern belle who dressed in ballgowns and lavish flowered hats. Her outfit had the audience laughing before she had a chance to open her mouth. I asked her to explain her unique theory of psychology, which maintains that the psyche is fed by four sources, like pipes: we have an anxiety pipe, a love pipe, a fear pipe and a sex pipe. To be mentally sound we just have to keep our pipes clean. "So if you get depressed," I said, "then you just call the Roto-Rooter man?" The audience was howling but Cleo kept right on talking as if we were in a meeting of the Viennese circle.

Next out was a young black singer making her talk-show debut. Her name was Aretha Franklin, and, needless to say, she left the audience breathless.

Then more comedy with Irish actress Pat Carroll, who fueled the show's momentum.

By the time it was all over, my mind was drained and my body drenched. However, the studio's setup made it hard for me to tell how I'd done. A ring of close-up cameras blocked my view of the audience, and the desk where I interviewed the guests was set to the side of the stage at a forty-five-degree angle from the first row. The whole setup separated me from the crowd, so when I walked offstage I didn't have much idea of what had gone through to the tape. I'll tell you, though, the format *felt* good, and I'd already tried radio, big bands, nightclubs, records, Broadway, movies and game shows—but hosting "Tonight" was the culmination of it all. On "Tonight" I was free to carry on conversations, crack jokes, sing and, in short, draw on all the different jobs as an entertainer I'd had over the 53 years. The format totally seduced me even though I couldn't convince myself the show had been a success.

Marty Kummer and Julann whisked me off to Danny's Hideaway, a show-business hangout where we had a late supper and waited for "The Tonight Show" to air. For the first time in my life I couldn't taste the food on my plate; I was just too nervous. Marty and Julann assured me the taping had been excellent, but I had hardly heard a word. Even when a couple of show-business types came to our table and told me word was around I'd done well with "The Tonight Show" I hardly heard them. I just sat and stared at the TV set on the wall.

The second the theme music for "The Tonight Show" started, my pulse quickened; I leaned back and tried to look detached. I'd done enough television by then to know that what you do in a studio often looks and feels different from what goes out on the air. During "The Tonight Show" I had been surrounded by cameras, microphones, technicians and stage managers waving signals at me; I was lucky to know my own name by the end of the show, much less have a sense of how it would all look on the air.

But as the show started playing, all of us at the table felt the electricity: it was *working*. The opening bit with Al Kelly, which I had thought would end my career on talk shows, made the crowd in Danny's Hideaway howl. Even I thought it was funny this time.

Suddenly people started coming by the table to pat me on the back. I stayed focused on the TV set, and for the first time of the evening I had a sense I actually could do this show.

What I didn't know, sitting there at Danny's Hideaway, was that certain other people were watching the show that night who felt I was handling it well, too, and these were people who could give me my own talk show. Marty had stood by the phones at the studio, and once I started the show and he knew it was good, he called programming and talent executives at NBC, members of the television press and executives of the advertising agencies who had bought commercials on "The Tonight Show." While I sat at Danny's letting my food get cold, I was becoming known to this exalted pantheon of people, the behind-the-scenes decision makers who can make a performer's hopes reality. In the near future I was to know and work with, and sometimes battle with, this elite corps of executives; at least for this introduction I had to agree I was hitting a bright note.

Next morning I didn't have to look in the paper or call my agent for reviews. When I stepped out on the street to catch a cab, the drivers slammed on brakes, made illegal U-turns and blocked traffic to try and give me a lift.

One stopped in the middle of the street and shouted, "Keep your pipes clean, Merv!" That's the moment I knew my debut was a hit.

The reaction of "Tonight's" producer, Paul Orr, to my appearance was curiosity. He thought maybe I was a pitcher with only one great game in my arm, so to find out he booked me to host the following Monday.

Again, I asked for Bob Shanks to handle the show, and again we were faced with the problem of no stars being available. But this time I had some ideas of my own. I'd seen a young writer-comedian who'd made a disastrous appearance with Paar on "The Tonight Show." After the comic did his stand-up routine, which was about as blue in content as television got in 1961, Jack apologized to the audience, promised to fire whoever booked the comic, and pledged he'd never again be seen on this show. But the guy made me laugh, and though he didn't click with Paar, I felt he would with me.

I said to Bob, "Can you get me the writer—you know, that comic Paar hates?"

"Merv, if Jack finds out . . ."

"He won't be around. The guy is a scream."

"All right. It's Woody Allen you want, right?"

"That's the kid, Woody Allen."

We booked Woody for my second appearance as host, and he was the hit of the show.   55

I was invited back for a third time.

I brought on two brothers Bob Shanks had interviewed but Paar didn't want to use—the Smothers Brothers. I was by this time developing a sense of which guests worked best with me, and I knew Tommy had the energy and mixed-up attitude to make for a funny interview. He came on and started acting so wild I just turned the show over to him; he moved me right out of my seat and brought my wife on stage and interviewed her. Now, Tommy and my wife are like the same person, vague but funny, so no one in the audience knew what they were talking about—and they loved it. While that was going on I chatted with another of my guests, an English actor named Arthur Treacher. I'd done a long interview with Arthur earlier in the show, and I'm sure we presented an odd picture, this elderly English gentleman being interviewed by a boyish entertainer, but the audience was charmed; there was an offbeat chemistry between the two of us that really worked.

When Tommy finally ran out of gas and went to commercial, I said to Arthur, "If I was ever fortunate enough to have a show like this, I would love to have you as my sidekick." He was delighted "Why you dear little fellow, I never knew anyone was interested in what I had to say." Neither of us was ever to forget that conversation.

With three "Tonight" shows and a packet of good reviews under my belt, I should have felt confident about what I was doing. But I wanted to know what Paar felt. He was the man I watched every night; he was the master. I wanted to know if *he* thought I was doing a good job. A television writer I knew called Jack after my first two appearances to get a quote, but Jack said he hadn't seen those shows. A few weeks later, however, he asked Bob Shanks to schedule Dr. Cleo Dawson for a midweek appearance, and that's when I knew Paar had looked at my opening show.

Jack Douglas, one of Paar's writers, gave a party several weeks after my initial appearances, and when Paar noticed me there he took me aside. He said, "Merv, you're doing the show well, very well. Just always remember one thing about talk shows and you'll be fine: *you* always be prepared, but let the show unfold, let it be chaos—planned chaos. Chaos pays off on a talk show. You want an electric undercurrent that keeps the audience from knowing what's going to happen next. You be ready with your next question, but know when to let the show run itself."

Jack's final form of approval came when I was given back-to-back nights, Thursday and Friday, while he went to England for a remote. This time his staff was there to work with me, but I said, "I appreciate you all coming this time, but I don't really know you, so it would be easier on me to keep working with Bob Shanks." I didn't want to insult them, but a talk show is an intimate, touchy format, and I can't face a bunch of strangers telling me what to do.

By this time it was known among the NBC affiliate stations that Jack Paar was retiring from the Tonight Show" in the fall. He felt he had talked himself out. Because of the high ratings I was pulling as guest host, and because of the strong press support, the affiliates were calling NBC and asking to have me be Paar's replacement. The network executives, however, had already signed a replacement, long before I showed up on the scene. This bit of news stayed inside NBC, while the TV press, particularly Jack O'Brien in the *Journal American*, kept pushing me as the logical replacement for Paar. Bob Aaron, head of daytime programming at NBC, called Marty Kummer and said it was time for a meeting. We listened to Bob explain that the network wanted a daytime version of "The Tonight Show." "I don't want you to change a thing from the way you handle it at night. We'll do a fifty-five-minute version of the show, with five minutes at the end for news."

Fortunately they had told me early enough about already having signed Paar's replacement—a comic and game-show host named Johnny Carson—so that I was only mildly disappointed. Besides, I was being offered my own show, and I jumped at the opportunity. 57

NBC was delighted to report to their affiliates about my future. They hooked into the closed-circuit feed to the affiliates and announced Johnny Carson's signing for "The Tonight Show" and the creation of "The Merv Griffin Show" for daytime television. In their haste to make the announcement NBC failed to actually negotiate a contract with me. We shook hands with Bob Aaron, but that's all. At that point I could have held out for a fortune. But I didn't. For my show to have a chance, the network had to be behind me all the way. I went with my attorney, Roy Blakeman, to meet with the NBC negotiator, Herb Schlosser, who said he wasn't used to having a performer run his own negotiation session. But I must have done all right, because when we finished, Herb said, "If you ever decide not to perform any more, I'd hire you in a second for our negotiating team."

"The Tonight Show" booked me once again during the summer, this time for two weeks solid. By the end of those two weeks I came away with a good idea of what to look for in putting together my own staff. I wanted people fascinated by new ideas, people who read constantly and who knew where to look in New York for undiscovered talent. And I knew just the person who could build this staff for me: Bob Shanks.

I asked him what the producer of "The Tonight Show" was making.

"About eight hundred dollars a week."

Bob was making two hundred a week at the time.

I said, "Bob, will you produce my show? I'll pay you a thousand a week."

His big eyes spun around behind those glasses, and I had myself a producer.

Pat McCormick, the redheaded giant who has worked on and off for "Tonight" over the years, came on as my head writer. We also hired a sharp young kid out of Yale by the name of Dick Cavett, and a third writer named David Lloyd, who went on to become the comedy guru

behind "The Mary Tyler Moore Show."

When I sat down with Bob Shanks to discuss the bookings for my new show, I kept in mind what I had learned from doing "The Tonight Show." Big stars won't make a talk show popular; as Jack Paar told me, you want an undercurrent of excitement, the possibility that something unusual will happen. To create these "events," a talk show must take chances with people who aren't constantly on other shows. So, along with the entertainment-world stars of the day—Joan Crawford, Danny Kaye, Harry Belafonte, Bob Hope—we booked exciting conversationalists like Buckminster Fuller, United Press White House correspondent Merriman Smith, British critic and wit Malcolm Muggeridge, Norman Mailer, White House press aide Pierre Salinger, and as many other informed, controversial guests as the staff could find. These people weren't often seen on afternoon television—we aired from two to three o'clock—but we were convinced the daytime audience wanted an alternative to the steady diet of game shows and soap operas they were used to seeing.

In deciding what format to use we were gambling with big stakes. Revenues from advertising on daytime television in 1962 were two hundred twenty-five million dollars. Women, who made up the majority of the daytime audience, spent one hundred sixty billion dollars a year on consumer goods, and each day twelve million of these consumers tuned in on daytime programming. Any decision we made about our show would be scrutinized not only by our audience but also by that same pantheon of television executives who had wooed me to the negotiating table; they would be looking at me with a very critical eye, with all those millions up for grabs.

"The Merv Griffin Show" debuted on NBC on October l, 1962, the same day Johnny Carson took the helm at "The Tonight Show." Our opening-day guests represented the attitude I wanted to bring to the show: comic Shelly Berman provided laughs, opera star Roberta Peters performed a lovely aria, and journalist Adela Rogers St. John sounded off on current events. As usual, I was a nervous 59 wreck during the opening and felt relieved when the stage manager signaled the first commercial, which was a three-minute sermon on behalf of laxatives. "Well, we're off and running now," I said, when we came back live, and was seduced by the first laugh of my own show.

When the ratings showed us reaching only three million viewers, NBC was less than ecstatic. The critics, on the other hand, loved me. One writer called our show "an oasis in the desert of daytime television"; another declared, " 'The Tonight Show' never looked so good as it does in the daytime with Merv." I was shocked. I've never been a darling of the critics, but this time around I could do no wrong. Because of the reviews, our studio tickets became a hot item in town, and we found ourselves playing to turnaway crowds every day.

Adding to the excitement was the music on the show. Each week we booked a different big-band leader as our guest conductor. Duke Ellington, Lionel Hampton, Xavier Cugat, all paid visits to the show. People working in the NBC building frequently turned up in my studio at show time just to hear the music.

I was learning something every day, particularly how to induce the "planned chaos" Jack Paar had told me about. For instance, we had Woody Allen and Eva Gabor on the panel one afternoon, and I said to Woody, "You are a fine playwright, Woody; if you were writing a play with Eva in it, how would you cast her?"

Woody looked her over and deadpanned, "As my mother."

Eva's face flushed red, and she threw her purse at Woody's stomach.

Sometimes the planning backfired, like the Christmas show for which we booked the esteemed poet W. H. Auden to do a reading. Preceding him on the show was a bit featuring Santa Claus. We invited a few dozen children to receive gifts from Santa, without realizing that once the kids got their gifts they weren't going to be interested in anything else. So while W. H. Auden tried to read his poem, kids were tearing open their packages and playing with toys. It was last time W. H. Auden visited us.

Danny Kaye did the first routine to be censored on my show. After watching a cigarette commercial by one of my sponsors, he launched into an unrehearsed skit about the pleasures of smoking, during which he coughed and wheezed every few seconds. NBC bleeped his routine and issued an explanation labeling Danny's humor "offensive and unjustifiably harmful to the product of a client." Feeling penitent, Danny burst onto my stage the next day dressed like a spy, with trench coat, derby, umbrella and attaché case. He introduced himself as the president of the "sponsor's protection agency" and said he was there to discuss the embarrassing behavior on the previous day's show, as perpetrated by the sinister Danny Kaye. Then he sat down, lit a cigar and proceeded to take over the show. I let him. And he gave us a marvelous hour of television. Danny quipped with Shelly Berman, sang with a confused Dolores Wilson and struggled through an interview with Dr. Cleo Dawson. The show was so good, Danny wanted NBC to release it as a prime-time special.

Since Johnny Carson's version of "The Tonight Show" had debuted on the same day as "The Merv Griffin Show," a natural rivalry existed between the two shows, intensified by the press. Clearly Johnny was in a difficult position. He came out of "Who Do You Trust" to replace television's favorite personality, Jack Paar, and that is no easy way to debut. Our show, on the other hand, was new and different, giving a fresh look to daytime television. So while the critics wrote me up glowingly, they were hard on Johnny, some even suggesting that NBC should replace him. What the press wasn't paying attention to, though, were Johnny's ratings. He was pulling higher numbers than Jack Paar ever did. A bad review sticks with a performer and his staff, so when one night comic Mickey Shaughnessy mentioned my show on "The Tonight Show," producer Perry Cross bleeped it. My secretary was watching that night and 61 was certain she saw Shaughnessy mouth my name. We requested a screening of the unedited copy of the "Tonight Show" tape, which proved my secretary's suspicion correct. I had been cut out of the show.

If it had been another network I wouldn't have given the incident a second thought, but to be edited out of a show on my own network was embarrassing, if not peculiarly petty. About the time I was going on the air the next day it started bothering me, and I announced at the top of the show that "Merv" had become a new four-letter word on "The Tonight Show," and I suggested that Perry Cross cut the sound on the entire show.

As you would expect, NBC executives were horrified by the crossfire and publicly called the edit a "mistaken, emotional reaction" on the part of Perry Cross. NBC's diplomat, Dave Tebet, jumped in to smooth everyone's feathers, but a cold war continued between the shows; we were getting certain stars, such as Danny Kaye, who weren't doing "Tonight" because they didn't trust Johnny yet. The problem ultimately resolved itself when our show went off NBC. Any personal chill between Johnny and me also resolved itself at a party a few months after the editing incident. After the expected amount of quiet growling across the room, we met—and discovered we actually liked each other.

To jump ten years ahead: Johnny later made a surprise appearance on my show. Doc Severinsen, one of my guests, announced he was introducing a new young singer, and out walked Johnny Carson. The final word on the subject is that Johnny's brother, Dick, became director of "The Merv Griffin Show." I brought Dick onstage during Johnny's walk-on and Dick did an impression of Johnny; he got the biggest laugh of the night.

Of all the remarkable guests on my NBC talk show, one appearance remains in my mind as the most memorable.

Montgomery Clift and I had been tennis friends since
the early fifties, when we played often at the Kirkeby Man-

sion that became famous as the home of "The Beverly Hillbillies," but by 1963 it was no secret to his friends that he was living a tortured, haunted existence, riddled with pills and liquor. The man was a walking nerve end. Few of his fans knew the state his life was in, so when I announced to our studio audience that Monty Clift would be the first guest, they went wild. His name alone evoked memories of so many brilliant performances on film.

He arrived at the studio while I was already on the air. At commercial, Bob Shanks told me Monty was in no condition to appear on television and an NBC official seconded Shanks's judgment. They said he was drunk, falling against the walls in his dressing room and singing an incoherent tune.

I took Bob Shanks aside and said, "Monty needs every bit of support we can give him. Walk him around, give him coffee, anything—but if we tell him he's not going on he'll be crushed. Bob, he's making this appearance as a gift to us, he knows he is a valuable name to the show. Just showing up is his way of extending his hand. I just can't brush him off; you don't know what that would do to him."

I think, perhaps, it takes a performer to understand what another performer is going through at a time of crisis in his career. When you're hot, everybody in show business is your friend, every executive is patting you on the back. When you are having problems, this business can turn against you just as quickly as it embraced you.

Bob Shanks dragged Monty to the side of the stage and whispered to me, "You don't want the public to see him like this, do you?"

I asked Monty, "Can you go on?"

"Hell, just bring me out. Of course I can do it."

The stage manager signaled me back to the desk, and I gave Montgomery Clift an elaborate introduction, even though I didn't know what manner of man would walk around the corner when the music started. But out walked a sober man; it was like he'd pushed a button inside his brain that brought self-control. He sat back in the chair 63 and gave a lucid, fascinating interview about Marilyn Monroe; at one point he even jumped up to reenact a touching scene from *The Misfits*. By the end of the interview I saw a few tears out in the audience.

We shook hands, Monty waved to the audience and strode offstage. As I looked into the wings I saw him collapse against a wall the moment he was off camera, the sound of applause lingering behind him.

In certain weeks our show received as many as a thousand letters, an unusually strong count for our time slot. But the ratings did not corroborate this response. NBC hired a ratings company to analyze what aspects of our show appealed to women. The test involved one hundred ladies sitting in a special studio with electronic devices at their fingertips used to signal approval or disapproval at any point during a program. Of several "Merv Griffin Shows" monitored, one received a particularly high rating. When I checked to see at which point in the show viewer interest was keenest, I learned it had occurred when Florence Henderson was chatting with me and I made some remark that caused her to whack me in the chest. According to the ladies, that was the high point.

Forget Monty Clift, Woody Allen, Bucky Fuller, Ogden Nash, Merriman Smith and the rest; to save the show I needed to get punched more often.

When one NBC executive told me we were aiming for too high a level in the discussions on the show—that I should go out into the audience on occasion and look through ladies' purses to get laughs—right then I knew we were in trouble. Comments like that, combined with dreary ratings reports, should have prepared me for a cancellation, but the show was generating so much excitement in New York itself that I ignored the danger signals.

January 29, 1963, was a bad day. I was in my office at NBC when Walter Scott, NBC President, called me. "Merv, we know we're doing an awful thing, because we know artistically the show is doing well. But the decision has to be purely economic. There is going to be a lot of gnawing at you from the press to take swipes at the network—I just want to warn you of that. But 'The Merv Griffin Show' is not going to be able to continue on NBC. I'll tell you this, though—we'll make it up to you in the future."

I sat back in my chair and looked out the window at the snow falling. Bob Shanks came in and we both sat there not saying much. We really felt "The Merv Griffin Show" was an interesting alternative to shows where the host looked through ladies' pocketbooks. But television is a numbers game and NBC was in charge of the numbers.

Television critics leaped to my defense. Not before or since have I received such support from the press. Each day sheaves of clippings full of complaints about the rating system and NBC's decision poured into the office. Then the letters started. In 1963, fifteen thousand letters of protest to a network was considered a major beef. Primed by the press, my viewers started writing in by the tens of thousands. I honestly didn't know what to make of it; I had to wonder if the Nielsen rating service had monitored *any* of those people who were writing. Sacks of mail were delivered daily to NBC, where secretaries simply forwarded them to my apartment. My den started looking like the mail room at the North Pole. We counted up to one hundred thousand letters and stopped after that. At the same time, my phone rang nonstop with reporters baiting me to come out and attack the network for the cancellation. While, based on the mail response, I did question the thoroughness of the rating services, I had no interest in bad-mouthing NBC. No other network had offered me a talk show. Of course, the cancellation was a bitter disappointment, but I'd been an entertainer long enough to know you either keep going or you quit. I chose to keep going.

So did the press. *Life* magazine sent a photographer over to my apartment and photographed me lying atop the mound of letters, and that picture generated more mail. Julann and I decided we'd take a trip to Europe after the last show and let the storm blow itself out.

For the final show I played one of the corniest scenes I've ever tried, but it worked. I said to the audience, "We worked here at NBC and we don't have windows to look out. We didn't know if people were watching us or not. We tried to do wonderful shows for you, and some of them, I think, were."

I put on an overcoat, sat on a suitcase at center stage and sang "Lost in the Stars":

> Little stars, big stars
> Blowing through the night
> and we're lost . . .

When I finished the song I lifted the suitcase, picked up an umbrella and waved to the audience. "Goodbye," I said, as the lights came down.

I knew the closing worked because an hour after the show played I received a call from Joan Crawford, who was a loyal viewer, and she told me she'd been in tears ever since "Lost in the Stars."

On April Fool's Day, 1963, "The Merv Griffin Show" went off the air after a twenty-six week run, replaced by— guess what?—two soap operas.

5

To ease the pain of cancellation and allow the controversy it caused to blow itself out, Julann and I flew to Italy, where we met a long time friend of mine, San Francisco *Chronicle* columnist Herb Caen, there with his new bride, Maria Theresa.

The four of us spent a memorable evening in Venice. It was spring, the air was warm and soft as we meandered through the canals in a gondola. We drank chilled chablis while the gondolier sang for us. Floating there under the stars, nothing in the world seemed important compared to the charm of Venice. When the gondolier tired of singing, we rode in silence for a long while, hearing only the lapping of water against the houses.

Then out of the blue my wife commented, "This must be what it feels like when the Red Cross picks you up in a flood."

Herb Caen laughed until I thought he might choke.

We pushed on to Paris, which I hated that year. The city was in a cold spell and its citizens were rude; I couldn't get out of there fast enough. (A few years later I returned to interview James Jones at his house on the Ile St-Louis, and fell in love with the city. But this time I couldn't wait to reach the border.)

Julann and I hopped on a plane to Ireland, where the earthy humor of the people and a steady supply of stout refreshed me.

In a pub in Limerick we met a sweet, red-faced little 67

Irish lady who spotted us immediately as Americans. Obviously she'd been at the bar long before we arrived, as her hat was sliding off the side of her head and her eyes didn't seem to move in unison.

She looked at my wife's fair skin and red hair and said, "Ah, look at ya' darlin'—you're Irish-American, aren't ya'?"

Julann smiled.

Then the woman whispered, "But why did you marry that Italian?"

"Italian?" I said. "Hell, I'm more Irish than me wife."

"Ya' are now, are ya'? Say, we know all about rich Americans with your furs and jewelry and cars. And we know how ya' get those fine things. . . ."

"Oh? How?"

"Ya' *charge* them."

We bought a round of drinks, cash.

Our new friend was excited about President Kennedy's upcoming trip to Ireland. "Now, I'm sure in the Lord's name you're both Irish Catholic, aren't ya'?"

"Yes, we are."

"Well, that President Kennedy, he's Catholic and Irish you know. And he's married to the most beautiful Irish colleen I've ever seen. . . ."

"Irish?"

"Sure, the beautiful Jacqueline Fitzgerald."

"No, no. She's not a Fitzgerald, that's the middle name of John Kennedy. Jackie is a Bouvier—she's French."

"Bouvier?"

"Yes."

"Well," the woman scoffed, "I didn't think she was so much, anyway."

It was President Kennedy who cut short my trip to Ireland. My friend Merriman Smith of the United Press wired us that the President wanted me to host the annual White House correspondents' dinner on May 23. Evidently the President and the First Lady used to catch my show now and then, and when he spotted my name on a list of suggested MCs he gave me the nod.

My agent, Murray Schwartz, lined up the entertainment for the evening. He booked Edie Adams, comedian Marty Brill and a young singer by the name of Barbra Streisand. I now have to make the painful *painful* admission that we'd turned down Barbra as a guest on "The Merv Griffin Show"; and I was still doubtful that she was right for this dinner.

I told Murray that John Kennedy liked bathing beauties, a category Barbra didn't exactly fall into. But Murray persisted on Barbra's behalf and I accepted the idea (thank God I'm not *too* stubborn).

You might guess from the kind of shape I was in before my debut on the Paar show that I was a wreck before hosting the White House correspondents' dinner. I brought Pat McCormick with me to write a funny monologue, and we paced the streets in front of the Sheraton waiting for my cue to appear. "Pat, the President is in there, his Cabinet, Supreme Court Justices, Senators, the entire press corps . . . Pat . . . suppose they don't laugh . . . suppose they just sit there with their coffee and cigars and stare . . . and don't *laugh*. . . ."

Pat shook his head thoughtfully. "If they don't laugh, just tell them they'd better *start* laughing or you'll reveal the name of the Unknown Soldier and blow the whole monument."

That put me away and loosened me up for the show.

During my monologue, which, thanks to God and to Pat McCormick; went well, President Kennedy kept jotting brief notes on an envelope. It's very flattering to think the President of the United States is writing down your jokes, but finally my curiosity got the best of me, as it always does, and I said, "Mr. President, you've been writing through my entire monologue. Are you adding up the check? Just what are you doing over there?"

I found out.

A lot of my lines had been about the Kennedy house at Rattlesnake Hill, which Jackie didn't like and had rented out. I did a lot of jokes about angry tenants calling the President in the middle of the night to complain about a 69 stopped-up sink. While I was doing the jokes, the President jotted down a quick retort to each one, and when it came his turn to speak, his impromptu lines topped mine.

The show-stopper of the evening, though, was Barbra Streisand. Washington's power structure sat mesmerized as this little girl from Brooklyn stunned them right out of their minds. When she finished, an awesome pause filled the room; then applause thundered toward the stage. Everyone in the room—even me—knew they were looking at a girl on her way to becoming a major star.

The entertainers then went to a foyer where we formed a receiving line. A White House aide cautioned us the one thing we should *not* do was detain the President as he came through the line. Just shake his hand and let him go. Fine.

Mr. Kennedy was jovial after the show and had kind words for all of us. When I introduced him to Barbra, she curtsied, then stuck a program and pen in his face and said, "May I have your autograph?"

An aide flashed an irritated look, but Kennedy grinned and signed the program, while press photographers elbowed each other to get the shot.

Next morning at breakfast I said to Barbra, "You were fabulous last night, you just floored everybody. But for God's sake, Barbra, did you *have* to stop the President for an autograph?"

"I wanted it."

"Well, I know, but they specifically asked us not to stop the President."

"But I wanted his autograph, Merv. How many times would I get a chance to have the President sign an autograph?"

"Well, did he write an inscription?"

"Yes. 'Fuck you. The President.' "

Not only did Barbra get the President's *real* autograph, but the picture of her getting it made all the morning papers.

Smart girl, that one.

6

EVEN THOUGH my talk show on NBC lasted only six months, it put my face in front of the people who hand out the jobs in show business, and there were other offers waiting on my desk when I returned from Europe. Television producer Irving Mansfield arranged for me to host the weekly "Celebrity Talent Scouts," an updated version of a similar show Arthur Godfrey had hosted years earlier. I also contracted to do two summer-stock plays, *The Moon Is Blue* at the Bucks County Playhouse in Pennsylvania and Neil Simon's *Come Blow Your Horn* with the Kenley Summer Theater in Ohio.

I knew I'd been signed for these plays because of my television exposure—not because I was a great actor. My acting experience was limited to two years as a contract actor at Warner Brothers, small parts in television variety-show skits and a role in the 1956 Broadway revival of *Finian's Rainbow*. I never had the awesome respect for the theater displayed by other actors and actresses I knew. I come from a different world, television, where an ad lib can save a show. So when I acted, if I didn't know a line, I'd ad-lib one; I'd change anything for a better laugh, or to suit my style of delivery. That attitude created problems for me as an actor.

In 1956 I had an audition with Rodgers and Hammerstein, who were casting the role of Prince Charming for a television special. I knew it was a big opportunity and I also knew I'd feel more comfortable accompanying myself at 71 the piano; just the thought of standing by a piano in an empty rehearsal hall with the legendary Rodgers and Hammerstein staring at me was enough to cause me to break out in hives. I arrived for the audition, and before I could say Hello, they wanted to know the whereabouts of my accompanist.

I pulled out one of my ad libs: "*Well,* you see, just as he was leaving the apartment his wife went into labor and they had to rush her to the hospital."

"Well, Mr. Griffin," Richard Rodgers said stiffly, "what do you plan to do?"

"Oh, I'll play for myself, that's no problem at all."

"You mustn't do that."

"I mustn't?"

"How are we to get a sense of your stage presence if you are sitting behind a piano?"

"Oh, I see, yeah . . . well, how about if I try it once behind the piano and if you like the way I sing, then I'll stand up and sing *a cappella* and you can judge from that."

Reluctantly they agreed.

I sat down at the piano and started "It Might As Well Be Spring."

Before I had three lines out Richard Rodgers stopped me. "Could you hold it a moment, Mr. Griffin? Are you singing 'It Might As Well Be Spring'?"

"A . . . yes. 'It Might As Well Be Spring.' Your song."

"We know it is our song, Mr. Griffin. However we never wrote it like that."

They thanked me politely and that was the end of Merv Griffin as Prince Charming.

I ran into a few problems in *Finian's Rainbow* too. This was 1956, and memories of Freddy Martin's orchestra were still fresh in my mind. I was used to having the orchestra follow me, which is not the way things are done in Broadway musicals. My co-stars, Helen Gallagher and Don Driver, had been rehearsing with the orchestra several days before I came into the picture, and by opening night I didn't have the songs down well enough to suit conductor

Julius Rudel. He rushed into my dressing room at intermission. "What are you *doing* out there?"

"Why are you yelling at me?"

"Because I'm conducting the orchestra and you're not staying with me."

Helen Gallagher wasn't too happy with me, either. I'd been warned about Helen, who supposedly once shoved an actor into the orchestra pit for upstaging her. By no means did I want to end my life impaled on a violin, so I kept an eye on her. When the reviews came out and I received particularly good notices, Helen began breathing fire. That I came late into the production, played around with the phrasing of the songs, and *then* pulled good reviews was all too much. So the next night as I was waiting in the wings for a scene where I chase Helen out on stage, then sing "Old Devil Moon," she socked me in the stomach as she ran by for her entrance. The blow knocked the wind out of me, and I limped out to my mark where the orchestra hit the cue for the song. I couldn't get my breath, and Julius Rudel stared up at me like "There goes that s.o.b. again." I forced myself to start singing the love song. Helen put her arms around me, with her back to the audience, slid a hand under my shirt, grabbed the short hairs on the back of my neck and yanked for all she was worth. I barely stopped myself from screaming and somehow plowed through the number, which I'm sure sounded awful. But then it was her turn to sing a chorus, and as she drew air for her big opening note I locked my arms around her like a vise. She couldn't get the note. Julius Rudel held the chord, and she whispered, "Let go."

"Will you ever mess me up out here again?" I whispered back.

"Let go!"

"No. I'll let you die, here and now." The audience started to murmur. "Will you ever . . . ?"

"I won't."

I let go and the note jumped out on a cushion of air.

Helen didn't give me any more trouble. 73

So with that background I signed for the two plays in the summer of 1963. Mike Ellis, who ran the Bucks County Playhouse in New Hope, Pennsylvania, booked me with the idea of drawing an audience unaccustomed to live theater (he certainly had an actor unaccustomed to live theater, so why not an audience?). It was a gamble on his part, but it paid off. He sold out every performance. And Mike knew he was drawing a new crowd because of their unusual response to the play; the audience carried on conversations with my character. I'm in the middle of a love scene and a lady in the twentieth row says, "Wait until his wife finds out about *this* one." At other times they answered questions in the script. It drove my co-star, Barbara Mattes, crazy.

Mike Ellis loved it, and he invited friends from New York's theatrical community to see what was going on. It was madness every night, but we broke the house record.

The Moon Is Blue closed in Pennsylvania on a Sunday night, and my agent, Murray Schwartz, who had been so wise in bringing Barbra Streisand to Washington, D.C., booked me to open *Come Blow Your Horn* on Tuesday. I had to spend all my afternoons rehearsing *Horn* in New York, fly to Pennsylvania in a seaplane to make the curtain of *Moon* and also make time to tape "Celebrity Talent Scouts."

I arrived in Ohio on Monday in no condition to open the next night. I just didn't know my lines, and I admitted to producer John Kenley that I wasn't properly rehearsed. "All you'll need is a walk-through," Kenley said, "and you'll have it down. It's just nerves. I'll have the stage manager walk you through your part right away."

I said to the stage manager, "Don't tell Mr. Kenley, but I can't remember one damn line of this play."

He came up with a plan.

Opening-night tension built backstage because my co-star, William Bendix, didn't like the idea of my being billed above him, and he knew I didn't have my lines down; the rest of the cast, too, expected me to blow lines left and right. The curtain went up to a full house and, thanks to my friend the stage manager, I didn't miss a cue or a line. The others suffered from the usual dose of opening-night jitters and flubbed their share of lines, but I was right on the money, because at every mark on stage where I delivered lines my script was pasted to a prop.

The chilly looks I received backstage from the cast turned to ice the next morning when one columnist wrote, "Merv Griffin was in perfect command of his lines, which wasn't the case on opening night for the rest of the cast." It was my turn to suffer the second night, when the cast took it upon themselves to remove my script from the props, and I had to ad-lib half my part.

What I really remember about that play was the opening-night party, because I still can't believe what happened to me. You see, it's common knowledge in the theatrical community that producer John Kenley is a registered hermaphrodite: he lives half the year as a man, then goes to another state where he has six months of life as a woman. People know this, but *I* didn't know it, and I didn't know it was customary for the leading man of John's productions to dance the opening song with him at the cast party. Can you believe how confused and embarrassed I was when John walked up to me at the party and asked for the first dance?

"I beg your pardon?"

"It's customary that I dance with the leading man."

"Oh . . . a . . . I see . . . well, I really should acquiesce to Mr. Bendix."

And so to the strains of "Tennessee Waltz" I stood there watching William Bendix dance with John Kenley; I couldn't wait to get back to New York and a television studio.

While I was working summer stock and hosting "Celebrity Talent Scouts," the lines to NBC remained open, with the hope of coming up with an idea to keep me working in the fall. Their promise was not an idle one; they offered me a game show called "Word for Word." But the offer was not just to host; I would also produce the show. When I mentioned the offer to a few of my friends, they turned their noses up: "Why go back into game shows, you were the host of your own talk show, don't lose your prestige. . . ." But I'd seen plenty of people with prestige who were out of work, and I've always preferred doing something to staring at a blank waiting for lightning to strike. I recalled 1957, when I *did* stare at a blank wall, because I had turned down offers to be the boy singer on television variety shows. By then I knew I wanted to talk, develop a personality on camera, so I spent that year forcing the transition. But in 1963 I knew enough to keep working, to keep myself in view of those powerful network executives I keep talking about. And by 1963 I was aware of the advantages of being a producer, as well as star, and of being in control of the finances and the format of one's show. Obviously, I wasn't ecstatic about hosting another game show, but this one gave me the opportunity to start my own production company. I grabbed the chance. Every performer wants a better hold on his professional destiny, but few want to put in the time to learn how to run a production company. I wanted to learn.

And besides, games come naturally to me. As kids, my sister Barbara and I constantly played word games in the back seat of the family car during Sunday drives. All those hours in a bus I spent on the road with Freddy Martin's orchestra I worked crossword puzzles and "hangman." To this day, the first thing I do in the morning is the crossword puzzle of the *Los Angeles Times.*

Like all successful games, "Word for Word" originated with a simple concept: We gave the contestants a master word, such as "rifle," and they formed as many other words out of it as possible (life, ire, lie, lire, etc.). The winner advanced to a bonus round of anagrams. The show ran only one season, but it was enough to get my production company off the ground, and during that season my wife gave me an idea for a game show that took the company from the ground floor right to the penthouse. Julann's idea was a twist on the usual question-answer format of the quiz shows of the fifties. Her idea was to give the contestant an answer (Rosemary Woods was this President's heavy-footed secretary) and they had to come up with the appropriate question (Who is Richard Nixon?) We called the game "Jeopardy!" and, with Art Fleming as host, it became one of the longest-running game shows in NBC's history.

My dream of a successful talk show never left me, though, even during the excitement of starting my own company.

Early in the sixties a new force in the business of television emerged called "syndication," a method of marketing television shows independent of the "big three" networks. Syndication works like this: a parent company, usually one that owns several television stations, buys rights to a show from an independent production company; the parent company (the "syndicator") then hires salesmen who travel the country and sell the show to stations on an individual basis. This allows the stations to place the show in a time slot best suited for the viewers in their area, and the station sells advertisements on a local basis. A syndicated show can be original programming, like "The Merv Griffin Show" or it can be the constant stream of reruns of shows cancelled from the networks: "I Love Lucy," "The Dick Van Dyke Show," etc. In 1964 syndication was not the billion-dollar business it is today, so I did not immediately think of it as an outlet for a talk show. Luckily, it found me. Chet Collier of Westinghouse Broadcasting wanted to bring "The Merv Griffin Show" back to television by means of syndication.

Sol Leon and Roy Blakeman were contacted by Chet. Roy mentioned their conversations to me, but in the initial stages of discussions there wasn't enough money in the deal to make me take much notice. Then one morning, as I was pulling into my parking space at work, I saw Sol and Roy standing in the lot waiting for me. Roy said, "Westinghouse is really after you, Merv." We went up to my office to talk, and I felt the adrenaline pumping as if I were about to walk onstage.

"But syndication, Roy . . . it's such a baby. . . ."

"Yes, but they are offering substantial money now, *and* you will own the show."

Every week I saw the good news on the balance sheet because I owned "Jeopardy!" so I knew ownership of the show could be more important than a big network salary.

"But, Roy, do they have any stations?"

"They don't own a station in New York, and they don't own one in L.A., but they do own stations in San Francisco, Boston, Philidelphia, Pittsburgh and Baltimore. And they think they can sell New York and L.A."

"What do you think of it?"

"It's worth sitting down with them."

I knew the next time "The Merv Griffin Show" went on the air it *had* to be a success; two cancellations in a row and I'd be back in game shows forever.

We asked the William Morris Agency for their opinion, and word came down from company President Abe Last-fogel, "The station they're offering in New York is Channel Eleven, and it's a graveyard. Don't kid yourself, Merv, if a show isn't a success in New York it won't generate the excitement necessary to sell it around the country. It could end your career."

I asked William Morris if they had any alternatives to the Westinghouse deal. They didn't. It boiled down to whether I thought *we* could make the show work: simple as that. The decision, finally, was in my hands. I instructed Roy Blakeman to make the deal. "They think I'm pushing myself right out of the business, " I said to Roy, "but let's try it and see what we can do."

I wasn't operating totally on instinct, however, because this time I was in control of the show, and I'd learned a few things since the NBC show.

First, I wanted to do the show from a theater. Talk shows depend on excitement, spontaneity, that "electric undercurrent" Jack Paar had told me about. Television studios

78

are fitted purely for function; they tend to be cold, stark and cavernous, and anything but exciting. This time I wanted my show to be part of the theater district, identified with Broadway. Just off Times Square, next door to Sardi's, the most famous restaurant in the theater district, I found my "home." Unfortunately it was occupied by a play called *The Subject Was Roses*. There weren't a hundred people in the house the night I saw the play, but enough people were buying tickets to keep the production going. Frank Gilroy, who wrote the play and owned the lease on the theater, got wind of my interest but said under no condition would he give up the lease. Thus, two famous words came to my lips: "How much?"

"Twenty-five thousand dollars and it's yours."

"I'll take it."

So I got his theater, while he took his nervous hit to the Helen Hayes Theater on Broadway, and there *The Subject Was Roses* suddenly became a smash and walked away with a Pulitzer Prize.

I should have asked for a rebate.

Now that I had my theater I was ready to discuss format with Westinghouse. We both agreed I should do the same show I did on NBC, but add a sidekick. And I had an answer before they could ask the question.

"Arthur Treacher," I said at a meeting with Bob Shanks, the William Morris representatives and Chet Collier.

They all stared at me. I hadn't seen Arthur since that spring of 1962. I had heard he'd gone on a road tour of *Camelot*, but hadn't worked much otherwise; his name didn't register an immediate impression in the room.

Someone finally said, "You mean, the butler from the Shirley Temple movie?"

"He's not a butler, he's an actor and we work wonderfully together."

You've never heard so much silence.

Then Sol Leon said, "It's a one-night joke. It just won't play week after week. You can't run your show with an English accent as announcer, people won't accept it."

"I agree you can't have an entire show with an English 79

accent, but you can *open* a show with one. It'll add a nice touch. And he's a wonderful character, trust me."

They didn't, and all voted against it. Even Julann, who loves wacky combinations of people, thought it wouldn't work. I put my foot down and said it had to be Arthur.

No one was more surprised at my decision than Arthur's agent. I called and asked him to offer it to Arthur.

"Are you serious, Merv? It's an interesting idea, but are you serious? Really?"

"See what he says."

Now what I am about to tell you may sound too poetic to be true, but this is the way it happened. After I talked to the agent, he picked up the phone and immediately called Arthur.

"Arthur," he said, "I've just had the strangest request for your services."

"Oh? Did that dear little Griffin chap call?"

When the agent lifted himself up off the floor, he said, "How the hell could you possibly know that?"

"I knew one day he'd call."

"Well, what he wants is you to work on his show, do the opening announcement like Hugh Downs did for Jack Paar. You would be Merv's sidekick, so to speak."

"Yes. I see. Well, he's a dear little man so I'll do it."

"The money . . ."

"It doesn't matter what he's offering, I'll take it."

"You don't want to hear the offer?"

"If I remember correctly, the lad has an honest face."

So I had a theater just off Broadway, my trusted producer Bob Shanks booking the show, and now Arthur Treacher, who I felt would bring a delightful touch to a talk show. "The Merv Griffin Show" was ready to try again.

Guess who just about stole the show on opening night? Mr. One-Night Joke, Arthur Treacher. The audience was crazy about him. A stately Englishman was the perfect counterweight to the wildness of an American talk show in the middle sixties; his honesty functioned as a funny foil to my enthusiasm.

If Arthur thought a question I asked of a guest too personal, he'd say, "Why you wretched little man," and turn his back on me. The audience adored him because they knew he wasn't kidding. Arthur did not pull punches. Once I coaxed him into doing a vaudeville number with English comedienne Tessie O'Shea, whom he loathed. They did the number and the audience leapt to their feet for the ovation. Arthur took his bow, and as he passed me on the the way back to his chair I said, "Gee, Arthur, that was great."

He whispered, "She's a prick."

Fortunately Tessie didn't hear the remark. She followed Arthur to the couch and propped her feet on his lap, basking in the laughter of the crowd.

Arthur removed her feet, carefully placed them on the ground and said, "You are a very vulgar woman," and turned his back, leaving me to conduct the interview with Tessie.

This same simple honesty, unsheathed in the presence of a network executive many years later, would have a devastating effect upon both Arthur and me.

The Westinghouse shows were good but the ratings on Channel 11 in New York were not, and we needed a New York success to motivate other stations to buy the show. Once more, nightmares of cancellation came into my nights.

But an executive of Metromedia, the company that owned Channel 5, WNEW, in New York stepped in to change all that. His name is Al Krivin, and he was to play an even larger role in my career years later. Right then, in 1965, he almost singlehandedly saved the show, because the moment we moved to Channel 5 "The Merv Griffin Show" streaked ahead in the ratings. Taxi drivers were cutting in to pick me up again, and then I knew we were headed in the right direction. By presenting guests like Bertrand Russell, Marlon Brando, Tallulah Bankhead, Bobby Kennedy, Nobel Prize-winning scientist James Watson, Dick Gregory, and discovering new entertainers like 81

Lily Tomlin, John Denver, Diane Keaton, Richard Pryor and George Carlin, "The Merv Griffin Show" became part of the sixties ferment. Soon one hundred fifty stations were carrying the show. All those nights on the Jack Paar show, the six months of my own show at NBC and the years as producer and host of games shows were finally paying off the way I had always hoped they would.

But when CBS stepped in with their fat checkbook in 1969 I walked away from the security of Westinghouse and plunged into the thin air of network television. And on that August night in 1969, after doing my shaky debut on CBS, I sat in the suite of my room in the Hilton Hotel and wondered about the wisdom of my decision.

PART TWO

Fat and Freddy

1925-1948

7

AFTER OUR GUESTS said good night and Julann had gone to bed, I sat up thinking about my first show on CBS. It is a lonely time for a performer, after a show, particularly when the show has not gone well. No matter how many people work with me putting the show together, or how many millions of people watch it on their television sets, doing the show is still an intensely personal experience; when the show is bad, such as on this night, I feel a sense of real loss. It was a precarious summit, that big contract with CBS. If the show wasn't a success, it would not just be a business failure for me, it would be a deep personal jolt. I sat wondering why the show was so essential to my happiness, and I was struck by the thought of how much of my life had been "shows." As my thoughts turned back to early memories, I realized there would be a second show on CBS and a third and fourth, and shows for a long time to come, because in my life there have always been shows.

There were the shows on the back porch of my family's home on Eldorado Street in San Mateo, California. They were *my* shows, these back-porch extravaganzas; from the age of four onward I was the P.T. Barnum and Billy Rose of my neighborhood. Every Saturday I had a show, recruiting all the kids on the block as either stagehands, actors or audience, and sometimes as all three. I was the producer, *always* the producer; I produced the curtain by raiding my mother's linen closet and borrowing a clothesline, swiped a milk crate to use as a podium, and made a megaphone out 85 of cardboard. My shows always had lavish openings and lavish closings, with very little attention paid to what came in the middle. The Barnum side of me created carnivals, complete with games, food stands and cages made from boxes where the freakier-looking kids could be coaxed into imitating wild animals. Peggy Holitz was my leading lady and chief ticket taker; if she reported one of the kids to me for failing to pay the ticket, we'd start a little fire by his house and see that he got the blame. I always seemed as a child to be pulling open the curtains and waving my arms to start a show.

Since a big part of show business is reviews, I started a newspaper to give them. And not just of my own shows, but of the activities of our neighbors. While I was running around the neighborhood doing my Sol Hurok number in search of talent, I picked up all the local gossip and put it in *The Whispering Winds*; I was only seven years old, but already I wanted to let other people know what I found interesting. My parents inadvertently put my paper in business by giving me a hectograph, which is a primitive mimeograph. Using the hunt-and-peck method of typing, I composed my stories on a stencil, pressed the stencil on a hardened, Jell-O-like compound and made dozens of copies. Because I printed gossip, *The Whispering Winds* always sold out instantly. One of my biggest sellers ran a story that began: "Did you hear all the noise at the Johnsons' house Tuesday night? Lots going on there. . . ." The Johnsons bought all thirty copies of that edition. *The Whispering Winds* sailed along happily until one day I printed a certain joke and my parents immediately put an end to my career as San Mateo's answer to William Randolph Hearst.

I kept boxes, mysterious tin boxes of many sizes and shapes, and in them saved old documents, coins, marbles and anything that made noise. I liked little bells and buzzers and chimes because their sounds caught people's attention, created a dramatic pause in the middle of a conversation. That's why, of all the nuns who taught me at
Saint Matthew's Catholic grammar school, I remember

only one: she kept a big brass bell on her desk, and the ringing of it sent us out to play or to go home; that bell's sound imbedded itself in my memory.

The nuns were kind, always willing to join us in the play yard and toss a ball around or organize games. But there was the feared Captain Carey, a retired military man who wore jodhpurs and puttees, in charge of physical education at the school; he insisted on being called "Captain" and made us stand at attention and marched us through ridiculously regimented exercise periods. Captain Carey instilled in me an early hatred of, and resistance to, regimentation.

Of those eight years at St. Matthew's I recall little. It was not a happy time of my life. Much of that time I spent alone, drifting, daydreaming, thinking and hoping life on the outside was more exciting than it was inside the classroom. Life in the classroom was dull indeed, and because I was fat, the playground didn't appeal to me either. School was never a pleasant experience for me because I don't have the patience to sit and listen to someone lecture. My life started at 3 P.M. every day when my favorite bell rang out, and I ran home to mastermind my backyard productions.

I took to music immediately. My mother's family, the Robinsons, were all amateur singers and musicians, and it was family tradition to spend Sunday afternoon around the piano, with everyone taking a turn at making up a song. When it was my turn to sing I insisted on turning my back to the audience, or I wouldn't sing at all; I was just too shy to sing to people's faces. I started playing piano at age four, not with any precocious aspirations; I just liked the noise it made when I banged on the keys. My mother's sister, Aunt Claudia, who lived near us, was a piano teacher. She decided to start teaching me and I was eager to learn. Since I was too small to reach the keys while sitting on a bench, I stood. And I guess I caught on pretty fast, because I remember friends of my mom standing around the piano to marvel at little "Buddy."

In 1930 we lost our house because of the Depression. My father was a tennis pro, and his students dwindled during those lean years, so we moved in with Aunt Claudia and Aunt Helen. That's when Claudia and I became inseparable friends. She never overburdened me with music. Some afternoons she took me fishing or roller skating, but whenever I wanted to play piano she was there to guide me. And though she adored me, she knew when I had progressed to the point of needing advanced instruction and placed me with another teacher. As I grew older and became a success in show business, I thought often of how crucial a moment it was when Aunt Claudia decided to move me on to advanced instruction; I was the light in her eye, and I know she would have liked to keep me at the piano with her, but she recognized my talent and made sure I had the best opportunity to develop it. My mother was a partner with Claudia in that goal. You see, my father came from a family of athletes, and his friends were athletes, and no son of his was going to sit around and play piano. For years he never knew I played, because Claudia and my mother knew he wouldn't like it if he found out. Claudia taught me in the afternoons when Dad wasn't around, and my mother set aside a bit of her grocery money each week to save for the day I would need professional instruction. Even during the worst of the Depression, my mother tucked away a few coins by selling cakes to a local bakery to go toward my musical future.

Over the years, whenever I went home I sat down with Claudia to play our favorite tunes and to test out my newest compositions on her. In 1978 when she died at age eighty-six I rushed home with my son Tony for the funeral. It was a typical Irish funeral, full of fond remembrances of Claudia, and I was asked to go to the organ and play some of her favorite songs; we all knew them by heart. I started playing, and with the songs came a flood of memories and it was as though I forgot I was at a funeral service because I kept playing and playing, and I even played a song of my own that Claudia had liked very much. When I finished *all* of us were in tears. Afterward I cried and cried and almost didn't make it to the cemetery; I suddenly realized how much of my musical life this woman had given to me, and now she was gone.

From Aunt Claudia I went to Madame Siemmens at Mercy High School, and then to a music conservatory in San Francisco. I played only classical pieces and considered anything "pop" shabby. Beethoven, Chopin and Grieg were all I played until one day I found the sheet music to "In a Little Gypsy Tearoom" lying beside our piano. It was a popular hit at the time and I tried it out. From that moment on I was "ruined"; it was fun and I could improvise chords to make it dramatic. I never seriously studied classical music after that.

Many times I played impromptu recitals for my mother's friends, and it was at one of these gatherings that my father finally found out about my lessons. He came home early from the tennis courts, and one of the guests said to him, "You must be quite proud of your son, he's really brilliant when he plays."

"Plays?"

"Piano, of course."

"Buddy doesn't play piano."

"You're not serious, are you?"

My father walked over to me "Do you play piano?"

"Sure."

He still looked doubtful. "Play something."

I played "Tea for Two" because I knew he liked the song. When I finished he said, "Play it again." I did, and he wouldn't let me go away from the piano for the rest of the party; I ended up playing "Tea for Two" ten times.

Pretty soon he got used to the idea that I was a piano player and before long started dragging me all over town to show his friends how good I was.

Most of the kids I liked were involved with music. Bob Murphy, who owned a dazzling mother-of-pearl drum set, lived a few blocks away and went to St. Matthew's and San Mateo High School with me. Bob had his sights set on 89 being a lawyer, but lost his patience with law school, went to work in real estate around San Francisco and ended up coming to New York in the early sixties, where he started with my game show, "Jeopardy!" moved over to "The Merv Griffin Show" and worked up to producer and now executive producer. My other childhood pal was Cal Tjader, of whom I was in awe because his family owned a dancing school in San Mateo. They even had a tiny theater for revues, in which Cal tap-danced and played drums and piano.

What took my musical abilities out of backyard shows and Sunday-afternoon recitals was our church, and in particular our parish priest, Father Lyon. From an early age I was caught up in the high drama of the mass; the solemn ceremony and powerful music were thrilling to me, and chills went up my spine when, as an altar boy, I rang those brass bells at the holiest moment of the mass.

Father Lyon was a heroic figure. He was a huge, powerfully built Irishman who treated each member of his congregation, whether rich or poor, devout Catholic or occasional visitor, with equal concern and warmth. During the Depression he arose every morning to make sure the tramps who slept in back of the church had money for a hot meal, and the money always came out of his own pocket.

When I was only fourteen years old Father Lyon put me in charge of the church choir and gave me complete creative control over the music used for mass. It was a bold, unconventional thing for him to do, but he trusted my musical talent and encouraged my innovative ideas. If I didn't like the music prescribed by the church for a particular Sunday, I'd toss it out and score an entire mass myself, bringing in entirely new melodic lines and vocal parts. What Father Lyon especially liked was my sense of drama; when he made his entrance at the altar I hit chords on the organ that made the second coming of Christ seem imminent. Sometimes my ideas shocked the congregation, like the time I placed my choir on a long flight of stairs that led from the belfry to the choir loft, and the eerie, mysterious echo-chamber sound we created caused the parishioners to gaze cautiously upward and start repenting for their sins.

I turned in my sheets, clothesline and milk crates for a pipe organ, choir and the drama of the church and my new role as Father Lyon's producer and conductor.

Because of my flood of ideas, I needed a lot of rehearsal for the choir, but they didn't want to spend two nights a week in church and then all day Sunday. I took my problem to Father Lyon. He thought it over a minute and said, "Here's what we do, Merv, we pay 'em." And he winked at me, nodded, then added. "Ten dollars a week for each, but that counts two rehearsals." The money came right out of Father Lyon's savings account.

That choir was really something—I never saw anything like it. I wasn't interested in the religious character of my singers, just their voices, so it turned into a real soap opera up there in the loft. During the spoken parts of the mass half the choir went into a back room to smoke and who knows what else, because two of the female sopranos ended up having babies out of wedlock. I did make a wonderful friend, though, a girl named Janet Folsom who sang alto. She was from a ritzy San Francisco society family, and though she was quite a few years older than me, she took a liking to me for my enthusiasm and invited me to parties where I met the cream of San Francisco society.

Through my wild ideas, and Janet's public relations, our choir developed quite a reputation. People from all over the peninsula were coming to St. Matthew's to hear us, and because we were bringing in the flocks, Father Lyon overlooked gossip about the unusual habits of my choir members.

Once in a while a visiting priest complained to Father Lyon about the "unorthodox" young man running the church choir, pointing out that the masses I was scoring on my own weren't sanctioned by the archbishop. "We don't interfere with Mr. Griffin's selections," Father Lyon always calmly explained. Without Father Lyon to champion my 91 cause, I'd probably have been excommunicated from the church and afraid to pursue my own musical instincts ever again.

For a while Father Lyon had thought I might have the calling of the priesthood flowing in my veins, but I think my record as an altar boy discouraged that idea. I had a problem trying to keep a straight face in the midst of solemn ceremonies. They always struck me funny. It was awful for me to serve at funerals when everyone was wailing and I was supposed to stand like a sentinel next to the casket and hold the incense canister. The whole situation was scary and unnerving to a kid, and my reaction was always to want to start laughing. The mourners saw me shaking and turning red and thought I was sharing their grief. I think it was a disappointment to Father Lyon when he realized I wasn't cut out to be a man of the cloth.

When I wasn't orchestrating his Sunday masses, he kept me busy by recommending me as an organist at weddings and funerals. He figured that as long as I was up in the choir loft I wouldn't lose my composure. For twenty dollars I played and sang at weddings and, for five dollars extra, at funerals.

One of my worst moments as an organist came at the funeral for Chief Burke, the Chief of Police of San Mateo. I'd known Chief Burke all my life because he was a friend of my father, and the one thing I remembered about him was his nose, which was very red and protruded far out in front of his face. I played at his rosary but made the mistake of looking up at the casket. The top of the casket was open, and from my angle all I saw was the Chief's legendary nose. I had one of those terrible thoughts a kid will have, that maybe it was only Chief Burke's nose that had died. And then I had the awful feeling that a fit of laughter was approaching; I tried not to look at the nose and I tried thinking of all the painful memories I could conjure up. But it was too late. My face turned red, my sides ached, and as I slapped a hand over my mouth, my other hand slipped off the keyboard and hit a switch controlling the chimes in the steeple. All over San Mateo beautiful bells started ringing. The funeral director rushed over to me hissing, "You're ruining my rosary!" No, I could never be a priest.

But Buddy Griffin, organist for hire, did a land-office business, especially during May and June when weddings were nonstop. My mother took the calls from people and wrote the times on a calendar for me (she was my first agent) and she always reminded me a day ahead of time— except once. A socially prominent family announced the June wedding of their daughter, Linda; the mother was an acquaintance of my mom, so she called to hire me for the wedding. The two women got to chatting and my mother forgot to write down the date. On the appointed day I was off to San Francisco to see a movie, and poor Linda had to walk down the aisle sans music. Needless to say, the family didn't speak to us ever again. And I forgot about the incident until a dozen years later, after I'd achieved a modest amount of fame as a vocalist and returned to San Mateo for a tonsil operation. The San Mateo *Times* did a front-page interview with me and I received lots of flowers and calls from old friends. In the operating room the anesthetist slipped the gas mask over my face, and I asked how long it would take before I passed out. I looked in her eyes for the first time, and noticed an odd cast to them that made me ill at ease. "Just count to ten," she said "and by six you'll be out." She started the flow of gas and said, "Don't you remember me, Merv? I'm Mrs. Smith. Don't you remember? You were supposed to play at my daughter Linda's wedding, but you never showed up."

That was the last thing I heard before passing out.

When I regained consciousness in the recovery room, my doctor was standing over me. He said, "Mrs. Smith's arm had to be treated."

I was groggy and I shook my head, confused.

"When you were going under anesthesia you grabbed Mrs. Smith's arm and squeezed so tightly you pinched a nerve. I've never seen anyone fight going under so hard in all my life."

When I told him the story he stormed out of the room, 93

and Mrs. Smith had hell to pay. But, just the same, I checked out of that hospital in a hurry.

Growing up I slowly became aware of a shimmering world of show business, glamour and wealth, a world much grander than the back-porch shows on Eldorado Street, and a world with even more drama than the religious ceremonies of Father Lyon. My father's brother, Elmer, opened the window of this world to me.

Because the family regarded him as a bit of a rogue, I learned about him by eavesdropping on after-dinner conversations. Like my father, Elmer was a champion tennis player, and he used the social channels of tennis to travel through an assortment of occupations and wives. Elmer sent us invitations to parties in Hollywood, New York and Washington, D.C., and friends forwarded newspaper clippings about Elmer to us. He became friendly with Vice President Henry Wallace and parlayed this friendship into a powerful position as a Washington lobbyist. But he didn't like staying in one place too long, and to satisfy this restlessness carried on various careers as a stockbroker, real-estate entrepreneur, and owner of a Hollywood nightclub. When he made one of his visits to San Mateo it was a major event in my life, and I would sit for hours to listen to him talk about movie stars and parties held at huge estates. Once I saw him in the Movietone News at the Baywood Theater playing badminton with Shirley Temple; it took me days to recover from the experience of seeing someone I knew up on that big screen.

In the late thirties Elmer opened The Westside Tennis Club in Beverly Hills and the movie community flocked to join. The biggest thrill of my summer vacation came when my family drove down to visit Elmer, and I could sit in the lobby of the club and watch the stars walk by. And *did* I sit —for hours. When Kay Francis bounced through the lobby and smiled at me I couldn't speak for the rest of the day. My sister Barbara and I begged our parents to drive us up and down Hollywood Boulevard so we could spot the stars.

94 Every two seconds my dad would shout, "Oh! There's

Mickey Rooney" or "There's David Niven." Of course, it never really was. But when you're twelve years old and starstruck, your mind sees what your eyes do not.

As soon as I was old enough to travel on my own, I begged my mother to let me visit Uncle Elmer in Hollywood. When she finally said yes I was packed and on the train before she could change her mind. It was no big treat for Elmer to have his fat, frumpy nephew hanging around, but I promised to just sit by the tennis courts and watch. By this time he'd sold his own club and was running the Copa de Oro Club at the Beverly Wilshire. I arrived to find him on the court with Gloria Vanderbilt, Pat DiCicco and Errol Flynn. Just seeing Errol Flynn was good for two hours of nonstop gawking. Flynn used Elmer's apartment as a way station between romances, and when my uncle brought me there, Flynn was already sitting in the living room, slouched in a chair chatting away on the telephone. Except for a towel over his wet hair, Flynn was totally naked. "Hi, kid," he said without looking at me. I tried to speak but sound wouldn't come out of my mouth; the kids on El Dorado Street would never believe this one. Later two beautiful girls arrived to fetch Flynn and whisk the great swashbuckler away in their convertible, and the sight of the three of them in that white convertible was like an apparition to me.

Sooner or later I knew I had to work up the courage to talk to one of these stars and get an autograph; I *had* to go home with some evidence. Elmer took me to Romanoff's restaurant in Beverly Hills, where I spotted my favorite character actor named Monty Woolley. I broke out in a sweat thinking about actually talking to him. "Just go over there and ask him for an autograph," Elmer said. "He'll be flattered."

Woolley, a heavyset jolly-looking man with a white beard, was hunched over the bar.

I shuffled over to him, carefully set a napkin and pencil on the bar and squeaked, "Mr. Woolley, may I have your autograph?"

Without turning around, he growled, "Fuck off."

I didn't ask for many autographs after that.

When my mom called to check up on me I was bursting with information: "There's stars all over the place and *Errol Flynn* is staying here for a couple of days and he's got the most beautiful girls. . . ."

As soon as I said "Errol Flynn" my mother cleared her throat and said quietly, "Will you put your uncle on the phone for a moment, Buddy?"

Next thing I knew I was back on the train, heading home just as fast as I'd left.

My eyes were opened wide by Hollywood and I yearned to become a part of it; I wanted someday to see my name on an invitation to one of those parties Elmer had told me about.

Something soon happened that made me aware of music as a means of entry into the world I fantasized about.

Janet Folsom, my society friend from the choir, introduced me to a Mrs. Lent Hooker, who asked if I might consider playing piano at a private party for twenty dollars. I'd play in a tree house for twenty bucks. Her home was anything but a tree house; in fact, it was an estate. The occasion was a Halloween costume party with most everyone wearing masks, so I scarcely got a look at the faces of the people I was entertaining, but they kept me busy with requests for hours. For most of the evening a man dressed as a ghost sat by the piano and sang along. He had a pretty good voice so I gave him a stack of sheet music to look through and select a song. "Let's do this one," he said, handing me the music to "I Had the Craziest Dream" from *Sun Valley Serenade* starring Cesar Romero.

I asked him if he knew the lyrics.

"I ought to," he said, taking off his hood.

I thought *I* was having the craziest dream, because *he* was Cesar Romero. And I knew right then I'd never have met Cesar Romero playing Chopin's etudes, so I was more firmly convinced than ever it was going to be show-business tunes for the rest of my life.

96

Enough people heard me play at that party to keep me busy on weekends for the next six months. A few of those people weren't as nice as Mrs. Hooker, however. Some sent me invitations to parties and when I arrived there were no other teenagers there—just a piano. I accepted a few of those invitations; I wanted badly to believe I was being invited as a guest. One woman did it to me three times and finally I decided to get even. I showed up for one of her parties with my arm in a sling. When she opened the door she was obviously quite disappointed.

"What happened, Merv?"

"I burned my hand."

"Oh—does that mean you can't play piano?"

"I can't play, no."

Her face fell. "Well, come in anyway."

Once I started high school it was obvious my studies weren't going to get me far in life; my first report card showed three Fs and a D. I was much more interested in becoming the class entertainer than in being a scholar. Even though I did struggle through elementary algebra and Latin, I flunked Algebra II and Latin II. And I certainly had no interest in the sports teams; I was five feet nine and weighed two hundred twenty-five pounds. Music and drama classes were all I lived for.

If I was behind everybody in reading, writing and arithmetic, I knew as much as the teachers when it came to music. I took up the string bass because the piano parts in orchestra class put me to sleep; besides, I could take the bass over to the window and play it out to the courtyard, where it echoed and rattled the windows. Kids watched from all the surrounding classrooms just to see what the funny fat kid would try next.

My lifelong block against memorizing scripts started in high school. I won a lead role in our drama-class production of an English farce and used the script throughout all the rehearsals. On opening night I ad-libbed my part, which threw the other actors off but won big laughs for me. When it came time for the curtain call I received the 97 most applause, because the crowd thought I was the only one who had bothered to learn his part. Afterward the teacher took me aside to say my performance had earned me an F for the semester. There wasn't any way to explain I didn't intend to mess up anyone's role; I *couldn't* do a play any other way.

Next spring we did *Family Portrait,* a twentieth-century version of the life of Christ. I was given two parts, probably because I was so fat. In the first act I played Mordecai, and in the second, Mendel. Our teacher decided she didn't dare entrust the key role of Christ's mother to anyone but herself. That would have been fine, but our teacher was no beauty-contest winner. She had a huge overbite, short-cropped red hair and mammoth breasts. Not your classic Madonna. I don't think she looked too carefully at her costume, either, because to me it resembled a potato sack. But she was the teacher and she called the shots. When she made her entrance on opening night I was already onstage. What a picture she painted! Her black wig didn't cover all the red hair, and the buck teeth reminded me of a come-dienne I'd seen in movies, Cass Daley. I started laughing —who wouldn't have? This unnerved her, and she backed into the candles on the set, igniting her costume. Instead of a religious play, the audience saw this fat kid using his hat to smother the flames on the leading lady's fanny.

Not long after *Family Portrait,* this particular teacher left school to become a totally cloistered Carmelite nun. I'll leave it at that.

I didn't think much about being overweight until it came time for my first high-school dance. As a kid I'd heard all the usual taunts: "Fatty, fatty, two-by-four, can't fit through the kitchen door," "Fat, fat, the water rat," and a lot more I can recite by memory but don't want to. The taunts hurt. But not as much as looking into a mirror when I was dressing for the dance and seeing enough of me to fill two people. For a moment I contemplated calling my 98 date and telling her I'd been hit with a case of flu; but I really did want to go to that dance. I went to my father's closet, collected all his belts and cinched them one by one around my upper body. Rolls of fat bulged through the belts, and when I put on my tuxedo I looked like a human accordion. Just the same, I went to the dance.

The one girl I was really wild about in high school was Gypsy Ernst, the dark-haired love of my life. I'll always remember one date I had with Gypsy, when we went on the spur of the moment to San Francisco for dinner at Solari's. While I waited for a table Gypsy went to the powder room. As I was sitting in the lobby Gypsy's father came striding in with a girl on his arm who could have been his daughter, but, since I was with his daughter, it must have been someone else. I can't tell you how crazy about her father Gypsy was, so when she came out of the powder room I grabbed her arm and dragged her outside and said I was suddenly ill and wanted to go home. Next day Mrs. Ernst invited me to have dinner at their home, and of course she had to ask what Gypsy and I did the previous night. Gypsy spoke right up: "We went to Solari's for dinner but Merv got sick before we even sat down." Gypsy's father nearly swallowed his soup spoon. Our eyes met for a moment, and I believe he might have signed the mortgage of his house over to me just then.

Gypsy liked me, blubber and all, and it wasn't until a few years later that someone else made me realize all that weight had to come off.

When the war hit I volunteered my services to the USO and put together a small musical revue for them. Three of the prettiest girls at San Mateo High all wanted to be singers so I taught them to harmonize; I knew having pretty girls behind me in a USO show meant a certain encore.

Getting to our performances was really a cloak-and-dagger affair. The army sent trucks to bring us to the bases, and since many of them were top-secret installations we had to ride in canvas-covered troop carriers. They would back the truck right up to the stage door, we would 99 do the show; then we had to climb right back into the truck, never knowing where we'd been.

I was a first-rate war bond salesman. The local fundraisers built a platform for me on a street corner in San Mateo, and there I played piano, sang songs and heckled pedestrians until they coughed up some cash. My experience as a backyard master of ceremonies came in handy there.

My one other contribution to the war effort was as part of a civilian watch team who scanned the skies at night looking for unauthorized aircraft. Everyone around San Francisco was sure the Japanese were going to try another sneak attack, so all the cities had watch units. Another kid and I were stationed once a week in a tower at San Mateo High School, and we waited endlessly, sometimes hoped for a sneak attack. But the only action we ever got was when my friend brought a bottle of vodka one night, and after we drained it he reported three planes coming in out of the west. About ten minutes later six Air Force fighters came roaring through the sky. After that, I don't think our command post was counted on as much help. And my friend was relieved from duty.

I took a day job as a clerk at Hunter's Point Naval Shipyard, and by night I entered talent contests and wrote songs. A girl named Barbara McNutt teamed with me for talent contests. Wouldn't you know she was almost as fat as I was, so our version of "Cuban Love Song" looked like a concert by Tweedledum and Tweedledee; but we did place second in "Buddha's Amateur Hour," and the host, Dean Maddox, booked us in shows all over the Bay area.

When it came to songwriting, my favorite partner was Janet Folsom. She landed a job as social director at the ritzy Pebble Beach Lodge on the Monterey peninsula, and she liked having me visit because I played piano and entertained the guests. The Lodge was owned by a man named Sam Morris, the father of Mrs. Lent Hooker, the woman 100 who first hired me as party pianist. She introduced me around to many of the San Francisco society people who spent weekends at Pebble Beach. The people I really wanted to meet were the Hollywood stars who stayed at the lodge. Janet introduced me to Ann Sothern and Joan Crawford, and once I saw Dinah Shore having breakfast there.

Janet and I traded off writing music and lyrics, and when we wrote one we really liked, we called Janet's friend Joan Crawford and sang it to her over the phone. "Miss Crawford? Listen to this one."

> Someone ought to kill me
> cause
> I'm honestly acting like a dilly
> I'm silly
> "Cause I'm in love
> I'm horribly, borably
> So in love . . .

It never made the top ten but Joan Crawford sure thought it was cute.

Then we wrote a tune called "Never Let a Day Go By" and Janet was able to arrange for me to audition it for a song publisher visiting San Francisco. It was just my luck that the guy was Italian, and when I sang, "Never let a day-go by, no, never let a day-go by . . ." he jumped up from his chair and said, "Stop! Just what do you *mean* by that song?" End of audition.

Almost thirty years after my songwriting weekends with Janet Folsom I purchased a beautiful home looking down on the Pebble Beach Lodge. I planned a big housewarming party and was excited because Janet was coming to see how far I'd come from the days of the choir. On the day of the party, however, Janet suffered a heart attack and died.

Writing songs, performing at parties, USO shows and talent contests, even meeting a few Hollywood stars, titillated my show-business senses, but I didn't have a clue as to how I would translate these interests into a career.   101

After high school I attended the College of San Mateo and the only thing I was interested in there was the music classes. I wanted to try someplace else.

My father arranged for me to get a clerk's job with Crocker National Bank. Can't you just picture the Billy Rose of Eldorado Street trying to help the customers balance their checkbooks? After about a month of this job I asked the middle-aged man who worked next to me how long he'd been with the bank.

"Twenty years."

"Really? Can I ask what you're making by now?"

"Sure. Thirty-two dollars a week."

Next day I quit. I was willing to tap-dance on street corners for the rest of my life if I had to, rather than work twenty years in a bank for thirty-two dollars a week.

By my eighteenth birthday I was rudderless, having given up school and banking; I loved music and anything to do with show business, but didn't know what to do with my life. I went for a walk that day, July 6, 1943, to clear my head. Whenever I wanted to be by myself I walked down the railroad tracks near my house and sat by Wisnom's lumberyard. I liked the rush of air when the Daylight Express blasted by on its way south, toward Los Angeles and Hollywood. On this day I was walking along the rails, wondering where my life was headed, and a profound sadness enveloped me. I felt as though I were out of my body, almost floating above the tracks, and I had a vision. I didn't actually see a picture, but the words came to me, "You will never again be a private person." I know it sounds a little crazy, but the feeling was distinct and so unsettling that I stopped and stood perfectly still. Nothing was happening in my life to explain the feeling to me, but I felt something was *going* to happen. And for some reason I cried.

A year later my friend Cal Tjader called me about an audition coming up at radio station KFRC in San Francisco. He had heard they were looking for a piano player and dragged me up to the city to try out for the job.

102

When we got there the program director, Alan Lisser, told us they were looking for a singer, not a piano player. I turned to leave, but Cal decided to be a wise guy and said, "Merv sings really well, Mr. Lisser."

"Oh, then why don't you sing something for us, Merv?" I could have murdered Cal on the spot. Singing in a living room with friends was one thing, but in a radio station? Not me. Cal poked me in the ribs. Well, I thought, what the heck, I'll never see this guy again. I sat down to accompany myself at the piano and did my imitation of Dick Haymes singing "I Was Taken for a Sleighride in July."

Alan Lisser walked out of the room and I wondered if I was *that* bad. But when he returned he said, "When that red light goes on up there, sing the song again, Merv." Then he left the room again. The red light went on and I did my song. Alan returned with a prosperous-looking man named Bill Pabst. "Mr. Pabst owns the station, Merv. He'd like you to play another song." I couldn't quite figure out what was going on. Why did these two executives want to listen to a two-hundred-forty-pound teenager sing? I did another song and Mr. Pabst said, "We have a show called 'San Francisco Sketchbook' and I'd like you to be a guest on it tomorrow, Merv. Is that all right?"

"To play the piano, you mean?"

"No, to sing with our orchestra."

My heart nearly stopped when I realized these men were serious; I'd always thought of myself as a piano player, and now someone wanted me to sing on the radio.

When I told my family I was going to be on the radio I was too excited to explain I'd be singing, and they all assumed I'd be playing piano. Of course my whole family drove up to San Francisco to hear me play, but what they heard was me singing "Where or When" in front of an entire orchestra. I should have been more nervous than I was, with Bill Pabst, Alan Lisser and the station public-relations man, Dink Templeton, all standing outside the studio listening. But when I got in front of that orchestra it was like nothing I'd ever felt in my life; once the music started I felt like I was floating above all those strings and horns.

My family just couldn't believe it; they looked at me and said, "You haven't sung since you were a choirboy, a soprano."

"I know . . . I know . . . I just did it."

Mr. Pabst took me into his office and on the spot the "San Francisco Sketchbook" show was dead and "The Merv Griffin Show" was born.

I was to do a fifteen-minute show five days a week.

Three cheers for Cal Tjader.

In a whirlwind two days I went from unemployed bank clerk and party pianist to KFRC and billing as "America's New Romantic Singing Star." Can you believe that? I *did* have a romantic voice, even if my body was anything but romantic, and female fans started writing the station for autographed pictures.

The station then decided I'd better become KFRC's "romantic mystery voice," and when someone wrote for an autographed picture they got the autograph, period.

On weekends, however, I did make public appearances as singer-conductor of KFRC's orchestra. We became a must at San Francisco coming-out parties and at country-club socials. I negotiated all my own fees for these appearances, and when I added up the weekend take with my salary at KFRC I suddenly found myself with a pocketful of dough. I remember one party we played at the plush Burlingame Country Club where the host, Templeton Crocker, liked my singing so much he didn't want me to stop at midnight and handed me one thousand bucks to keep going. Being a kid from the wrong side of the tracks, this kind of money made my eyes spin. And it kept getting better. The show increased in popularity and so did my weekend bookings, so much that by 1946, when I was twenty, I was making as much as five thousand dollars a month. I spent it just as fast as it came in, joining a country club (even though I hated golf), and buying a new convertible. My father thought I was selling drugs or *some*thing illegal, because he was struggling to get by on tennis lessons and his kid was hauling in several thousand bucks a month.

Even though I had my own radio show and a wallet full of money, I still had one big problem: two hundred and forty pounds. How can you have a career beyond a radio station when you weigh more than a drum set? The idea that my weight was holding me back started getting through when a movie producer listened to my show and decided anyone with such a romantic voice belonged up on the silver screen. His name was Bill Dozier, and he picked up my show in L.A. on Mutual Broadcasting, so on a visit to San Francisco he put in a call to me. When I walked into his suite at the Fairmont Mr. Dozier's face fell; he could not believe *I* was Merv Griffin. But I was—all of me.

A week later I was standing in the lobby at KFRC when a woman walked in and said to the receptionist, "I've got to see Merv Griffin."

"Do you have an appointment with him?"

"I listen to his show all the time and I just want to meet him."

"Oh, well, I'm sorry but he's in the studio and they don't allow an audience."

"Then I'll just look through the window at him."

"No, I'm afraid that won't be possible."

"But I'm here all the way from Fresno and listen to Merv's show every day. . . ."

While this conversation was going on another secretary walked out of the back office and shouted to me, "Telephone call for you, Merv."

My fan whirled and looked at me in disbelief.

"You're Merv Griffin?"

"Hi, how are you?"

". . . the romantic mystery voice?"

She burst out laughing and went rushing down the stairwell; I could hear her laughter echoing in the hall. I still hear it echoing whenever a waiter asks me if I want to see a dessert menu. That woman's laughter, coupled with the 105 arrival in San Francisco of a singer named Joan Edwards, who gave me some hard advice, put me on the first of one thousand two hundred forty-one diets.

Joan Edwards, star of "Your Hit Parade," was one of the most popular radio singers in the country, and she prided herself on knowing the voice of every male singer in the business. She heard me on the radio in her hotel room and called KFRC to find out who I was. When I called her back she said, "Honey, I don't know who you are but you sing like an angel."

"Then come sing on my show tomorrow."

"I'll be there."

She walked into the studio, took one quick look at me and pulled out of the orchestra's earshot. "Merv, honey, you sing great but the blubber has got to go."

She was right. For the next four months I ate nothing but steak and salad, skipping my customary three bowls of puffed rice covered with honey and bananas for breakfast, and the daily trips to Blum's soda fountain for hot fudge sundaes. I dropped twenty pounds a month, and at the end of my diet weighed in at a svelte one hundred sixty pounds.

At twenty-two I was making fifteen hundred dollars a week, pulling top reviews in the papers and, most important of all, I still weighed only one hundred sixty pounds. Now I was really ready for a change.

I first heard about Freddy Martin and his orchestra when I was fifteen and working part time as a pinsetter at the Burlingame Bowling Alley. This had to be one of the world's most boring jobs. The pinsetters, perched on narrow walkways behind the lanes, jumped down to reset the pins and return the ball. My only joy in the job was listening to the alley's jukebox, and the big hit that summer was Freddy Martin's "Tonight We Love," an adapation of Tchaikovsky's First Piano Concerto. They played that song night and day at the Burlingame Bowl and I knew it by
heart.

In those days I still tipped the scales at two hundred forty pounds and I didn't win awards as the world's nimblest pinsetter. I moved a little too slowly one afternoon and a used-car dealer let his second ball go before I was out of the way. After that, I spent a couple of days in a hospital bed with my leg elevated and I lay there listening to Freddy Martin on the radio. My Uncle Elmer visited me and said Freddy played frequently at the Cocoanut Grove in Los Angeles and was known in Hollywood as the orchestra leader the movie stars came to see. That image alone placed Freddy in a lofty position in my mind.

When I started doing my radio show for KFRC, Freddy turned the tables and started listening to me. My show aired from seven-fifteen to seven-thirty each evening in Los Angeles on KHJ, which was the exact time Freddy spent driving to the Cocoanut Grove. I guess he grew to like this unseen voice, because when his singer gave notice that he was quitting the band after their next San Francisco engagement, he had his secretary, Jean Barry, give me a call. She asked to have lunch with me, but I assumed it was because Freddy owned song-publishing companies and wanted to pitch me to sing his songs on my show. I didn't have a clue he might want me to sing with his band.

Jean and I talked about the music business over lunch, but she didn't mention the band until I was getting ready to leave. She put it simply: "Stuart Wade is leaving us, Merv, and Freddy would like you to be his singer."

I stared at her.

"He loves your voice, and now that I've seen you I know he'll like your appearance, too."

"You mean he wants me to go on the road with his band?"

"Yes."

It was a possibility I hadn't considered. I liked working right where I was. "What's the salary starting out, Jean?"

"A hundred fifty."

"A day?"

She laughed. "A week, of course."

"But I'm making that much a day right now."

"We could never come close to paying you that. But think about something else, Merv. You're a big deal here in San Francisco—but what happens next? What's beyond San Francisco? I'm not just offering you a job that pays a hundred fifty a week, I'm talking about a job where you'll be playing the Waldorf Astoria and the Strand Theater on Broadway. You'll be recording on RCA Victor. And you'll be playing the Cocoanut Grove in Los Angeles. It's exposure, Merv."

"I don't know, Jean. Give me a little time to think about it."

I didn't sleep that night. With all the money coming in and the fun of being a local celebrity, I hadn't given much thought to what would happen once San Francisco was through with me, when another young romantic voice came along. Singing on Broadway and in the Cocoanut Grove was a thrilling thought. But riding on a bus and playing one-nighters, that part didn't sound too exciting.

Jean Barry arranged a ringside table for me at the St. Francis to see Freddy's orchestra, and Freddy stopped by my table during a break. I told him I was interested in his offer.

"Really? I thought you'd already turned it down."

"No, I'm really thinking about it."

"Come on back a couple of nights and get a feel for the band."

I did, and each night the music sounded better and better; I was hooked.

When I told Jean Barry I wanted the job she said, "Can you start next week?"

I thanked Bill Pabst at KFRC for what he'd done for me and started packing.

My family and friends wondered if I was doing a wise thing, taking such a cut in salary. I wondered the same thing myself. But I knew as long as I stayed in San Francisco all the money in the world couldn't buy me a spot center stage at the Cocoanut Grove.

Still, it wasn't easy leaving home. Driving from San Mateo to San Francisco to meet the band for my first road trip, I cried. I knew the family house on Eldorado Street wasn't going to be my home anymore; I was leaving my parents, my sister, Aunt Claudia and Aunt Helen. My sadness came from a sense of finality; I knew my life was headed in a direction that meant "home" would be a long way off from now on.

PART THREE

Let's Raise

Some Eyebrows

1962-1970

8

My FIRST TALK SHOW on NBC in 1962–63 generated attention from the press and at least from a certain portion of the public. But it wasn't until 1965, when Westinghouse Broadcasting decided to bring back "The Merv Griffin Show" and syndicate it across the country, that I made a mark as an interviewer. On the NBC show we had booked journalists, politicians and controversial personalities to mix in with the actors, singers and comedians, and the television critics cheered us for bringing topical issues to afternoon TV. The issues themselves, however, didn't start making news until 1965, when one nationally syndicated columnist questioned my patriotism because of an interview I did. That's when I knew "The Merv Griffin Show" was going to make it; we were causing trouble.

The sixties, tumultuous for America and the world, created a natural climate for talk shows. Sparks leaped off the tongues of dissidents and politicians. Cocktail parties were charged with controversy. Each day's papers reported a new crisis, but before the ink dried on the headlines another story broke, bigger than the last. We were surrounded by social and cultural upheaval, and in the middle of it stood a younger generation engaged in a sincere, though often confused and chaotic, search for summits, high ground from which to sort out changing values. Institutions were under attack. Government, school, religion, family—they were all under attack; nothing remained sacred. Dinner tables turned into forums for debate. For the 113 first time in more than a decade, America was passionate in its confusion. Talk shows flourish in such times.

The opportunity for my first big political interview came while we were in England doing a location show with Bob Hope. Hope was there shooting a movie and I did an interview with him on the set. But I felt, since we were over there, we should try to get an English perspective on current events. Someone suggested Bertrand Russell, the Nobel Laureate and world-renowned philosopher. We found him simply by looking in the phone book. Russell's personal assistant, a young American named Ralph Schoenman, informed us Lord Russell would consent to the interview on condition that I would not ask questions about his personal life; Russell was wary of American interviews, because he was often asked more about his four marriages (two to American women) than about his political opinions. Lord Russell's political opinions were what I was after. He had indicated to the press a dislike of American foreign policy, so when he greeted me at his modest home in Chelsea I asked him if he could possibly be as anti-American as the press painted him to be. The ninety-three-year-old philosopher smiled and said, "How could I be? Fifty percent of my wives have been American."

I began the interview by asking him if the cold war between America and the Communist bloc countries would ever be settled.

"Yes, it will be settled, one way or another. Probably the most likely way will be by the extermination of all combatants on both sides. Then somehow it will be settled."

Then I asked the question which caused Lord Russell's eyes to start flashing: "What *would* be the necessary steps toward world peace?"

"Of course, the first thing would be for Americans to give up aggressive war, give up the habit of invading peaceful countries and torturing them. I think that is a first step."

He caught me off guard. Nineteen sixty-five was a time

when most Americans felt there was a right side to the war

in Vietnam and a wrong side, and clearly we were on the side of right; this was before the weekly death toll underscored color films of bloody battles on the six o'clock news.

"Is that what you believe, Lord Russell, that we are conducting aggressive wars?"

"Yes, you are. It's not that I believe it; it's plain fact. You're conducting an aggressive war in Vietnam. And you're on your way to conducting a similar war in the Congo."

I was stunned, on America's behalf, at the charge.

"Aren't they protective skirmishes?"

He slapped his fist on his chair's armrest.

"*No!* Now, look, ordinary Americans believe that they are conducting a protective war, protecting non-Communists against these wicked Communists. And that is not the case. They're conducting a war against people who were, until they were attacked, entirely in favor of neutrality. And now they've learned what American troops are. . . ."

Russell's eyes were fiery, his voice increasingly sharp.

". . . The Geneva Congress decided, I think very sensibly . . . that Vietnam, north and south, as one, should have a general election and should have whatever government the general election showed the country wanted. The Americans were not part of the Geneva Conference but did announce when it arrived at its decisions that they would support it on the whole. They sent, first, advisers to South Vietnam, and the advisers sent back word to America that the country was not in a state where a general election was possible. . . . They [Americans] then sent troops to advise the advisers, and they made friends with the tiniest minority of people in Vietnam. They set them up as a puppet government, and about nine-tenths of the population disliked this puppet government. So they put the peasants into strategic villages where they were prisoners, where they were exposed to forced labor, where they had *no* freedom, where they had to do as they were told, and where they were from time to time murdered whenever a soldier felt like it. Now, Sir Robert Menzies, in 115 sending off troops to support this regime, said they were going to defend one of the 'frontiers of human freedom.' Well, now what do you think happens in South Vietnam? What sort of human freedom do you think there is? Who gets the freedom? *Well,* I'll tell you. This is a quotation from a paper in Dallas. Dallas is generally not considered in the forefront of revolution. . . .

"It says: 'Supposedly the purpose of the fortified villages is to keep the Viet Cong out. Barbed wire denies entrance and exit. Vietnamese farmers are forced at gunpoint into these virtual concentration camps. Their homes, possessions and crops are burned. In the province of Cantong some villagers were led into the town square, their stomachs were slashed, their livers extracted and put on display. These victims were women and children. In another village expectant mothers were invited to the square by government forces to be "honored." Their stomachs were ripped open and their unborn babies removed.'

"I could read you any number of extracts from any number of newspapers, saying *this* (he slaps the newspaper article) is what America is doing. *This* is the action of America. *This* is its war for liberty. And I think it's the most disgraceful thing I've ever heard of. Horrible! That they should take these innocent people who don't care a damn what government there is, as long as they're left alone, and torture women and children. . . . Apart from these sorts of things, they drop Napalm and other defoliants on people. They issue notices at the villages saying, 'Don't let your children run out, because if you do our helicopters will kill them.' That sort of thing. Most Americans don't *know* that's the sort of war that's going on. If they knew, I think well enough of America to think at least some of them would think it was perhaps rather regrettable. . . .

"They drop Napalm on a *child*. Napalm eats into you. You can't stop it. The children die of it in great agony, terrible agony. That sort of thing is going on all the time."

I sat stunned and sickened by the extract he'd read from the Dallas newspaper; I couldn't believe such an article hadn't caused a national scandal.

"I'm amazed that there was an investigation and this was printed in the Dallas paper . . . Americans have great conscience about that, sir."

"I don't remember that anybody was punished."

"They should have been."

"They should have been, yes, but I don't think they were."

I asked Lord Russell if he didn't admire America for our freedoms of speech and religion. He bristled once again.

"Those things were commonplace until America took to infringing them. When I was young everyone took them for granted. But since America has come in, it's quite different. Freedom of religion? Well, Communism is a religion. You don't allow freedom to Communism. You made it a criminal act to be a Communist in America [in reference to Senator McCarthy's investigation].

"Communism is a religion?"

"Certainly."

"It's a godless religion, though."

"Yes. So is Buddhism. Everybody admits Buddhism is a religion."

My mind kept flashing back to the atrocities he talked about in Vietnam; I turned the conversation again to the subject of world peace. "The peoples of every country, I am sure, desire nothing but peace."

"That's a slogan," he said, "and I think you should get rid of that slogan. They desire peace, but they desire peace on *their* terms. You see, this recent offer the Prime Minister is making . . . he won't meet the Viet Cong. He wants peace, no doubt. But he wants peace on his terms. That is, he wants the enemy, if you call him the enemy, to give up all his own demands and simply accept the demands of America. That is the sense in which he wants peace."

"On what terms *can* we have peace? Peace at any price?"

"Peace at any price only encourages the other folks who don't want peace. So that is not peace at any price. You've got to have a government, *one* government, for the world. That's the only way you can secure peace. One government 117 for international affairs. The national affairs would have a national government. You shouldn't insist on all national governments being of the same sort. If some people want a monarch, let them have it. If some people want a dictatorship, let them have it. You must let them have whatever they like."

I decided to ask about the CIA. It wasn't a subject many Americans were aware of in 1965, but I asked Russell his feelings about it.

"It's a band of organized assassins. That's what I think about it."

Again he caught me short. I had sought the interview to get a unique perspective on America, but by this time I realized the tape I was bringing back would be shocking to my audience.

"Do we, as mankind," I asked Lord Russell, "deserve to survive?"

"If you use God as judge, *that* God [of the Old Testament] judged at the time of Noah. He thought only eight people deserved to survive. A definite exaggeration." [Laughter.]

". . . But I don't think anybody *deserves* to survive, or hardly anybody. . . . We don't want to be dealt with according to our sins. We should have a very bad time, if so. I'd like to say just a little about how glorious the world might be if only the people would forget that they hate each other."

"That's what we want to hear."

"I think this is a matter where science comes in. Science has made it possible for everybody to be happy, unless they have some incurable disease. It only requires that people should stop hating each other. They should aim at their own happiness and not at the unhappiness of others. You see, all of us spend the bulk of our income and the bulk of our energies on making other people miserable."

"Lord Russell, let me leave you with one quote—of Thornton Wilder's. He was the one who said, 'Governments should be small and funny.' Do you agree?"

118

"Yes. And I should point out that the whole armed might of Monaco is on my side."

Immediately upon our return to the States we checked out the article in the Dallas newspaper Russell had quoted from. It turned out to be a "letter to the editor" written by a Vietnamese businessman, and not a piece by an investigative journalist. Still, the effect of Lord Russell's reading it on the air was devastating.

We played the interview into our show, and the studio audience was grumbling when it was over; some booed. I read a prepared statement: "Many of you, I'm certain, disagree with what Lord Russell had to say. I know I did. You are perhaps shocked and angry, not only at him but at me for providing him the platform of this show on which to make his remarks. But nothing would be easier for me than to book this show with people who have ideas that are carbon copies of my own, or no ideas at all. But I don't think it's an easy world or that my primary responsibility on this program is to take it easy. You'll continue on this show to see people of every persuasion who have hard things to say, and I don't think you can get at any truth without hammering out on the anvil of everyone's right to disagree. I believe the vast majority of Americans are committed to that principle."

As soon as the show aired I heard from hundreds of Americans who *weren't* committed to the principle of free speech. I received letters and telegrams labeling me a Communist, traitor and antireligious crusader. Even members of the national press lashed out at me, including my old friend Bob Considine, who contended I shouldn't provide a platform for such outrageously anti-American statements at a time when our country faced an internal struggle because of the war. It was as if *I* had attacked America. (The funny part about Bob Considine's article was that Bob's son, who worked as a cameraman on my show, caught hell from his dad, too.) Can you imagine the outcry that would be generated by the press if I went on the air and suggested certain columnists not write articles about Vietnam because 119 it was too sensitive an issue? I would have had to wear a flak jacket to work if I did that.

But there is no denying it was good for the show to be the center of controversy.

We couldn't get away from the Vietnam war in the sixties, either on television or in our daily lives. United Press White House correspondent Merriman Smith became a regular guest on my show, just as he'd been when I was with NBC. It shook us all when his eldest son, Merriman, Jr., was sent to Vietnam as a soldier and was killed in a helicopter accident. That was a turning point in my own attitude toward the war; it became evident to me how futile and wasteful our military efforts in Vietnam were. Because Merriman was close to President Johnson and Vice President Humphrey, the death of his son cast a pall upon the White House. I think it was the first Vietnam death of a boy the President knew personally. There was a private funeral in Washington on a rainy day. At the cemetery I stood across the grave from President Johnson, and in his face saw the awful responsibility a President carries. There were no reporters there at the cemetery, but because I was a broadcaster President Johnson looked at me with a complex, almost stern, expression, as if he felt I was judging him, holding him responsible for the war and young Merriman's death. And I remember the compassion in the face of Vice President Humphrey, and the quiet, compassionate tone of his voice when he spoke to Merriman.

Several months later I attended with Merriman the annual Gridiron dinner in Washington, where Vice President Humphrey delivered the keynote address. Afterward we went to a party hosted by *Look* magazine. All the well-known columnists and journalists were there, along with the owners of *Look*, the Cowles family. The Washington media power structure was out in force. When Mr. Humphrey arrived, flashbulbs started popping and everyone wanted to get in a few words with the Vice President. He noticed Merriman and me standing in a corner talking with

Merriman's youngest son, Timmy, and he worked his way

over to us. We congratulated him on his speech; then Merriman introduced Tim.

"I haven't met you before, Tim," the Vice President said, "but I'm very glad to meet you now. In fact, I would like to talk with you in private for a few minutes if I may."

So while Merriman and I stood there with our mouths open and America's media heavies watched enviously, the Vice President of the United States took young Tim Smith to a quiet corner of the hotel suite for what appeared to be an earnest conversation.

For fifteen minutes Tim spoke with Mr. Humphrey, then they shook hands and returned to the party.

Tim didn't say a word about it when he rejoined us. Here were the dean of the White House journalists and an inquisitive talk-show host both trying to keep their mouths shut and let Tim Smith make the first move.

Finally, on the way home, Merriman asked, "Tim, I know it must be personal because you haven't offered any information, but *what* did the Vice President want to talk about for all that time?"

Still staring out the window at the rain, Tim answered, "He wanted to talk about Merriman, Dad. Mr. Humphrey saw him in 'Nam a few weeks before the accident. I guess Mr. Humphrey had made a point of looking him up to say hello, and he wanted to tell me all the things they talked about."

Halfway through Tim's answer I saw tears in Merriman's eyes. There was nothing else to say.

We drove home in silence.

A few years later, as a Senator, Hubert Humphrey guested on my show. We were in the middle of a discussion of his most recent Senate bill when I suddenly remembered the story about the *Look* magazine party and Tim Smith. I said, "I know you are a great champion of civil rights, Senator, and have done much for improving the life of the common man in this country. But one thing I saw you do truly stunned me. It happened a few years ago. . . . He looked at me cautiously, the way all politicians 121 do when caught off guard. I told the story about Tim Smith.

When I finished I saw tears in Mr. Humphrey's eyes. "Yes," he said, "now I remember that."

For years Merriman Smith let his son's death eat away at him. One day he went to the Pentagon and looked up the official report on his son's death. It was a frightening account. A few days later he called me in my dressing room. He told me about looking up the awful report, then we talked of family and friends and exchanged news. It was time for me to do my show, and Merriman said he was taking his family out for Chinese food.

After the show Julann called me. From her voice I knew something was wrong. She called to tell me Merriman Smith had put a gun to his head and killed himself an hour ago.

To me, Merriman's death seemed like one more useless casualty of the Vietnam war.

Bertrand Russell's allegations about atrocities in Vietnam and the use of assassination by the CIA as a political tool, which sounded so inflammatory and unsubstantiated to us in 1965, proved in later years to be sadly close to the truth.

In order to keep my credibility as an interviewer I try to keep my political opinions private. But on the issue of Vietnam I offered the opinion that we should have held a national referendum on whether to fight it out or get out. The war was tearing our country apart from within, not to mention the horrors it was causing in Indochina; it was an issue too large for a President who wanted America to "save face." I said on my show, Let us vote. But we didn't, and the war dragged on.

By 1969, when "The Merv Griffin Show" was on CBS, network officials warned me that too many guests were speaking against the war, and we should offer more guests stating support of our military efforts. But responsible
122 spokesmen in favor of the war were hard to find; I

suggested to CBS *they* find the hawks and I'd be glad to put them on. I didn't hear from them on the issue again.

I must admit my show did display a penchant for irritating the Nixon Administration during the sixties. It started in December of 1967, before Nixon formally announced his candidacy but clearly was preparing to jump into the New Hampshire primary. We invited him to the show, specifying that there were to be no "out of bounds" areas in our questioning. This is not necessary to stipulate with most guests; but politicians like to set ground rules for their appearances and I don't like to work that way. (The extreme example of such a situation came later, in 1972, when Senator Thomas Eagleton was selected by George McGovern as his running mate on the Democratic ticket. The day Tom Eagleton was to appear on our show the story of his being under a psychiatrist's care broke. He called and said he would still do the show as long as I didn't ask about the story. Of course I would have looked like a village idiot if I had interviewed him and never asked about one of the major news stories of the year; we told him no restrictions or no interview. He relented and gave me a personal, moving show.)

Nixon said all questions were fair game. However, on the day of the taping, Bob Howard, a comedy writer who had worked on my staff and was then in Nixon's employ, sent me a list of jokes Mr. Nixon wanted to be set up for. I wasn't about to play straight man to a Presidential candidate, and besides, I knew Nixon didn't have the verbal dexterity to make the jokes come off as unrehearsed. Most politicians coming to our show have comedy writers in their entourage, but I couldn't ever remember having a request to feed them jokes. So I dismissed that idea and Nixon went along with my decision.

Preceding Nixon on the program was David Susskind, who was as anxious as I to hear what Mr. Nixon would have to say. When the interview started it became clear, as is so often the case, that Nixon was carefully prepared for 123 each of my questions. But when we moved to the subject of Democratic strength at the polls, things changed.

David asked Mr. Nixon how he expected to oust the incumbent Democrats when such a disparity existed between the number of registered Republicans and registered Democrats.

Nixon was prepared for that one, too. "I'm sure the same situation would happen that happened in the nineteen-sixty Presidential election with Mr. Kennedy. Many disgruntled Democrats came over and voted for me on the Republican ticket."

Susskind was prepared, too. "Yes, Mr. Nixon, but didn't a Michigan state study prove that many of those crossover voters were religious bigots?"

Nixon's eyes flashed angrily, and for a moment I thought he would leap at Susskind. Then he regained control of himself and launched into a heated challenge of Susskind's statement. Obviously, and for the first time that evening, his remarks were extemporaneous. We were seeing a rare side of Mr. Nixon, unrehearsed, speaking from the heart; he came close to brilliance.

When he finished we went to commercial.

Nixon was still steaming; he wouldn't even look at Susskind. "I'd like to leave, Merv."

"If you leave during commercial people will know you've had an awful disagreement, and that you walked out on it."

"How do we work it then? Because I really do want to leave."

When the stage manager cued us back into show, I announced Mr. Nixon had another speaking engagement to get to. He waved to the crowd and left hurriedly.

Backstage, he was still bristling. Storming down the hallway to his car, flanked by aides, he said, "That son of a bitch. It's much too early in the campaign to get into conversations like that."

Next morning Nixon's press representative, Herb Klein, 124 called me, sounding much too cheerful. I knew a request was coming. "Merv, about your interview with Mr. Nixon —we would like to edit it, along with you, of course."

"Herb, we never do that."

"Mr. Nixon would like to, if you would make an exception."

"I'm sure he would, but he agreed to come on the show without restrictions. Fair is fair. Just like in politics."

"But, Merv, Mr. Nixon is in a sensitive . . ."

"Herb, listen to me for a second. I sit out there every night and I've listened to all of them. And that's the best interview I've seen Nixon give on a talk show, and you know why? Because he showed genuine emotion. You're a public-relations expert. Come over to my studio and watch the tape. Just do that."

He did. Several times. Then he called me. "Merv, don't touch that interview."

Three weeks later *Life* magazine called. They were doing a piece on Nixon, and he had recommended that they get a transcript of his interview with me.

Evidently Nixon liked our theater, because when it came time to film campaign commercials his committee booked studio time there. I used to amuse myself by sitting in my dressing room and watching the monitor while the commercials were being taped.

One afternoon a young writer from *TV Guide* by the name of Joe McGinniss was interviewing me in the dressing room when the monitor caught his eye.

"What's that all about?"

"Mr. Nixon has rented the studio to shoot some commercials."

Joe couldn't believe what he was seeing. Nixon's media people had assembled a group of phony constituents chosen to look like real heartland Americans. They were given prepared questions for which Mr. Nixon had prepared answers. If the director thought the exchange might appear phony, he reshot it until it looked spontaneous.

By the time I finished explaining the process to Joe McGinniss, he'd forgotten all about the Merv Griffin story. 125

"Hey, Merv, do you think I could get down there in the studio?"

"It's a closed set. They probably don't know I can see what's going on in this monitor. I'd have to take you down there myself."

"Would you?"

He was so excited about it, I thought, Why not?

I had met the Secret Service agents with Nixon, and I introduced Joe to them, and to a few of the campaign officials. Joe is a gregarious Irishman who makes friends fast, and he managed to get himself invited to come back for the rest of the week and watch the commercials. Then he went on the road with the campaign. Nixon's staff all thought him a fine young Irish lad who would write glowing prose about the next President.

He did write a book, a best seller, in fact, called *The Selling of the President,* which detailed how Nixon manipulated the media during his campaign to dispel his old image and win back the confidence of the electorate. When the book hit the best-seller lists all over America it sent Nixon's staff into disarray. If his press relations were shaky *before* the book, publication of McGinniss' research sent shock waves through the President's staff. When they started tracing back the appearance of Joe McGinniss on the campaign trail, wouldn't you know somebody finally remembered it was another damned Irishman by the name of Merv Griffin who'd introduced him? I was told television sets all over the White House immediately went to the "off" button when my show came on the screen.

9

A WEEK DIDN'T GO BY in the sixties that we weren't contacted by at least one dissident group wanting national television exposure. One group offered to clandestinely arrange an interview in Algeria with Black Panther fugitive Eldridge Cleaver, but I turned it down in fear of inadvertently leading authorities to Cleaver's hideaway. Another group literally seized air time on my show by standing up at a prearranged signal and blowing shrill Mau Mau whistles. A spokesman for the group alleged we weren't using enough black jazz musicians on the show, a charge that simply wasn't true. I also pointed out to the group they picked a poor day to disrupt the show, because my guests were Dick Gregory and the ambassador from an emerging African nation.

One "invitation" I did accept came from a group of young American Indians who had taken over Alcatraz, the island prison in San Francisco Bay. The Indians cited a treaty which stated that all Federal lands abandoned by the U.S. government reverted to Indian ownership. Newspapers around the world carried the story on page one, but no one could get an interview—nothing more than a list of demands.

My crew and I arrived by boat at Alcatraz' landing at the agreed-upon hour and were greeted by a small group of stony-faced youths wearing war paint and ragged clothes. Their leader, David Lynch, looked like he stepped out of Central Casting. His features were spare and handsome, 127 his long, thick black hair was held in place by a colorful headband; he looked at us with dark, icy eyes. The Indians took us on a tour of the island, outlining their complaints against the U.S. government as we walked. I detected a sense of infighting among the leaders and suspected their occupation wouldn't last much longer. It would have been difficult to find fault with the logic of their arguments— the treaties had been broken—but I also felt an unspoken realization on their part about the futility of trying to turn back the clock. They knew they couldn't win their war, but wanted the nation's ear just the same.

When the tour ended and we loaded our equipment, six of the Indians decided to ride back to the San Francisco wharf with us. The Alcatraz takeover was major news, so all those sitting in the restaurants on Fisherman's Wharf dropped their forks when they saw us coming. It looked like Merv Griffin was being brought in for ransom. We hopped out near Scoma's Restaurant, where I planned to eat and visit my old friend Joe Scoma. I invited the Indians to join me. The idea of a hot meal sounded pretty good to them, but they were worried about being thrown out. "The owner's a friend of mine," I told them "He'll be glad to have you. San Francisco loves a good argument." When we walked through the doors, the place stopped dead; you could hear fans whirring in the kitchen. The Indians were dressed in their feathers and headbands and the diners didn't know what to expect from them. Joe Scoma waved to me from across the restaurant. I waved back, then turned to the Indians and shouted, "All right, *take the restaurant!*" For a moment the patrons went into shock. But Joe started laughing, and I said to him, "Do I know how to make an entrance, or don't I, Joe?"

Dinner was on the house that night.

The takeover of Alcatraz fizzled out a few days after we left and the Indians dropped out of the news for almost a year. Then one morning on the way to work I heard a report of an attempted Indian takeover of Ellis Island in New York's harbor. The broadcast didn't carry many details, other than that Dr. Spock had been involved. An hour after I arrived at the office our receptionist called me. "Mr. Griffin, the hall down here is full of Indians."

"What?"

"Yes, sir. I believe they are . . . *real* Indians."

"What are they doing in our office?"

"They'd like to see you."

"Just ask if one of them is named David Lynch."

She did and I heard David speak up.

"All right, send 'em up."

A dozen kids festooned in leather vests, jeans and war paint swarmed into my office; a couple of them grabbed phones immediately and started making calls to the press. I put up my hands, "No, wrong, put down the phones. I'm not Dr. Spock and you're not going to use my office as headquarters. David, it's nice to see you again. Sit down and we'll talk."

"Merv, we messed up the takeover this morning and we've gotta do something. What are we gonna do?"

"Rent an airplane, parachute out and scream 'Geronimo!' over Manhattan. Look, David, cool it awhile. Let this thing blow over."

"We have to think of something."

"Try something more responsible."

"That doesn't work. No one pays attention. We should go back and take over the island."

"I'm sure Federal marshals are waiting out there by now, so I'd take it easy if I were you."

I sent out for hamburgers and milk shakes and by the time they were through eating they were more interested in seeing the sights of Manhattan than in reclaiming it. Except for David. He stayed around the office all afternoon, venting his frustration at being unable to get the ear of Government officials. Once people acquired power, he told me, they became insensitive and unapproachable; he felt America was headed for hell in a handcart.

"If that's the way you feel, David, let me make you an offer. My wife and I are giving a cocktail party tonight and 129 there'll be quite a few prominent people stopping by. Why don't you come and meet a few of them? You might be surprised."

"I don't go to cocktail parties. I've never been to a cocktail party, and I wouldn't know what to do at one."

"Just order a drink and start talking. Come with a good attitude, leave the rhetoric home and we'll see what happens."

David left and I went down to the studio to do my show and forgot about Indians, politics and cocktail parties. By the time I got home I didn't think to mention to Julann I'd added another name to the guest list.

We were giving the cocktail party in honor of John Lindsay, who was running for reelection as Mayor of New York. John is the only candidate I've publicly endorsed, simply because I felt strongly about New York in the sixties needing a young, fresh image; though a series of strikes and the constant battle with government bureaucracy had tempered John's enthusiasm for the job, I was again supporting his candidacy in 1970.

I was introducing John around to some of my guests when the doorbell rang and I saw the butler showing David Lynch into the entry; it took me two seconds to realize I'd really made a blunder. All my favorite candidate needs is to be seen hanging out with radicals at cocktail parties. John Lindsay saw the direction of my gaze. His first reaction was curiosity. "Merv, I didn't know you were friends with any Indians." Then as John looked over David's buckskin outfit and saw the hunting knife dangling from his belt, he put a hand on my shoulder. "Now, Merv . . . he is *not* one of the Indians who tried . . ."

"Listen to me a minute, John . . ."

"You wouldn't do this to me . . . this is a joke, isn't it? . . ."

"I forgot all about it, John. I forgot I even invited him, he's one of the kids I interviewed . . ."

"For God's sake, Merv, I'm *running*. If the press picks this up . . ."

"This is a cocktail party. No press. And he's a nice kid, sincere, just a little frustrated is all."

I went to the entry and greeted David, quietly suggesting he leave the hunting knife in the closet.

"What am I doing here? These people hate me . . ."

"Just relax. I've got a surprise for you. Mayor Lindsay is here. I'm going to take you over and introduce you to him. Now, don't give any big speeches. Remember, he's off duty. Do some listening for a change and see what you can find out."

First I introduced David to Julann and Mary Lindsay, then I brought him over to the Mayor. David and John squared off and looked each other over, the politician and the radical, one wearing a three-piece suit, the other in deerskin. They looked like a picture right off the front page of the *Daily News*.

"So you're the young man who led the attack on Ellis Island this morning."

"I'm the one," David said.

"Poor Dr. Spock was stranded out in the bay with a dead motor in his boat."

"It wasn't a good morning."

The Mayor reflected a few moments, looking down at David's moccasins. He perked up suddenly. "Ellis Island —that's Federal property, isn't it, David?"

David nodded.

"Well I guess it's Mr. Nixon's problem, then. But tell me about it anyway. . . ."

Five minutes later I look over at David and John and see them chatting away like it's a high-school reunion. It was the first time I'd ever seen David smile. Pretty soon there was a crowd around the two of them.

Even my parties turned into talk shows.

Another year went by before I heard again from David. He called me from Wounded Knee in the midst of the Indian takeover there.

"Merv, we need your help."

"In what sense?"

"We need money, and I have to be honest, we need it to buy guns. This is the real thing. We have to make a stand."

"Do you want some advice?"

"We don't need advice, we need guns. It's the only thing the Government understands."

"Then I'm sorry, David. I can't help you."

John Lindsay brought me the idea for one of our most unusual shows. This was spring of 1968 and John was worried about the coming summer, having spent much of the previous summer trying to keep Harlem from erupting in riots. One quality I admired in John was the sincerity of his attitude toward New York; he was mayor to *all* the city, not just to the business community. Many steamy summer evenings John walked the streets of Harlem and let the people living there know he was their mayor, too.

We met at Sardi's for lunch one day in May, and he asked what I planned to do for New York come summer. I wasn't sure what he meant.

"Merv, I'm worried about Harlem. You've got a lot of viewers living up there, and if you did something for them it could mean a lot to the city."

"What if I do a show from there?"

"A television show?"

"Right from the street. We'll build a stage and do a show. You give me your assistance and I'll bring in a bunch of entertainers and put on a special show. But you've got to let me pick the street. This can't be a pure public-relations job for the city. We have to show Harlem like it is, right from the roughest street."

"You choose the street and my office will do whatever you ask."

We started work immediately and within the week settled on a date in August and confirmed the guests: Muhammad Ali, Gladys Knight and the Pips, Burt Lancaster (who was born in Harlem), Godfrey Cambridge, James Brown and Mahalia Jackson. Muhammad Ali came into 132 town a week early to help us work out the details for the show. He was battling the Government over his refusal to fight in Vietnam ("I ain't got nothin' against no Viet Cong") and I offered him the platform of our show to give his side of the story; the networks were giving him short shrift. I suppose he appreciated the gesture on my part, because he worked hard for the Harlem show and we could not have done it so well without him.

You wouldn't have believed the heat the night of the taping. It was one of those New York summer nights when all the fresh air is sucked right out of the city and you're left with a hot, wet blanket of air so thick you feel like you're walking under water. With ten thousand people jamming the streets around our stage we were looking at a potentially explosive situation. I introduced Muhammad Ali and the crowd roared until windows rattled all around us; his every word and gesture brought cheers. Mayor Lindsay, being the lone politician on stage, heard a weak welcome; the crowd wanted soul singer James Brown. Midway through the show we received a call backstage from Brown; he wasn't coming to the show. Already the crowd was growing restless waiting for him, and I knew we'd have a riot on our hands if he didn't show. I grabbed the phone and asked him what the problem was.

"John Lindsay snubbed me at the airport one time. So I'm not comin'."

"This show isn't for John Lindsay, we're doing it for the community here. We're just trying to let them know a few people in show business care about what's going on here, and we're giving the rest of the country a look at it. Forget John Lindsay."

"Listen, I'll come, but I want Lindsay to send police cars to escort my limousines from my house, and I want all those police cars to have their lights flashing and sirens going, all the way to the stage."

"You'll get the police cars."

By the time Brown's screaming, flashing fleet of cars arrived, the crowd was in a frenzy; when he walked onstage a mass scream filled the air and the crowd surged toward 133 the stage, arms raised and swaying. The scene looked like a great religious festival. He did three songs, then jumped into the back of an equipment truck, which was parked flush with the stage, and the truck blasted away with a police escort.

Harlem held together that August, and the mail we received on the show indicated it was the first look at an inner city by thousands of viewers around America.

Another of our most-watched shows of the sixties came out of a cocktail party given by my press agent, Henry Dorman. First let me tell you one thing about Henry; his public image was better than that of most of his clients. He had a Fifth Avenue apartment furnished with priceless antiques, a beautiful wife and children right out of a storybook, and a wardrobe of tailored suits accented by walking stick and homburg. This guy was a class act. Unfortunately, he and I didn't always agree on the nature of *my* public image. He planted column items like "Merv Griffin was seen buying a pair of $600 snakeskin shoes." I'd call him and say, "Henry, please don't plant items like that. I wouldn't wear a pair of six-hundred-dollar shoes if I had all the money in the world."

"But, Merv, Nelson Rockefeller wears them."

That was always his answer.

". . . Merv Griffin has just relined his den with priceless Tibetan parchment . . ."

"Nelson Rockefeller."

He drove me crazy. But he did give fascinating dinner parties.

Julann and I arrived late for this particular party. The living room was already full. I looked for a familiar face and spotted Walter Cronkite; who can think of a more familar face than Walter's? We said hello to Walter and Betsy, and he introduced us to Ambassador so-and-so—I didn't catch the name at first. After a while the Ambassador and I started chatting, and I asked where he was from.

"Hyde Park, Long Island, " he answered in his thick accent.

I laughed. "I meant, what country do you represent?"
Reaching into his pocket he pulled out a card and ceremoniously handed it to me. It read:

PROFESSOR NIKOLAI FEDORENKO
AMBASSADOR TO THE UNITED NATIONS
REPRESENTING
THE UNION OF SOVIET SOCIALIST REPUBLICS

My first Communist! "I'm sorry I didn't recognize you, Mr. Ambassador, because I know your name quite well."

"I know you too, Griffin," he said gravely. "I know you very well."

"That's a surprise."

"I watch your show quite often."

By now Walter is leaning over to hear what is going on.

I said, "Are you serious, Mr. Ambassador?"

He nodded slowly, "I know Treacher, I know Lindsay the orchestra man. I know the guests you put on your show. You see, my daughter was here visiting for the summer and she became, as they say, 'hooked,' on your television show. Now I must send her special summaries of what is being said and what is happening on your show. She is what you call a 'fan.' "

"I'm flattered, Mr. Ambassador."

"You probably want me to be on your show."

"That would be too much to hope for in this political climate. Would you consider it?"

Now Walter is really wilting next to me.

"We will consider it this evening," the Ambassador said, tightening his thick dark eyebrows. "We will see how the evening goes. Now I want to ask you questions about your show to tell my daughter."

From the questions he asked about the technical setup, the music and the guests, I knew he did indeed watch the show. While we talked, a small man in a dark suit lurked around us; the Ambassador referred to him as "my commissar." Right out loud the Ambassador said, "You are a 135 bad spy. Mingle with guests. Listen to what is being said and tell me."

The little man moved off to mingle.

At the dinner table Julann and I were seated near Walter and Betsy Cronkite and the Ambassador's wife, who resembled a blond Kewpie doll. She didn't speak English as well as her husband, but seemed to understand the conversation anyway, because she was always laughing. The Ambassador, seated at the other end of the table, kept peering down at us because we were laughing, and the people around him kept asking serious questions. As dessert arrived I told a joke that brought down our end of the table, and the Ambassador couldn't stand it any longer.

"Griffin, I see you're having a good time down there. What is it that is so funny?"

I said, "Your wife just asked for political asylum."

You've never heard a room stop dead so fast.

Walter lowered his spoon from his mouth and stared at me in disbelief. Mrs. Fedorenko looked like I had stabbed her in the heart. All of a sudden it was the cold war come to life. Everyone looked down at his plate, waiting for the Ambassador's response. And in the meantime my entire life was flashing in front of me.

In an explosion of motion the Ambassador threw his arms in the air, leaned back in his chair and burst out laughing, his whole body shaking with delight. "You see?" he boomed, "You see? What do you expect? He is the same devil in person as on television."

We all sank back in our chairs and laughed politely. Talk about life after death . . .

After dinner the Ambassador said, "Griffin, there will be a call. I don't know when, but we will call you. I will come to your studio and do your show the same day I call. It must be that way. You will be allowed to ask whatever you like."

"I'll wait for the call."

Walter said, "Now do you see the limitation of doing hard news on television? We simply haven't the time these 136 kinds of men want on a TV show. He wants to come on your show and make his points, take his time. He doesn't like being interrogated by reporters. We have to pop him the tough questions right away because that's all the time our show allows for, and that hurts the answers. I envy you your format."

Julann and I rode the elevator down with Mr. and Mrs. Fedorenko and his "commissar." A crowd of cloak-and-dagger types wearing overcoats and hats pulled low over their eyes were skulking around the lobby.

I remarked loudly, "Mr. Ambassador, are these yours?"

"No, Griffin," he boomed, "these are *yours.*"

Fedorenko's limousine pulled away, and three unmarked cars roared off behind him.

I really thought America could come up with a better bunch of spies than that lot.

I told Bob Shanks about my booking, but he didn't believe the Russian government would allow the Ambassador to make an appearance. Tension over Vietnam was running high between our two countries, and Bob felt the Russians would fear a slip of the tongue by their Ambassador.

But just one week after the party the Ambassador's office called me and said, "Tonight's the night."

A bustle of aides and security officers signaled Fedorenko's arrival. And spies from *our* side started showing up and standing around the back of the theater. You'd think they would all get sick of following each other around town.

Fifteen minutes before showtime Fedorenko asked to see me. He was pacing in the hall outside his dressing room.

"Ah, Griffin, now you can tell me what you are going to ask on show?"

"Mr. Ambassador, you told me there were no conditions on the interview."

I was afraid he might say something interesting backstage and then decide he shouldn't talk about it on air; I wanted to get him right out on the stage and let the chips fall.

"You won't tell me what you are going to ask?"

"It would ruin the spontaneity. I've done a lot of research. I know what to ask."

He looked toward the doorway like he was thinking of leaving; then he cracked a wide smile. "I just wanted to test you under pressure, Griffin. Let us begin the show."

And I'll tell you what—he was a good guest. Didn't dodge a question, never wrapped an answer in rhetoric, just said what he felt. We discussed Russia's nuclear policy, its attitude toward Vietnam and China and its economic policies; he bragged a bit about his country, but you expect that from an Ambassador.

And he knew how to charm the audience. He'd seen guests on my program show pictures of their families, so he took out snapshots of his wife and daughter. And he held up a copy of his political science text, just as he'd seen other authors do on my show. The texts he showed were Chinese editions, however, so I suggested to him not to expect a leap in sales.

Only once did he lose his temper—when I remarked the Chinese "Red Guard" reminded me of youth groups in Nazi Germany. Fedorenko whirled and said staring directly into the camera, "Communists are not fascists, and Communists do not *act* like fascists."

The most talked-about moment of the interview turned out to be Fedorenko showing the pictures of his family: a man who thinks about his wife and kids isn't a man willing to jump into war. By showing those pictures he cut through layers of propaganda we heard in those days about the awful Russians; he accomplished in two minutes what a thousand speeches could never do.

Now let me tell you a short story which distills what *I* think of Communists. A few weeks after the interview with Fedorenko, I and several friends visited the World's Fair in Montreal, and the Russians invited me to have lunch at their pavilion. I didn't want to become known as Russia's best friend, but a little lunch couldn't hurt.

138   There were six in my group and we were joined by ten

Russian officials. The entire time I was trying to eat, a correspondent from Radio Moscow kept pushing a microphone in my face and asking me questions about my interview with Fedorenko.

"Which of your questions to the Ambassador were supplied to you by your government?"

"My government had nothing to do with the interview."

"But your government must have called you after interviewing Lord Russell (those Russians really do their homework) when he spoke so critically of America. Were you not reprimanded for that?"

"By some members of the press, yes, but I never heard from the government."

"You were not admonished?"

"No. The only time I hear from the government is when they want a spokesman for some government agency to make an appearance."

All the Russians leaned forward at this statement. "And what do you tell the government when they make such a request?"

"That the people they recommend are usually boring and I don't want them on my show."

When we finished the interview, they brought *me* the entire bill for lunch, including the Russians'.

Some Communists.

Several months later I was at some official function in New York, and ran into Ambassador Fedorenko there. We were talking when Governor Rockefeller strolled by and said hello. He hadn't met the Ambassador so I performed the introduction. The Governor smiled. "Well, well, well, my first big Communist. How do you do?"

Fedorenko bowed and replied, "And you are my first big, *big* capitalist."

The next week I received a case of Russian vodka from the Ambassador, which made up for his comrades in Montreal.

10

ANY TIME I am interviewed the one question I can count on being asked is, "Who are your best guests; who are your worst?" Foreign actresses and writers are usually the best —foreign actresses because they aren't running public-relations campaigns like most American actresses—they are more open and say what's on their mind; writers like James Michener, Irwin Shaw, Gore Vidal and Jimmy Breslin, because they brim with ideas an interviewer can get his teeth into. Politicians are usually my worst interviews. They've heard every question you can think of, and call upon prepared answers meant to keep the voters happy, which makes for boring television. But in the sixties I interviewed plenty of politicians, simply because there were so many hot issues to discuss. Of all those politicians, one man stands out in my mind as the most genuine—Bobby Kennedy.

I met him by coincidence. Our apartment at 135 Central Park West was on the same floor as that of Jean and Bill Vanden Heuvel. Jean became one of New York's most interesting hostesses; she gave the famous party for Leonard Bernstein and the Black Panthers, which was later the basis for a best-selling book, *Radical Chic*, by journalist Tom Wolfe. Ours and Jean's were the only apartments on the floor, and since we didn't have numbers or nameplates on the doors, Jean's guests were always knocking at our door.

One Sunday in 1966 Jean and Bill were having several 140 of the Kennedy clan over for cocktails, prior to dinner in celebration of Teddy Kennedy's birthday. Julann, Tony and I were spending the evening relaxing in front of TV. About seven o'clock the doorbell rang and I trotted out to answer it in my T-shirt and Levi's. I opened the door and there stood Bobby and Ethel Kennedy along with Pierre Salinger. Ethel was in a formal gown and Bobby and Pierre were wearing tuxedos. I knew Pierre from my show, but it took me a moment to recognize Bobby and Ethel, and they me.

They looked up and down at my jeans and T-shirt and Pierre said, "Merv . . . ?"

I looked at my watch. "You're very late for the party—and why are you dressed like *that*? No one else is."

They looked nervously past me to see who was in the apartment.

Pierre winked. "Aren't you going to invite us in?"

"No."

"Why?"

"Because the Vanden Heuvels live across the hall."

Ten minutes later my bell rings again. This time it's John Kenneth Galbraith.

I did my act again, then pointed him in the right direction.

Arthur Schlesinger, Jr., was the next caller. After about an hour of this I could have written down their entire guest list. Finally Jean came over and asked Julann and me to come over for a cocktail. We didn't feel like getting dressed up, but we went for one drink and I did get a chance to talk with Bobby and extend an invitation to him to do my show.

He made the appearance in the fall of 1967 when he was readying to run for the Presidency. His schedule called for him to arrive about a half-hour into the show, and by the time he reached the studio, after a full day of meetings, speeches and handshaking, he felt worn out, and sent word through Bob Shanks that he'd like a word with me at the next commercial.

"I'm a little worn out, Merv," he told me, "I've been 141

pounding the pavement all day. That's a large audience out there. . . ."

"But I've already announced you're the next guest, Bobby."

Then he looked directly into my eyes with that steady gaze of his and asked what I knew about the legislation he currently had in front of the House.

I'd done my homework and described the content of the bills to him.

Bobby smiled and said, "Let's go out there and do it, Merv."

Interviewing Bobby was unlike interviewing any politician in my experience. With most, I watch them reach into their mental file and pull out answer 6-B to go with question 1-A. Not so with Bobby. He didn't mind leaving a few seconds of dead air while he considered his answer; he listened to the questions and *thought* about his answer.

We started out on the state of the country following the trying summer of '67: "Senator, there is rioting, labor unrest, young people revolting . . . what is this country facing?"

"It's difficult to talk in generalities, Merv, but it would seem the situation will continue to grow worse in many of the areas you've indicated. I think the war adds to it . . ." —he shook his head sadly—"the fact that there's violence in the world, and the fact that it is accepted as a way of dealing with human beings, this has an effect on young people and on our country as a whole. . . ."

Then he hit on an issue that I think freshly crystallizes the attitude of many Americans right now.

". . . Another great problem within our country, with all these groups and particularly the young people, is, everything has become so impersonal. Everything is so large that you don't play a role any more, you can't *affect* things. You can't affect what government does, it's so big, so large, and so far away. It spends a great deal of money, but you are just a small cog. You have very little to say about how 142 universities are being run, and what you're being taught.

You're just a number in a large university. In schools you don't have any relationship with the teachers . . . I think that has an effect. . . .

"I think labor unions are so large they've become impersonal. Management is the same way. So for the individual it is difficult for him to associate with anything, anybody or any institution. Therefore he begins to move, perhaps, in a different direction. I think that is really the explanation of the 'hippies.' They've reached the conclusion they can't affect their own lives and they can't affect society. They see terrible things going on within our country and around the world. This distresses them, but they can't *see* their ability to change the course of events. So they turn off. They pull the curtain down and say 'We can't get off the earth but we're going to leave it as much as we can.'

"That's the major problem we have within government. But I think it is the great problem that all of us have in society: How we're going to come back to the idea that the individual is important and that society exists for *him*, government exists for *him*. . . ."

Because of riots in many cities during the past summer, we discussed the "inner city." Bobby had a clear idea of how to put big business to work rebuilding the cities, rather than relying on government welfare programs.

"I don't think the Federal government can do it. What you have to do in the last analysis . . . is realize you're not going to have the *money* to do it. We should face it, we're not going to have guns and butter. We can't fight the war with 2.5 billion dollars every month and do this other thing, too. . . .

"The whole poverty program is equivalent to about three and a half weeks of the war in Vietnam. . . . I therefore think we have to bring the private sector in, the businessmen who have been successful and effective in other areas, and make it attractive for them to invest in the ghetto. I don't think it is sufficient to say to them you should do it from a charitable point of view. They have to report to their stockholders. I think you have to make it attractive 143 through tax credits and in other ways, through tax write-offs, for them to invest in the ghetto. We made it attractive for them to build defense plants. We made it attractive for them to build grain-storage bins. We made it attractive for them to build oil wells. We made it attractive for them to invest in Israel. I think we should do the same for our cities. . . .

"It's much less expensive [to rebuild the ghettoes this way]. We could do housing at a much less expensive rate, dollar for dollar, if we did it in this fashion . . . than if we do it through rent supplements or other housing programs which are not effective and have not been successful, expensive as they may have been. I think it makes all the sense in the world to call upon the private sector to build a factory, build a plant in the ghetto; make it *attractive* for them to do so. If we make it attractive for them to build an oil well or storage bin, why can't we make it attractive for them to do this as well? We've never done it—but I think we have to face the fact that what we've been doing for the last thirty years hasn't been right. There are a lot of Government programs which I support and will continue to support. But Government programs are not enough. It's *not* just a question of putting more money in—that is *not* enough, it's not the answer. But we can do what we've done and supplement it by bringing in the private sector and using their ingenuity, their brains, and their effort in this area."

As Bobby spoke I saw the sincerity of his statements mirrored in his eyes, and the thought occurred to me: Why does he keep a sixteen-hour-a-day schedule, why run around the country making speeches, eating rubbery roast beef and drinking lukewarm coffee, why put himself through the paces of a politician? He'd lost a brother to war, another to an assassin—why did he feel such a driving responsibility toward America? I asked him about this.

He pondered the question and obviously was a bit embarrassed by it. When he answered, his voice was just above 144 a whisper, and he wouldn't look at me or the camera. "I think we [the Kennedys] are extremely lucky. My parents felt we're extremely lucky. They felt since money was not a problem because of what this country had done for us, and because of the ability of my father, we had an obligation to try and repay that . . . we should continue to try throughout our lives to do something for those less well off than we were. . . ." Then Bobby straightened up, eyes twinkling. "In addition," he said, "my father told me to stay busy."

After the show I sat in my dressing room thinking, There was a man who meant what he said, who *could* change the country. Several months later, on that awful day in June of 1968, all the hope came to a terrible halt. I remember that Tony, only eight years old, came running into our bedroom at seven in the morning. He shook me by the shoulder, and Julann said to him, "Tony, go watch the cartoons. Your dad was up late last night, let him sleep."

"You know that President Kennedy guy?" Tony said, waking me, "they shot him."

And I said, "Oh, Tony, that was five years ago."

"No, no. The President Kennedy that comes here. They shot him on the television."

I looked over at Julann, and she flicked on the television set by our bed. There was the camera at the Ambassador Hotel, and there were pictures of Bobby. Most Americans probably felt the same awful, hollow feeling I did at that moment.

Just a few months before that, we'd all been through the death of Martin Luther King. Like Bobby, he'd made an appearance on my show shortly before his death. To this moment I can see Dr. King's eyes. He was the most peaceful man I ever met. As I interviewed him and he spoke of a day when black children and white children would walk together to school, leaving behind the hates and prejudices of their parents, I was struck by the peacefulness of his eyes. Having seen those eyes and talked with Dr. King, and having interviewed and known Bobby Kennedy, made 145 their deaths that much more bitter to me, because I knew firsthand when Martin Luther King said, "I have a dream . . ." and Bobby Kennedy said, "I see a day when . . ." that Dr. King *did* have a dream and Bobby *did* see a day.

Sitting in my host's chair day in and day out, year in and year out, is like having the stream of history flow in front of your door, and it is easy to pick out the truly exceptional people along the way. They were two.

Because everyone, from Shakespearean actors to rock stars, was frothing with issues during the sixties, one of the toughest parts of our job was presenting a balance of opinion. When too many guests spoke out against the war, we heard about it, as I said earlier. Network lawyers sent me memos: "In the past six weeks 34 antiwar statements have been made and only one pro-war statement, by John Wayne. . . ." I shot a memo right back. "Find me someone as famous as Mr. Wayne to speak in favor of the war and we'll book him." The irony of the situation wasn't wasted on me; in 1965 I'm called a traitor by the press for presenting Bertrand Russell, and four years later we are hard-pressed to find *anybody* to speak in favor of the Vietnam war.

Then there was the marijuana issue: "Several guests on your show have talked in favor of marijuana legalization. Please balance. . . ."

Have you ever tried explaining to a corporate lawyer that our show isn't rehearsed, that I don't control what someone might say in conversation? Besides, I explained to them, people were commenting mostly on the severity of marijuana laws, not campaigning for dope smoking.

To get our balance, we went right to Nixon's health officer, Dr. Roger Egeberg, Assistant Secretary of Health, Education and Welfare for Health and Scientific Affairs. He had been personal physician to General Douglas MacArthur and Dean of the University of Southern California School of Medicine, and was now a Government expert on health matters, including the use of drugs. The network was delighted at our choice. Here was a man who would tell the truth about marijuana.

We booked him on the show and I got right to the point.

"Dr. Egeberg, what do you think about the marijuana laws in this country?"

"Ridiculous."

"I beg your pardon?"

'Antiquated and ridiculous. It's foolishness."

In the back of the studio a battery of network lawyers started reeling in their shoes; young people in the audience cheered.

"Now, Dr. Egeberg, I'm not getting the interview I expected to hear from you, being one of the government's top health officials."

"Mr. Griffin, let me tell you the marijuana laws are outright foolishness. Why are we locking up decent American youths? For what crime? Let me give you an example." He told the story of a Vietnam veteran who returned to America with one ounce of pot in his possession, and for this he was arrested and sentenced to five years in prison, leaving his wife to fend for herself and their infant. "Now, does that seem like the American way to you, Mr. Griffin?"

"Well . . . no . . . it certainly doesn't. But you are the Government, Doctor. . . ."

"No, I'm part of the current Administration. And I am the part who has been trying for three months to get an appointment with our Attorney General, Mr. Mitchell, so I can recommend new legislation on this issue. So far I can't even get past his secretary."

My phone rang at four in the morning the night after the show. It was Merriman Smith, calling me from the western White House at San Clemente.

"What the heck went out on your show tonight, Merv?"

"Why?"

"There's hell to pay around here. You had some Government official on."

"Dr. Egeberg."

"Merv, I have to have a transcript of his interview in the morning."

"You don't work for the Government, you're a reporter; who wants the transcript?"

"Nixon's people are putting pressure on me. I've got to do them a favor and get a transcript."

"Let them get their own transcript."

"Then tell me what Dr. Egeberg said."

"Why don't you watch the damn show? You're on it enough."

"Now, come on, Merv, play ball with me. . . ."

I told him about the interview, and Merriman commented, "Between that Joe McGinniss book and this thing, Nixon is going to start cringing whenever your name is mentioned."

A few weeks later Dr. Egeberg's office called to inform me that due to our show Dr. Egeberg got his appointment with John Mitchell, and, after lots of arguing, Mitchell was going to recommend a change in the laws to Congress.

Only once was a political interview actually censored by the network, and they'll never live it down. We booked Yippie radical Abbie Hoffman and he showed up for the interview wearing a shirt network censors judged to look too much like Old Glory; by wearing the shirt, they claimed Abbie was defaming the flag. So, if you can believe this, they used an electronic device in the control room which blacked Abbie's image right off the television screen. On the air it looked like I was interviewing a black hole in the universe, and the black hole was answering in the voice of Abbie Hoffman. We go to commercial, a car advertisment featuring Roy Rodgers and Dale Evans, and Roy is wearing the exact same shirt as Abbie Hoffman.

Ah, the sixties.

11

I SAVED THE STORY of one particular guest I interviewed during those years until last, because she has nothing to do with the cultural revolution or politics of the sixties. Instead, she was the greatest entertainer I've ever seen: Judy Garland.

Growing up I didn't miss one Judy Garland movie. Most of them I watched several times, crying when she cried, laughing when she laughed; I always thought one day I would go to Hollywood and marry her. When I did move to Hollywood in 1953, as a contract actor for Warner Brothers, Judy was there making *A Star Is Born*. Everyone in the show-business community knew her life was awash with demons, imagined and real, and I saw firsthand the mess her life was in one night in Ciro's nightclub.

I was there drinking with several friends, including another of my favorite singers, Peggy Lee. Judy and her husband, Sid Luft, were sitting at the bar, both on the downside of a long night of drinking. The bartender was keeping the place open past the normal 2 A.M. closing just for us.

Judy had an eight o'clock call at the studio and wanted to go home; Sid wanted to stay and drink. She kept telling him how tired she was and how badly she needed sleep to be fresh for the morning's shooting. But Sid ordered more drinks, and when Judy complained again he swung around and threw the back of his hand at her face, catching her square in the jaw and knocking her to the floor. I stood to 149 help but Peggy Lee grabbed my arm. "Stay away from it, Merv. This is what they do. Believe me, I've seen it before." I watched Judy pull herself up to the bar stool, and Peggy eased me back down to my chair.

I was also present for one of her great triumphs. Who could ever forget her first big comeback concert at Carnegie Hall in 1960? Nothing in show business will ever touch it—no Broadway opening, film premiere, nothing. Garland—performer and legend were one that night, and magic. All New York turned out to see her, and Judy left us standing on our chairs, weeping and cheering and totally drained.

In 1963 I met her for the first time, and then only because she had a bone to pick with me. Liza Minnelli had done an interview on my NBC talk show the previous winter. When I asked who her favorite singer was, wink-wink, Liza said, "Ella Fitzgerald." That next summer I was hosting "Hollywood Talent Scouts" at CBS, and Judy was there doing a show. We ran into each other in the hallway and she said, "Merv, I thought that was unfair, what you asked Liza on your show, who her favorite singer was. Liza thought it was unfair, too."

"I hate to tell you this, Judy, but that was a rehearsed answer on Liza's part. It was her idea of a joke."

Judy didn't say anything to that; she nodded and walked away.

After some good years and some bad years for Judy, she called me in 1968 from a private hospital in Boston where, registered under an assumed name, she was drying out from a bad bout with alcohol and drugs.

She said, "I'm getting myself straightened out here, Merv, and I'm going to come to New York. I really need to work. But who's going to hire me? I have no arrangements, Sid's taken them all. I have no wardrobe. I'm down to nothing. But I have to work."

"Then do my show."

"That's what I was calling you about."

"Judy, any time."

150   There was a long pause, then she said, "I meant it when

I said I'm down to nothing, Merv. I don't have a penny. I have enough to get on a train and come to New York."

"Do you want me to have someone meet you at the depot?"

"No, don't do that."

"Then I'll make your hotel reservations for you. We'll get you a suite at the Americana." Judy was famous for running up enormous bills at hotels and leaving them unpaid, so I said, "There will have to be a limit on expenses at the hotel."

"I got ya, Merv. I'll be fine."

"Now, we have to get you something to wear on the show, so I'll have a designer get your sizes and we'll make a gown. We'll get a fur for you."

She started crying. "What am I going to do for music? I don't have one arrangement . . ."

"Judy, Mort Lindsey is my conductor."

Mort had conducted for Judy for several years, as well as for Barbra Streisand; he'd take care of the music.

"Just get yourself on that train and go to the Americana and we'll put you on the show day after tomorrow."

"This means a lot to me, Merv."

"They'll be expecting you at the Americana."

"I'll be there tomorrow."

We made the arrangements with the Americana's manager, called Christian Dior for a gown and alerted Mort Lindsey to write some arrangements for Judy.

Her train arrived late Wednesday night in Manhattan and by the time she reached the Americana the manager was gone and the night manager was on duty. No one had told him about Judy's arrival. When she walked in the door he recognized her immediately and pointed right back at the entrance. "You're not staying here, Miss Garland. You owe a large bill at this hotel and until it is paid you will not be registered here."

She explained to him that "The Merv Griffin Show" had made a reservation for her and the show was paying the bill.

"I don't care who made your reservation. You are not 151

staying here until that bill is paid. That is hotel policy. Now please leave the premises before I have you removed."

She walked back outside and had to bum some change from a passerby in order to make a phone call. Her pride prevented her from calling any of her friends in Manhattan and she didn't have my home number, so she called a friend in Brooklyn and took a subway out there to spend the night.

I arrived at the office in a great mood next morning, anticipating Judy's performance on the show. My first call changed all that. It was Judy and she was in tears. When I got the story out of her I could barely hold the phone, I was so upset. In two seconds I had one of the Americana's owners on the line and told him the cruel situation that had taken place at his hotel. Of course he was very apologetic, but I didn't take another chance with them and booked Judy into the Hilton. Next I messengered over an envelope of cash so she could have a facial, and her hair and nails done. You couldn't send her a check, because the Internal Revenue Service was standing over her shoulder all the time waiting to confiscate any money she made.

By showtime Judy had herself together. She sang two show tunes and the audience gave her a standing ovation. Afterwards she was in tears. She'd proved to herself she still had the magic. And I said to her, "Why don't you take over my show one night while you're here? I'm going to Switzerland for Christmas and I'm taking a few days off to get ready."

She looked shocked. "You'd let me do that?"

"You bet I would. You've done ninety-minute concerts, so just come on the show and sing your brains out, sing "The Man Who Got Away," "Swanee," "Life Is Just a Bowl of Cherries," sing anything and you'll be great. Bring on a few of your friends and interview them. Do whatever you want. Who should we invite to come on with you?"

"Well . . . Liza, of course . . . and Burt Lancaster, we've been friends forever . . . James Mason, he'll do it . . ." and she ticked off the names of friends she adored.

152

What transpired stunned me and will stun you. First we called Liza, who said she absolutely had to be out of town. A famous leading man said, "I wouldn't trust that drunk on the air." Another singer said, "I'll be conveniently busy." It was turndowns all around.

By showtime we had Margaret Hamilton, who had played the wicked witch in *The Wizard of Oz*, and Moms Mabley. Judy did a lot of singing to carry off the show, and of course we never told her the derisive answers of many of the stars we had invited.

Just before leaving for Switzerland I rented out Sybil Burton's Arthur discotheque for a staff Christmas party and invited Judy to join my professional family for the evening. That was a mistake, because she took a few drinks with Mickey Deans, the manager of the club, and called me over to her table. She had Earl Wilson on the phone and said he wanted to talk with me.

"About what?"

"To confirm Mickey and I are getting married."

"Confirm *what*? You just met . . ." I picked up the phone. Earl said, "Merv, is Judy marrying Mickey Deans?"

"I don't know, Earl, I just showed up and that's what they're saying."

And that's what they did, in London a few weeks later. Shortly after that, Judy died.

Most of the people who refused to go on the show with Judy were at her funeral.

PART FOUR

Goodbye Hollywood, Hello New York

1948-1957

12

I WAS TOSSING the dice in 1948 when I left KFRC and home to join Freddy Martin and His Orchestra; here I was, twenty-three years old, making a substantial income and living in my beloved northern California, throwing all that to the winds in the hope of making a mark in Los Angeles and New York. My vision of the Cocoanut Grove and Broadway seemed remote when I boarded the band's bus in San Francisco and high-balled it to the site of my first appearance wtih Freddy's orchestra in Eureka, California. That had to be the longest bus ride of my life; halfway to Eureka I started thinking how much I enjoyed driving my convertible to work each day. But it was goodbye convertible, hello all-night bus rides; when I mentioned to Jean Barry how slow the bus was moving, she said, "Better get used to it, Merv. It never goes any faster."

The ballroom we played in Eureka didn't look anything like the elegant Mural Room of the St. Francis hotel in San Francisco, where I was used to seeing Freddy's band; and the crowd wasn't the champagne-and-society set Freddy attracted in the city. But you know what? I didn't care. It was a thrill to be singing with a big band in front of a live audience.

My big numbers were "Wilhelmina," "Never Been Kissed," "Am I In Love?," "I've Got a Lovely Bunch of Cocoanuts," and an original number appropriate to our profession called "Back on the Bus."

From Eureka, we embarked on a tour of seventy-four

consecutive one-nighters in seventy-four different cities. A typical day meant performing from 9 P.M. until 1 A.M., load the bus, then have supper and hit the road about 3 A.M.; by noon we reached the next stop in time for breakfast and a few hours sleep before heading for the ballroom to start the cycle all over again. I did this for two and a half months without a day off, and guess where the day off came? Fargo, North Dakota. I spent the day doing my laundry.

As the months rolled on in an endless medley of ballrooms, bus rides, noisy hotels and middle-of-the-night meals, I saw the big-band era winding down in the face of a new invention called television. It was backstage at the Riverside Theater in Milwaukee when I got my first look at the funny little box; an RCA dealer brought a set to demonstrate for us. He showed us a fuzzy picture of the "Milton Berle Show," but it was already enough to keep people in their homes and out of the ballrooms.

I began wondering if I had made a horrible mistake.

Then all the one-nighters and bus rides started making some sense when I caught my first glimpse of the Manhattan skyline. We were coming into town from the New Jersey side at six in the morning. The gray sky slowly turned rosy with dawn, and the dark buildings cut a skyline I'll always remember. Suddenly I was wide awake, cleaning the moist window with the cuff of my shirt. We were headed for Broadway.

The film *Johnny Belinda,* starring Jane Wyman in an Oscar-winning role as a deaf-mute, was opening at the Strand Theater on Broadway, and we were booked to play five sets a day in between screenings. As the big moment drew near, my stomach started tying itself in knots, and I paced the hallways backstage trying to calm down. Jean Barry came by to tell me the house was sold out and we were going on in five minutes. Broadway was an awfully long way from the back porch on Eldorado Street and I hoped my knees would hold up just long enough to get me onstage.

"And now, Freddy Martin and his Orchestra, featuring Merv Griffin on vocals . . ."

Adrenaline surged through my system as the band hit the first few notes of "Tonight We Love." I tried peeking around the curtain at the audience but the spotlights were too bright; then the stage lights dimmed for my cue and I charged out to the microphone and started my medley. Everyone in the band felt the electricity of the Broadway opening and played for all they were worth, while I sang my heart out for fifteen straight minutes. At the finish of "Because of You" the band, suited in their finest whites, stood and held the final note as I sang the last line and then stood back from the microphone to hear the tidal wave of applause for our thrilling finale.

Not one person applauded.

The house lights came up. A thousand people were staring at me. All at once they started lifting their hands and making signals, as if working invisible marionettes. I squinted in the light and looked back at them, bowed awkwardly and then hurried off stage. The manager of the theater was waiting there to embrace me. "Fantastic show," he said. "Wonderful, you were wonderful." Talk about the "twilight zone" . . . I stared back at him, my jaw slack and eyes dazed. "The audience," I mumbled.

"Oh, you weren't told? We brought in groups of deaf-mutes for the opening . . . *Johnny Belinda* is about deaf-mutes . . . we thought it would . . ."

I held up a hand to cut him off, wandered down a narrow hallway to my dressing room and sat in the room's single chair. I sat in silence, staring at peeling paint on the walls.

If we forget about the opening, our run at the Strand Theater went beautifully. What seats *Johnny Belinda* didn't fill we did.

We were working next door to the Ethel Barrymore Theater, which featured a new play by Tennessee Williams with the unlikely title *A Streetcar Named Desire*. I assumed it 159 was a San Francisco musical. I'm not kidding—you see, my idea of Broadway came from watching movies starring Peggy Ryan, Donald O'Connor and Judy Garland. The thought of introspective drama being popular on Broadway never crossed my mind.

One of the young stars of *Streetcar* finished work the same time as I each night, and we often talked in the alley between theaters while he warmed up his motorcycle. He was especially interested in music, particularly jazz with lots of percussion in it, and wanted to know all about Freddy's band. You've never heard such a scream as when I asked the actor if he had any songs in *Streetcar;* he promised to arrange for tickets for me to see the play when Freddy's run at the Strand finished, and I took him up on the offer.

Streetcar stunned me; I'd never seen such emotionally taut theater. And the young actor was superb, portraying his complicated, powerful character so intensely the audience hardly breathed during his scenes. I knew I was watching a monumental talent at work.

After seeing the play I left with the band to head for Los Angeles, but Streetcar was not the last I'd see of the young actor named Marlon Brando.

Everything my Uncle Elmer had told me about the Cocoanut Grove at the Ambassador Hotel in L.A. turned out to be true. It was elegantly styled, with a Moroccan flavor: stucco arches ringed the room, with red clay tile eaves jutting from them; the tablecloths were white and the carpet a rich red. The booths did fill up with stars when Freddy Martin came to town. Jane Powell, Gary Stephan, Richard Long, Ricardo Montalban, Roddy McDowall, Barbara Hale, William Reynolds, Elizabeth Taylor, Bing Crosby popped in now and then, and the secretive Howard Hughes appeared regularly in a back booth of the Grove.

Let me tell you about Howard Hughes. Each night when I drove to the Ambassador in my new Buick convertible, which I proudly left with the attendant, I saw this ten-

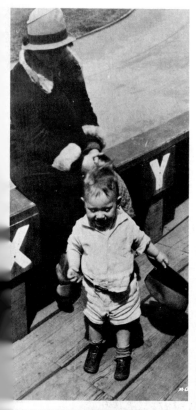

Above left, with Mother at two
years old
Above, sitting on my first piano
bench
Left, high school graduation
picture

Opposite, singing at San
Francisco Press Club at age
19
Opposite below, my Uncle
Elmer, the lovable rogue,
with his pal Errol Flynn
Above, Lena Horne, Café
Rouge, Statler Hotel, 1951
Right, Gertrude Lawrence,
1951
Below, singing with Freddy
Martin at the Statler Hotel

Kathryn Grayson, *So This Is Love*

The Moon Is Blue, Bucks County Playhouse, New Hope,
Pennsylvania, 1963
With William Bendix in Neil Simon's *Come Blow Your Horn,*
Warren, Ohio, 1963

Julann, Tony and me at
Teetertown Farm in Califon,
New Jersey

UPI

ELLEN GRAHAM

MICHAEL L. HITCHCOCK

Opposite top, with Clint
Eastwood at tennis
tournament, La Costa,
California
Opposite center, three
generations of Griffins:
Uncle Elmer, me, Tony
Opposite below, three tennis
legends, Pancho Segura,
Pancho Gonzalez and me
Right, at spring training in
Palm Springs with Gene
Autry's California Angels
Below, golf with John
Lauderdale, Clint and Tony

ANNE ZANE SHANKS

Above, Robert Kennedy, 1967
Left, JFK at White House
Correspondents' Dinner, 1963. Writer
Pat McCormick in background
Below, Secretary of Defense Melvin
Laird and Chief Justice Warren
Burger with Tony

On the streets of Harlem with Mayor Lindsay

Martin Luther King, 1967

Above left, Paris, on location
Above right, James Jones on the banks of the Seine
Below, Jane Fonda, then Mrs. Roger Vadim, the day she arrived
at her new farm outside Paris

Maurice Chevalier at home

Fernandel at the Ritz in Paris

Left, England: The Ritz
Below, Hyde Park, its own
talk show

Leslie Caron on the Thames

English pub

Beatle John Lennon in Cannes. His first talk show.

Bob Hope in England

Zero Mostel in Spain filming *A Funny Thing Happened on the Way to the Forum*

Margaret Rutherford at home

John Huston in the west of Ireland

Alan Bates, set of *Far From the Madding Crowd*

Julie Christie, *Far From the Madding Crowd*

Sean Connery, 007, Cannes

Arthur Treacher

Jack Warner, my former boss, the last Hollywood mogul

Tony Curtis

Burt Reynolds

Burt Lancaster,
streets of Harlem
show

Opposite top, Anthony
Quinn, Charlton Heston
Opposite middle, Henry
Fonda
Opposite below, Rex
Harrison, Michael Caine
Above, Walter Pidgeon,
Bette Davis
Right, Gene Kelly
Below, Elke Sommer, Liza

Liv Ullmann

Beverly Sills

Ethel Waters

Peter Ustinov

Above, Tennessee Williams
Below, Richard Burton on location

Upper left, Dick Cavett
Lower left, Johnny Carson
Upper right, cameras and "boom" microphones are placed not
to intimidate guests or block view of studio audience
Lower right, Dick Carson, Emmy-winning director of
"The Merv Griffin Show"

Opposite top to bottom: Bert Lahr, Groucho Marx, Red Skelton, Jimmy Durante

Jack Benny

Cast of "The Carol Burnett Show," left to right, Vicki Lawrence, Carol, me, Harvey Korman, Lyle Waggoner, Tim Conway

Top, Bertrand Russell,
London, 1965
Above, Clint Eastwood,
me, Maharishi Mahesh
Yogi
Left, the Shah of Iran,
President Gerald Ford

Spiro Agnew

Henry Kissinger

Ronald and
Nancy Reagan

year-old, beat-up Chevy sedan parked right out in front of the hotel. One night I asked the attendant why he allowed that junk heap the best parking spot, and he said, "Because that's Mr. Hughes' car." It made me feel good to own a better car than Howard Hughes, until I started thinking about how many millions he had. What is hilarious to me is I saw more of Hughes than Edmund Granger, who was running RKO Studios for him. Hughes would meet Granger on the corner of Fountain and LaBrea in Hollywood to give him instructions, then he would vanish into the night. Well, the place he was vanishing to was the Cocoanut Grove. Each night he showed up with a different girl, all of them gorgeous. I learned from one of Hughes' dates that he kept girls in apartments all over town; they drew a payroll check, lived with a chaperone and were on twenty-four-hour call. She told me Hughes rarely said a word to the girls and never wanted to take them to bed; he just liked dancing. I'll tell you another thing: he *did* wear tennis shoes. Here's one of the richest men in the country showing up at the fashionable Cocoanut Grove in slacks, sport jacket and dirty tennis shoes. He was the only person allowed to eat during our show; every night he ordered ice cream. He had a ritual with the waiters. As soon as the dish of ice cream was on the table, he took one taste and invariably said, "It's too soft." From the stage I could see the word being passed from busboy to waiter to maître d' to the kitchen, and in short order Mr. Hughes would get his ice cream hard. Then it was time for dancing. And did that man dance! One number after another, always directly in front of the bandstand, and always with his eyes cast toward the floor. Sometimes he'd turn to me and request a number, and it was always a rhumba, preferably "Misirlou."

The only times I was nervous playing the Grove were when my uncles showed up and announced to the crowd I was their nephew. After a few drinks, Uncle Peck fancied himself an orchestra leader and liked to come up on stage and conduct the band while I cringed in the corner. Elmer 161 had even bigger ideas. There was a woman who came to see our orchestra every night at the Grove; she always wore black and sat in a side booth, alone. I asked the maître d' about her, and he explained she was a wealthy widow from Milwaukee, spending time on the West Coast to ease the grief of her recent loss. Elmer noticed her there one night; I told him the same story the maître d' had told me. Well, two nights later I see the widow's booth is empty and I ask the maître d' if she has a reservation. "Oh, she is here already, Mr. Griffin—dancing." He pointed her out on the floor. Guess who she was dancing with? Gone was the black, on was a new red dress, and she was whirling around the floor with none other than Uncle Elmer. After the show he approached me with a note pad and said, "Now, Mervyn, how much will band uniforms cost?"

"Band uniforms?"

"And equipment—how much equipment will you need?"

"Equipment, band uniforms—Elmer, what are you talking about?"

"Why, Mervyn, I've met a lovely woman who wants you to start your own band. Now, how much will uniforms be? . . ."

"I don't *want* my own band, Elmer, there will be no uniforms—forget about it."

At least he got her out of mourning.

One of the strangest engagements we played at the Grove was a private party celebrating Louella Parsons' fiftieth anniversary as a writer. All Hollywood turned out for her—they had to. Louella ruled Hollywood by her column; if she didn't like an actor, she could keep him from working, period. Only Clark Gable and Bing Crosby were beyond Louella's reach, so they didn't bother showing up for the party. But the rest of Hollywood's glittering elite was on hand, including Marion Davies, William Randolph Hearst's mistress, who was seated at a table directly in front of the bandstand.

One of the evening's distinguished speakers was Earl
Warren, then Governor of California and later Supreme
Court Chief Justice. What a speech he made! Governor
Warren couldn't find enough flowery adjectives with which
to massage Louella's large ego. His buckets of praise persisted until Marion Davies, reeling from champagne, grew
weary of the speech.

The next time Warren took a breath, Marion shouted,
"Oh, shadddup, Earl."

A sticky silence followed, then the Governor plowed onward, refusing to look at Miss Davies.

She yelled again, "Play, Freddy! Earl, you're going on
toooooo long."

He kept speaking.

Then Marion delivered the finishing blow. "Earl, I put
you *in* office, and I can take you *out*."

The Governor quickly wrapped up his speech and sat
down, while Marion's friends carried her out. As she went
out the door she was still yelling, "Play, Freddy!"

I recorded lots of songs with Freddy Martin's orchestra,
and a few of them pushed their way up the charts—"Wilhelmina," "Never Been Kissed," "Am I In Love"—but in
1950 we struck gold with a novelty tune called "I've Got a
Lovely Bunch of Cocoanuts." To tell you the truth, I didn't
like the song when we recorded it, because it wasn't a
singer's number. But the novelty tune exploded to number
one on the Hit Parade, and sold three million copies. So
even though big bands were waning in popularity, we were
suddenly a hot property.

Freddy had never played for popular prices in Los Angeles; it was always the Cocoanut Grove. But with the hit
record we were offered an engagement at the Hollywood
Palladium for a concert. I'd never seen such a crowd; a
sold-out house of six thousand people pressed toward the
stage, shouting "We want 'Cocoanuts.' " They were crazy
for that song. When I stepped forward to sing it, a lot of
people looked shocked, because on the record I sounded 163

like a little old man and in fact I wasn't much older than any of the kids in the audience.

We added a couple more dates at the Palladium and sold them both out.

My fan club turned out in force each night. With today's singing stars being the likes of Rod Stewart singing "Do Ya Think I'm Sexy?" and "Tonight's the Night," it's hard to imagine a bunch of teenage girls getting worked up over Merv Griffin singing "I've Got a Lovely Bunch of Cocoanuts," but, believe me, they were there. The President of my Hollywood fan club, a large-toothed girl with pigtails and a perky personality, came backstage at the Palladium after each concert to fill me in on the details of the club. Her name was Carol Burnett, and it didn't take her long to get out of fan clubs and into the spotlight herself.

The owner of Ciro's nightclub, Herman Hover, called the MCA Talent Agency to book me for an engagement because of the popularity of "Cocoanuts." She told them I was under contract to Freddy Martin and performed only with him. So Herman booked the whole band.

Being booked into Ciro's was a big thrill to me; it had been one of the places I made my parents park in front of when we came to Hollywood on vacations. There would always be a dozen photographers stationed outside Ciro's, and I loved watching the battery of flashbulbs pop when stars arrived. You can imagine what was going through my head when I arrived for the afternoon sound check at Ciro's and saw my name on a banner above the door. Unfortunately, my name was larger than Freddy's on the banner, so when I went into the club Jean Barry intercepted me and whispered, "Don't say a word about the sign, Merv. Don't get in the middle of it. Let Freddy settle it with Mr. Hover." That banner went down in a hurry when Freddy threatened to cancel the engagement if it wasn't changed to "Freddy Martin and His Orchestra, featuring Merv Griffin."

But guess who still has the original banner in a closet at home?

Just as I had to make a decision in San Francisco about going on the road with a band or staying in the city as a radio singer, the time came either to leave Freddy and pursue offers coming on for club dates, records and shows or to let my career coast comfortably along as a band singer. Since the heyday of big bands was obviously over by 1951, I knew it was time to move on, and I did so with Freddy's blessing. I headed for New York to talk with RCA about a recording contract.

My girl friend at the time, Judy Balaban, moved back east with me. I had met Judy in Hollywood during the time I was playing at the Cocoanut Grove; in fact, Elizabeth Taylor introduced us one Sunday afternoon at Roddy McDowall's house. We hit it off so well she went on the road with me two weeks later. Normally, Freddy didn't allow girl friends or wives on road trips, but he liked Judy so he made an exception. That girl was nineteen going on thirty-five and we fell madly in love. Her parents weren't too pleased about the idea. Judy's dad, Barney Balaban, was one of the owners of Paramount Pictures and wielded enormous power in the film industry. If I had had any acting ambitions I would have stayed on the good side of Barney and paid attention when he sent Leonard Lyons, the New York show-business columnist, to talk to me about the differences in Judy's and my religious background. We couldn't have cared less, and we intended to marry. I was booked for an engagement in Las Vegas at the Last Frontier, and Judy was out in Hollywood on a visit, so we decided over the phone to meet and be married in Las Vegas. Dorothy Kilgallen somehow got the story and ran it in her column. Judy's parents were vacationing in Europe, but they heard about the item from one of the executives at Paramount and their vacation was over in five seconds. When Judy went to the studio cashier at Paramount to pick up a ticket to Las Vegas she got nothing but a curt "I have instructions not to issue you any money or tickets, Miss Balaban." So I flew out to Hollywood, while the Balabans 165 were landing in New York. Meanwhile, Dorothy Kilgallen was tracking all four of us like it was a spy movie. She printed items about the Balabans' return to New York and their immediate repacking for Los Angeles; then she mentioned the fact that Judy was still in L.A. while I was in Las Vegas. Anyway, time and diverging careers stepped in on behalf of the Balabans. Both Judy and I ended up moving to New York, but we met other people and the romance cooled, though we remained friends. What's really crazy is my introducing Judy to Jay Kantor, the agent I worked with in New York, and she ended up marrying *him*.

When the girl who started the entire Judy Balaban episode, Liz Taylor, came back to New York in 1952 for her first extended visit there, I volunteered to show her the town. Gallant of me, don't you think?

First I took her to Asti's Italian restaurant in Greenwich Village, which had a nice neighborhood feeling and where the waiters sang opera while serving pasta. It's not the kind of place where you expect to bump into a movie star. And Liz Taylor is not just any star; from the moment we walked in the door every head in the restaurant turned in her direction. Her effect upon people amazed me. They stared at her as if she were from another planet; no one seemed to be smiling, just staring. People were just too taken aback to ask for autographs; they sat in enraptured silence watching Liz eat ravioli. What really threw me was Elizabeth appeared unconscious of the attention. I shoved dinner down my throat so we could get out of there, while she casually tasted the different dishes we ordered and chatted about the nice atmosphere in the Village.

From Asti's we were off to Broadway and *Catherine the Great* starring Mae West. We arrived three minutes late, but even in the darkness of the theater people recognized Elizabeth; a wave of excited whispering followed us down to our seats. Suddenly I had the uncomfortable feeling that every eye in the audience was on us rather than on the stage. I could see a few of the actors peering down at Elizabeth, including Mae West, who wore a look not of anger

166

but of curiosity, just like everyone else. We didn't dare move at intermission, and when the play finished we stayed in our seats to let the house clear out. Hardly anyone left. "Elizabeth," I whispered, "there must be an encore . . . no one's leaving . . ."

"I'm afraid that's not it."

When it became pointless to wait any longer, we headed for the aisle. Elizabeth was calm and cool, smiling at the hundreds of curious onlookers.

She knew she could get away with anything. She loved to belch just loud enough for the fans to hear, but discreetly enough for them to whisper, "That *couldn't* have been her."

We went backstage to see Mae West. She was wearing a white satin robe and sat amidst a rain forest of flowers; she looked like a pagan love goddess getting ready for mating season. I did not catch all of the conversation between Mae and Liz, but I did see Mae look deep into Elizabeth's violet eyes and heard her say, "I was once as beautiful as you are, dear."

Next stop was Lindy's, a famous Broadway hangout where the comedians gathered to top each other with jokes. But Elizabeth didn't want to go there for laughs, she just wanted a piece of their legendary cheesecake. I tried to talk her out of it. "Lindy's is jammed on Saturday. You'll never get out of there alive."

"I hear about that cheesecake wherever I go. I've got to try it."

Lindy's star fixture was Milton Berle. Uncle Miltie had the number one show on television; movie theaters across America hardly bothered to stay open on Tuesday nights when his show aired. Milton owned New York, and Lindy's was his throne room. Jack Carter, Jack E. Leonard, Joey Bishop and the rest were often there, but Milton was the top banana.

When Elizabeth Taylor and I walked into Lindy's what we saw was a massive double take. A few heads turned in my direction ("Oh, he's the band singer, you know . . . Herb Griffith . . .") but when they realized who was on my 167 arm, Lindy's came to a screeching halt. Jaded waiters stopped in mid-step, forks dangled in front of lips; the only sounds to be heard were the electric fans gently turning above us.

We took the first empty table, and the host fell all over himself to bring us menus. Gradually the sounds of the restaurant resumed. But you knew who everyone was talking about.

"Why don't they just keep eating, for Godsake?" I said.

"We'll be fine, Merv. Let's order some of that cheesecake."

Elizabeth had the oddest effect on other women. As they walked past, they reached down to touch Elizabeth's fur coat, never saying a word.

The cheesecake arrived and it was everything Elizabeth dreamed it would be. Suddenly I was aware of another hush in the room. King Milton had risen from his booth and was heading for our table. His usual routine with me was "Hi, kid" as he looked elsewhere and walked on. Tonight was a different story. Halfway to our table he yelled, "Merv, baby, good to see you. How *are* you?"

You can guess what I was thinking. I let him stand by the table a few seconds before saying to Elizabeth, "This is Mr. Berle. Milton, this is Elizabeth Taylor."

Liz peeked up from her cheesecake long enough to smile, but then resumed eating.

Mr. B. had the surprised look of someone who had just been zapped in the face with a Lindy's cheesecake, but he knew everyone in the restaurant was watching so he sat down and plunged ahead as if Elizabeth wanted to chat. She didn't. The truth is, she just didn't know who he was because she never watched TV. He sat there nervously trying to make conversation, while she continued to savor the cheesecake. After he left I tried explaining how famous a man Milton Berle was.

"Oh, that's nice," she said. "You know, Merv, this *is* the greatest cheesecake on earth."

• •

At the same time Elizabeth was in New York, two other friends from Hollywood were also there: Jane Powell and Roddy McDowall. So I called Roddy and we decided to give Jane and Elizabeth a party to introduce them to some of our East Coast friends, including Eddie Fisher, who refused to believe I was having a party for Elizabeth Taylor.

In fact he roared with laughter. "Well, well, well . . . Liz Taylor and Jane Powell . . . you do get around."

"If you'd like to come, it's two o'clock Sunday afternoon, I've got a suite at the Meurice."

"Oh, I'll be there," he said.

On Sunday I ordered several trays of food from room service and tried ordering liquor from a store around the corner. I'd completely forgotten New York is dry on Sundays, so I had to run over to Carlos Montalban's (Ricardo's brother) apartment with a handcart and borrow whatever I could.

I guess Eddie's curiosity got the better of him; he showed up Sunday at one forty-five.

"You're a little early, Eddie."

"Liz Taylor and Jane Powell?" He winked, waiting for me to admit the joke. "I suppose they'll be here soon?"

"Elizabeth is here now."

"I don't see her," he replied, rocking on his heels.

Eddie's girl friend was looking bored. I said to her, "Will you excuse us a moment? Eddie, will you come with me?"

We walked into the bedroom and saw Elizabeth sitting at the vanity combing her hair out. She turned around and focused those famous violet eyes directly on Eddie, and old Eddie went pale and started wobbling. I could have sold him a thousand acres of Florida swampland that afternoon.

I'll tell you what resulted from that little introduction. Elizabeth was coming off her divorce to Nicky Hilton and she'd just met Michael Wilding, whom she married in February of 1952. But she and Eddie struck up a frienship, which resulted in Eddie's introducing her to Mike Todd, whom Liz also married. In the years after Mike's death, the 169 friendship between Eddie and Elizabeth turned to romance and, as you all know, marriage.

During the year after I left Freddy's band I spent my time waiting to be drafted and sent to Korea. I went through the physical when the dreaded notice arrived. Packing up clothes, furniture, records, everything I owned, I shipped it all to California. My friends in New York threw a pre-induction party for me, and we drank the entire night away. I showed up at the induction center hung over and depressed. A grim clerk looked for my name on his list. When he found it he shook his head; I thought, my God, are they sending me straight to the front? Or maybe they are going to nail me for back taxes?

"You're not going to be inducted today, Griffin. The board overfilled your age quota; you're on the 'stop' list here. You can go home."

"Say that again."

"You don't have to go, we're over the limit . . . you can go home. *Next!*"

My hangover vanished like magic, and I skipped singing and dancing down the street like a crazy person. I had no idea what to do with myself when I got home; all my thoughts had been geared to spending the next two years in the army. I called Judy Balaban to tell her the good news. She asked me to join her and her new-found friend, Montgomery Clift, for dinner. "Monty is a little intense, Merv, but he's an interesting guy." That may have been the greatest understatement of Judy's life.

He was already a major star, and Judy told me people on the street stopped dead in their tracks when Monty walked by. These days, I was more interested in food than in making the acquaintance of another movie star. We met at Daly's on Lexington Avenue, and you can be sure Monty was the center of attention. He inspired that same sort of awe in people Elizabeth did; the other diners whispered and stared but were afraid to speak to him.

170   Monty and Judy were both dieting, but the famous Grif-

fin sweet tooth spotted a specialty of the house on the dessert menu, lemon-meringue pie.

"My God, that looks good," Monty gasped when the pie arrived.

I suggested he order a piece.

"No, I just want a taste," he said, sticking a finger into my pie.

Now that kind of thing really annoys me, and my reaction was not wasted on the actor in Monty. Playing to the staring crowd, he leaned over and started licking the meringue off my pie.

Film star, friend of Judy's, whatever, I failed to find this amusing. So with both hands I shoved Monty's face flush into the pie. He looked up, the face that thrilled America on the screen a gooey mess of meringue and lemon filling. Slowly he wiped the pie off his face. He said quietly, "Yeah, that's good pie, Merv. You're right, it's real good pie."

From that moment on we were friends.

I saw Monty on many social occasions in New York, and also in Hollywood after I'd moved west and signed as a contract actor with Warner Brothers. Monty came out to do Alfred Hitchcock's *I Confess*. I had the role of the voice on the unseen end of a telephone call. So I was on the set the afternoon whispered reports of Monty's arrival started circulating. I looked around at the awestruck faces; even the technical crew was abuzz when the legendary Monty Clift strolled onto the set for the first time.

He arrived with Mira Rostova, the renowned Russian acting coach who had given up her own acting career to devote herself to coaching Monty; he trusted her totally, relied on her judgment of his craft more than he ever did the judgment of a director.

As all took their places, Mira found a seat out of Hitchcock's line of sight, but in a place where Monty could see her. After each take Monty glanced at Mira for a signal of approval. Just how much Monty counted on Mira's judgment became clear to me as I watched the third scene of the afternoon's shooting. It was between Karl Malden, portraying the police investigator on the murder case, and Monty, playing the priest who refused to break the seal of confession to reveal the murderer's identity. Even in the bare surroundings of the sound stage, Monty and Malden played the scene so intensely it stunned us all. The crew burst into applause, and the characteristically impassive Hitchcock was visibly moved. Hitch jumped up from his chair and proclaimed, "Brilliant! Print it."

Clift neither heard or saw Hitchcock; he looked at Mira, who made a signal by putting a hand to her left ear. When the applause died down, Monty said, "I'd like to do the scene over, Hitch."

Hitchcock whirled, trembling with rage, and glared at Mira.

But the scene was shot again. And, somehow, improved.

My own film career began, surprisingly, when Freddy Martin called me one evening in 1952, after I'd left the band, and explained his orchestra was opening the next night at the Last Frontier in Las Vegas and their singer had been called out of town on a family emergency. Twelve hours later I stood onstage in Las Vegas rehearsing with the band, and a few hours later we opened to a full house. In the audience that night was America's leading lady, the number one star in Warner Brothers' stable, who was also a former band singer: Doris Day. You couldn't walk by a newsstand or into a drugstore without seeing Doris' picture on fifteen different magazine covers. But with all the confusion of opening night, no one told me she was there.

After the show there was a knock on my dressing room door, and a little kid poked his head in the room. "My mother and father liked your show, Mr. Griffin, and would like to sign you."

I told him to thank his parents for the interest, and sent him on his way with an autograph.

How was I supposed to know he was Doris Day's son? And how was I supposed to know she wanted to put in a good word for me at Warner Brothers?

Well, she did go back to Hollywood and tell the casting department at Warner Brothers about me, and this occurred at just about the same time that my manager, Bullets Durgom, was pitching me to Warners' casting director, Bill Orr. I wasn't burning to be an actor, but Bullets explained to me that movies could open doors to almost any area of show business I might want to pursue.

It turned out my Uncle Elmer knew Bill Orr quite well from the days when Elmer owned a nightclub on the Sunset Strip called the Sports Circle. When Bullets called to tell me Bill Orr was granting me an audition, I called Elmer to find out about Bill Orr. "Oh, he's a fine chap, Merv, you'll like him. He worked in my club as the emcee and did impressions. He's married to Jack Warner's stepdaughter, you know, Joy Page." I felt a little more comfortable knowing something about the man. I arrived for the audition accompanied by Bullets and a pianist. A few of Bill Orr's assistants were waiting in the rehearsal hall for me, but no Bill Orr. We waited for over an hour, which is a terrible thing for a performer to endure when he is primed to go; I grew more irritated by the second. Finally we heard footsteps approaching down the hall and one of the assistants whispered, "That's his walk."

I jumped and told my pianist to hit the last three notes of "Night and Day." Just as Bill Orr walked into the room I belted out the end of the song, bowed to the gathering, said, "Thank you all for coming to my audition," and bustled out of the room.

Bill and I brushed shoulders in the doorway.

When he realized I was on my way out of the building he yelled, "Merv, where are you going? *I'm* Bill Orr."

"Oh. Well, you're an hour late, Bill. I just gave your staff an entire concert. Am I supposed to do my whole act over again?"

He started mumbling an apology.

173

I cut him short. "If you want to see me perform, you'll have to come to Las Vegas. I'm very busy right now."

"Now, Merv, come on. I was held up in a meeting."

"I see. By the way, Bill, my Uncle Elmer tells me he has some dirty pictures of you from goings-on in your dressing room at the Sports Circle."

For a second he looked shocked. When I burst out laughing he looked relieved.

"Is that old devil really your uncle? If you're anything like him you're the world's greatest actor. Hell, let's forget the audition and go right ahead and set up a screen test."

Just prior to the start of *I Confess* Monty Clift had called me to ask a question about the script. He felt the writers were missing part of the point of the seal of confession, which is the crux of the plot, and since I was Catholic he sought my advice. I agreed with him about the point he felt was lacking, and the change was incorporated into the script. So when the date was set for a screen test, it was my turn to get a little advice from Monty. He and Mira both offered suggestions to help me out, and I tried to keep their advice in mind when I arrived at Warner's for the test. I did a scene from *The Hasty Heart* and a musical number, "I Don't Want to Walk Without You," with Phyllis Kirk.

The only thing I liked about the test was Phyllis Kirk; I was impressed by how smoothly she slipped in and out of character. If nothing else was to come of my screen test at least I'd get a date with Phyllis.

We had a brief relationship, brief because Phyllis was always talking about how busy she was. One night in Dominick's Restaurant she got to talking about her busy schedule and pulled out her appointment book to show me.

"Now, you're *not* going to read me all your appointments, are you?" I said.

First she looked hurt at my lack of interest in her career, then she started getting angry; she picked up her plate of
174 spaghetti and dumped it over my head. It's very difficult

to argue with someone when you have spaghetti and marinara sauce all over your head. Phyllis and I didn't date a lot after that. In fact, I made a private vow to myself not to become enamored of actresses in the future.

One evening, a few days after my screen test, I walked through the editing bays at Warners, having a look around the lot, and I heard my test being run. Producers and directors on the lot were asked to use the contract players as much as possible, so I stuck my head in the screening room to see who was having a look at me. It was Monty and Mira. "You know, Merv," Monty said, pointing to the screen, "you're doing something good up there. It's raw, but you're doing something."

I would have liked to agree with him, but using Monty himself as a measure, I knew I lacked the brooding intensity great actors draw upon. Monty possessed that quality in spades, to the point of obsession. For instance, Monty called me after he'd signed to do James Jones's *From Here to Eternity* under the direction of Fred Zinnemann. He wanted to know where musicians bought their horns in Hollywood, and mumbled something about preparing for his role; I said I'll pick you up and take you there. I drew up a list of stores and away we went. On the way Monty explained he was searching for a trumpet mouthpiece. The description in James Jones's novel of the mouthpiece used by Prewitt, Monty's character, was so vivid that it became an obsession with Monty to find one precisely matching it. We spent hours searching for it, visiting stores and studying dozens of mouthpieces. They all looked the same to me, but not to Monty. Finally, at the end of an all-day quest, he found Prewitt's mouthpiece.

I watched with fascination as he gradually let the picture take over his life. Fred Zinnemann, probably on the recommendation of Alfred Hitchcock, told Monty that Mira would not be allowed on the set. Clift agreed to this condition, but held up shooting on a number of occasions to telephone Mira for advice. They were staying at the Chateau Marmont during the Hollywood portion of the film- 175 ing, but Monty didn't like the noise at the hotel and asked if they could use the house I rented from Bullets to rehearse scenes. I told Monty to use it whenever he wished. One afternoon I stayed around to watch him work with Mira. He was rehearsing a simple scene. But Monty must have rehearsed it fifty times before he felt satisfied; each movement was planned and practiced in the minutest detail. I wondered how he had any energy left over for the actual filming.

That kind of intensity needs release, and when I came home early one day I found them still at work, but I smelled liquor. Monty was slurring his words and his eyes were cloudy.

"We're all going out for dinner, Merv," he announced suddenly. "I'm driving."

"I don't want to go, Monty," I told him.

Mira added, "I'm not riding with you."

He was furious; that anyone ever questioned his ability to do anything infuriated him.

"You don't think I can drive?" he said, grabbing my keys and charging past me.

It was an ugly scene and I was amazed as he stormed out the door. I'd seen him angry before, but never this out of control. From the look on Mira's face I judged this behavior wasn't new to her.

He started my car, raced the engine, and threw it in reverse by accident. Mira turned her back while I stood in the doorway and watched Monty knock the garage door in, lurch the car forward through a hedge, across the lawn, over the mailbox and away.

Eventually he brought the car back, repaired, and he paid for the house and yard damage. But he never mentioned the incident again.

Bill Orr liked my test and Warner Brothers signed me to a contract. Bullets Durgom brought me to Warners for the official signing. There was a photographer, and Bill Orr and I posed over a phony piece of paper. Then they dragged me over to a publicity office and somebody interviewed me for a studio biography, took a few more pictures, and all of a sudden I was an actor.

Once the ink dried on my contract and I knew I'd be around Hollywood a while, I rented an apartment just off Hollywood Boulevard in the Commodore Garden Apartments. The building was occupied primarily by high-priced hookers, with the notable exception of another young actor who lived on the first floor. He was a tall, square-shouldered, blue-eyed fellow whose bold features were soon to be known around the world. We exchanged pleasantries each morning as we left for work; soon he was making enough money to move to a better address. But I admired and liked the young Charlton Heston, and the same holds true for today's mature version of the man.

So we had God in the front apartment, the boy singer upstairs, and hookers and con men everywhere else.

The girls weren't too friendly, and since their business was strictly call-out, I didn't see much of them. I only got to know one, a sad, sensitive girl named Ann who moved to Hollywood from the Midwest filled with dreams of movie stardom, but who found herself trapped in a destructive lifestyle she couldn't shake. She talked constantly of doing away with herself. Once or twice she tried overdosing, but it was characteristic of Ann's life that she tried overdosing with vitamins instead of sleeping pills, and ended up healthier after the suicide attempt than before. Another time she drew a steaming hot bath and contemplated slitting her wrists. But she sat so long thinking about it she fell asleep and almost drowned; she came away from it with only temporarily wrinkled skin.

I do have one gruesome memory from my life at the Commodore. Actually, the incident occurred one morning just as I was leaving the apartment to go to work. I pulled into traffic on Franklin Boulevard and stopped for a red light. A tiny blue sports car stopped in front of me. I'll never forget the thick, gorgeous blond hair of the young woman driving it; next to her, buckled into a special seat, 177 was her infant daughter. In front of the sports car a large dump truck loaded with steaming asphalt was stopped at the crosswalk. When the light changed the truck driver somehow hit a wrong lever when he went to shift into gear, causing the bed of his truck to rear up. It wasn't possible for the woman to maneuver her car out of the way, and the hot mass of asphalt poured down on her and her child. It took only seconds to bury the car. I saw the mother struggle to protect her child but the dark wave kept pouring down, and it was all over as suddenly as it started. People leaped out of their cars to try to help, but mother and daughter were both killed. For years after the incident I'd awaken shivering in the middle of the night. I still am unable to put it out of my mind.

My favorite part of the day as an actor was driving each morning through the gate of the Warner Brothers lot and waving to the guard from my white Buick convertible. "Good morning, Mr. Griffin!" he'd shout as I rolled by; it made me feel like Clark Gable.

My day went downhill from there. I went to my nine-by-twelve dressing room, sat in the room's single chair and waited for someone from the casting department to call. That phone didn't do much ringing. Most of the time I spent thumbing through movie magazines sent over by the publicity department containing fabricated articles about my glamorous Hollywood-bachelor life. Some life. Lunch in the commissary was the only big moment of the day.

Bill Orr did toss a "welcome to the family" party for me at his stately Beverly Hills home. It was quite an eye-opener for a kid from San Mateo. In the back yard a huge green-and-white-striped canvas tent housed a dance floor, orchestra and buffet table. White-jacketed waiters passed an endless stream of hors d'oeuvres and drinks. I wandered around trying to look as blasé as everyone else, but I don't think I was convincing. Bill stuck me in a receiving line and I pumped a lot of hands and forgot a lot of names. A few of the actors and most of the songwriters I recognized, but the directors, producers and executives were all new to me. Then in walked Gordon MacRae, Doris Day's leading man. He was quite charming toward me, but seemed unaware of what this party was *for*. "Merv, I'm happy to meet you. I know you as a singer. But I didn't know you were here in Hollywood. I was under the impression you were New York based."

"I'm living out here now."

"I didn't know that. What are you out here to do?"

I thought I was here to do movies with Doris Day, but it dawned on me that might not be the best thing to say to Gordon. I didn't have to. Sammy Cahn, the songwriter and movie producer, did it for me. Thrusting his impish face into our group, he poked Gordon in the ribs. "Why do you think we're here, Gordie? Merv is with Warners now. So you'd better behave or he'll be starring with Doris!"

The color drained out of Gordon's face; he threw an icy stare at Bill Orr.

People around the lot had mentioned Doris was having problems with Gordon, but to hear Sammy say it out loud was not my idea of how best to meet Gordon MacRae. The thought occurred to me I might have been signed as a silent studio threat against Gordon, a message to him to straighten up or else.

In any case, I didn't want any part of the mess.

Well, the Hollywood rumor mill being what it is, movie magazines picked up the story of a feud brewing between Gordon MacRae and Merv Griffin. If a problem did exist, it was between Gordon and the studio; he was friendly to me next time I ran into him.

However, I did expect to get a part in a film opposite Doris.

One problem with that, though, was that I looked about eighteen years old on the screen, a little too young to be romancing Doris Day. But the call finally came from casting that I had a part in *By the Light of the Silvery Moon,* Doris Day's newest movie. I knew the movie had been shooting for two weeks already when I got the call, but the casting 179 girl told me not the worry about the script, just to show up at wardrobe next Monday morning. This struck me as an odd way to treat Doris' future leading man.

Monday morning I ran into Gordon MacRae in wardrobe and wondered what he was doing in *my* picture. But when I finally found the director, David Butler, I was in for a few surprises. "I'll be with you in a minute, Merv," he said, ". . . costume looks great."

I was wearing layers of winter clothing.

"What about my script, David?"

"Oh, don't worry about it."

After two hours of sitting around, the assistant director gave me my instructions. The set was a winter scene built around an ice-skating rink. "What you do, Merv, is stand up on that box over there and when the stage manager cues you the skaters will come into the rink and you say, 'All you figure skaters grab your favorite girl and skate to your favorite song!' You use a bullhorn."

"And then what?"

"Then you're done."

"What?"

"That's the part."

"What about Doris?"

"You won't have to worry about her. You just have to say your line."

Doris and Gordon and the other actors arrived on the set and David Butler explained the scene to them.

I did my one line and managed to get it right on the first take. Everyone laughingly cheered my dramatic reading. When the movie was released I was upstaged by the bullhorn in front of my face.

The next picture I tested for, *So This Is Love,* brought my first featured role. My part was that of Buddy Nash, actor-manager-fiancé of Kathryn Grayson, who portrayed the opera star Grace Moore. The part put me on the screen for twenty minutes, which beat *By the Light of the Silvery Moon* by nineteen minutes and fifty seconds.

180   Doris Day dropped by the set on the first day of shooting

to congratulate me and offer encouragement. And I assumed I would need all the encouragement I could get, word around the studio being Kathryn Grayson was a terror to work with. She was supposed to fight constantly with her leading men, forcing their faces out of scenes, giving them acting lessons and generally wreaking havoc on the set. When I ran into her ex-husband, Johnny Johnston, on the lot and told him I was in the new film with Kathryn, he shook his head. "You're in for a lot of trouble, pal. Good luck."

When I first met Kathryn I must have looked like a boxer sizing up an opponent. But from day one she popped all my preconceptions by being the most charming, helpful person I'd met in the business. Perhaps she sensed I was a fish out of water on a movie set because she patiently guided me through scene after scene. Once she stopped a scene in midtake just to explain, "How will you ever be a star, Merv? You keep turning your face away from the camera and losing your key light. Now make sure to talk to me from this angle (she turned me around) so your face will be on the screen, for heaven's sake." I didn't seem to know where the camera was or where the "key light" was coming from; I just knew how to find the commissary. But Kathryn slowly taught me the bare essentials of film acting.

Some of the first sequences we filmed were kissing scenes. I can be very romantic in the privacy of my own home, but the idea of playing a love scene in front of a camera crew petrified me. So what does the picture's publicist do for the first day of kissing scenes? He invited a college football team from Texas, in town for the Rose Bowl, to watch us film, without saying a word to me. We were on the set rehearsing a tender love scene in which I whisper a few endearments in Kathryn's ear, then kiss her passionately, and as I'm getting my courage up for the first take I see a mob of large men slowly surround the set. The crew accepted it as normal procedure, so I tried to take it in stride. The players had been instructed to be perfectly 181 quiet during filming, but when fifty large men attempt to be quiet they begin breathing in unison, like some primeval monster lurking beyond the lights. Could *you* feel romantic with fifty football players surrounding you and breathing heavily? Sweat rolled down my forehead and onto Kathryn's nose; the makeup man stood by with lots of cotton swabs to use between takes. And there were *lots* of takes. I kept kissing her head-on, my nose leaving a dent in her face. Director Gordon Douglas quietly prodded me: "Merv, you're putting your nose in her eye. Turn your head, exaggerate it." She tried to help me but I was having a terrible time transporting myself from being Merv Griffin to being Buddy Nash, master kisser. After ten takes the football players started mumbling. "What's the matter with this guy?" "Give me five seconds and I'll show her a kiss." "He's gettin' paid for *this*, jeez." At take twenty-five Gordon Douglas was ready to play the scene himself. It was eleven in the morning, but to save me he called for lunch break.

I eventually managed to make it through the kissing scenes, and they actually received quite a bit of attention when the picture was released; in one of the scenes our mouths were open when we kissed, and believe it or not, in 1954 that raised a few eyebrows.

I have to tell you about one silly sidelight of working with Kathryn Grayson. She was, perhaps, the most generously endowed actress of her era, a fact Warner Brothers took great pains to conceal (a few of those pains were Kathryn's because wardrobe mistresses were always binding her in). She made Marilyn Monroe and Jane Russell look like Campfire Girls. But that was not the image the studio wanted for Kathryn, particularly not in *So This Is Love,* so our intrepid wardrobe mistress concealed Kathryn's breasts beneath layers of unrevealing gowns. When she showed up for rehearsals wearing a tight sweater, I saw why she had such a problem; if they didn't bind Kathryn in for our film, I might never be *able* to get close enough to mess up the kissing scenes.

• •

The next epic in my film career was *Three Sailors and a Girl*, which starred Gordon MacRae, Jane Powell and Jack E. Leonard. If you sneezed while watching that film you'd miss my part. In fact, I was little more than an extra in that one, spending most of my time blocked by Jack E. Leonard's bulk; in one scene I look like a second head growing out of his shoulder. The one good line of the film belonged to Veda Ann Borg, who read a newspaper review of George Givot's performance in a show contained within the movie: "The audience forgave Mr. Rossi for forgetting his lines—but not for remembering them."

Next I did a western. Having trouble picturing me as a cowboy? Well, it happened under the guidance of one of Hollywood's legendary directors, Michael Curtiz, the man who brought you *Casablanca, Yankee Doodle Dandy,* and *Charge of the Light Brigade.*

He stopped me on the Warner lot one afternoon. "Greefen?" he said in his thick Hungarian accent, "I'm Curtiz. Michael Curtiz."

I knew him by reputation; he'd won an Oscar for *Mildred Pierce.* He was an anxious man with dark, intense eyes. Clearly he carried a thousand things on his mind at once.

"I'm just coming from viewing room where I run your test. You can do anything, anything, I see that."

"Really?"

"Yes, yes."

I detected an odd aroma around Curtiz, spicy.

"Listen," he said, "I be in touch."

"Terrific."

As he walked away I saw a huge salami protruding out of his back pocket.

Two days later casting called. Curtiz wanted me for *The Boy from Oklahoma*, which starred Will Rogers, Jr., and Nancy Olson, along with some of Hollywood's great wranglers, Sheb Wooley and Slim Pickens among them. I was to play a deputy sheriff who had an eye on Nancy Olson, who in turn had her eye on Will Rogers, Jr.

"Much riding?" I said to casting.

183

"Yeah, but not right away."

"Good, I'll need a couple of weeks to brush up on riding."

"Fine. But you start the other scenes next Monday. Seven for makeup and wardrobe, shooting at nine."

Makeup and wardrobe did their best to turn an Irish altar boy into a cowboy, and I reported on location to Curtiz for his assessment of the transformation. "Ah, Greefen, you on time, good boy . . . you look just like cowboy, good. Now what you do this morning is lead the posse down that hill and stop at this mark, then pull your gun . . . that's whole scene. No trouble. Got it right?"

"Lead a posse down the hill at full gallop?"

"Yes. Big scene."

"Mr. Curtiz, I was supposed to have two weeks before the riding scenes started. I can't lead a posse down a hill. . . ."

He waved away my concern. "Anybody can ride, my daughter can ride, my wife can ride. Don't be chicken. Get up there and do your job. You're actor. Actors ride. Go be an actor and ride."

Curtiz didn't want to diffuse the drama of the scene by rehearsing it. The crew was set up and the cast assembled on top of the hill. Slim Pickens and Sheb Wooley sat comfortably atop their mounts, reading racing forms, while ten other seasoned wranglers took positions behind them. And there I was in my woolly chaps and ten-gallon hat looking like Spanky McFarland, trying to remember which side of the horse to get up on.

Curtiz called "Action" and I started my horse with a light kick. Hollywood horses know immediately if their rider is experienced, and mine got the message right away and moved at his own leisurely pace. The rest of the posse thundered past in a furious gallop. When the dust cloud cleared I was last to reach the mark, and Curtiz stood with his hands covering his face. "Oh God, help me, please God, help me. . . ."

I took him aside. "The wranglers are going to kill me if we have to do this over and over."

Curtiz moaned, "Oh, actor bum stinking on the goddamn horse . . . how come I get these goddamn actors? . . ."

He talked this way to everyone, however, even his star, Will, Jr., to whom I heard Curtiz say, "You are son of actor bum and you stink. You can't do more than one line, you're crazy in this business. Quit the business with your hat and your rope." One day, when he thought the horses looked tired, he took their keeper aside. "What's the matter with these horses? They are sweating like pigs, tongues hanging out, they trot like old ladies. They are the worst fucking horses in Hollywood." Then Curtiz realized a script girl was standing behind him, he turned and in a gentle voice said, "Pardon the 'fuck' for now," then turned back to the trainer and continued cursing.

In the interest of time that first morning, Curtiz substituted a stunt man for me in my riding scenes, but needed me for a closeup where I was to shoot a bad guy on a stagecoach. Simple enough. My horse trotted next to the stagecoach and on cue I fired the gun, but the explosion made me grimace and shut my eyes, which in turn caused me to "shoot" my victim in the back.

"*Cut!*"—Curtiz was in shock—"*Cut!* You don't shoot him in the back, Greefen. Wait until he turns at you. Are you crazy? You are *good* guy, good guys do not shoot anybody in the back. Oh, where do I get these actors?"

All day Curtiz cut slices for himself from the salami in his back pocket, but when it came time for us to have lunch he complained actors were lazy bums who never do an honest day's work without lunch break every time the director wants a scene shot. One day he told me about filming *Charge of the Light Brigade.* "I sent the actors to their goddamn lunch because the scene we do look fake. Twenty men on horses jump wall in attack, but it was fake. Like a movie, no one believe the scene. I have a trench dug on other side of wall while actors eating their goddamn lunch, big deep trench, and I don't tell them. Then we shoot scene again and it was like nothing you ever see on film. 185

Horses and actors flying all over the place. Killed a man. Unbelievable action. Great scene in the picture. Now your actor unions ruin everything . . . stand-ins . . . pooey!"

I should have learned more about acting from Curtiz than I did, but he was just so unpredictable I never knew if what I was doing was good or bad. For instance, he didn't like the way I was playing a certain line to Nancy Olson so he tried to help me with it. "Greefen, you must look tender and sound hopeful, like this: 'Could I take you to the dance tonight?' " His Hungarian accent made him sound like Count Dracula.

So I did it his way. Exactly like Dracula.

The crew broke up but Curtiz ignored them. "Perfect! Greefen, you finally get the idea. Print it."

I rushed over and had to explain to him I was just joking.

"Joking? That is your best scene in the picture."

"My accent . . ."

"What accent?"

I managed to leave my mark on *The Boy from Oklahoma*, but not as an actor. We were filming a shooting contest involving Will and Nancy. I tossed the plates into the air, then the camera stayed on me for a reaction when the guns were fired. Even a simple little scene like this took hours to film, and my attention span never went past the first take. Bullets Durgom was on the set that afternoon, cutting up by doing some of Jackie Gleason's famous takes. The one that caught my attention was Jackie's famous exit move, where he lifts his arms into a big "M" and says *"Away* we go." The devil in me got the upper hand, because after the fifth take I did the famous Gleason move when Will and Nancy fired their guns. The crew loved it as much as my Dracula impression.

Curtiz wasn't sure what to make of it. "What are you doing there with that move?"

I shrugged. "Just reacting to the scene, Mr. Curtiz."

"Very interesting move. I like it."

It stayed in the picture. Now if I come across *The Boy from Oklahoma* on the late show, and I mean the *late* show, I still get a laugh from the scene.

After finishing the picture I saw Michael Curtiz only twice. Driving down Sunset Boulevard one afternoon he pulled up next to me at a red light. Evidently the young blonde in the car with him was supposed to be a secret, because when the light changed and I yelled "Hiya, Mike, it's Merv," he drove right off the street and through somebody's begonia garden. The last time I saw the legendary director was on the Warner lot. He stopped me one day on the way to the commissary. There were tears behind his sunglasses, and I asked what was troubling him.

"How many years I am here making movies, Greefen? How many years? Jack Warner just walked by and did not say good morning. Not hello. How many movies I make? How many years?"

Then he walked away, shoulders sunken in, with a large salami still protruding from his back pocket.

When I wasn't working on a film, which is to say most of the time, the studio kept me busy with voice-overs and radio promotions: the phone call in *I Confess,* a dramatic death rattle for *Charge at Feather River,* a radio plug for the Duke's latest, "*Hondo! Hondo! Hondo!* John Wayne is *back* in . . . *Hondo!*"

The publicity office kept my name in the papers by sending me off to premieres with studio starlets, who for the most part were a parade of airheads. When I dated an actress from another studio I heard about it right away. "Why are you promoting RKO? Please take out *our* girls. . . ."

I first met the great Jack Warner himself over the phone; he called to personally advise against one girl I'd taken out. "Griff," he shouted gruffly, "what the hell are you going out with her for? You don't need a cheap dame like that. She's no good for your image."

When the publicity office complained about my dates, I laughed; when Jack Warner complained I immediately forgot the girl's phone number. He was Hollywood's last absolute monarch. While other studios were being taken over by accountants, lawyers and boards of directors, Jack Warner remained king of his studio, wielding his clout to make a career or end one. I was with his studio six months before actually meeting him. The meeting was arranged through a formal invitation.

Jack Warner employed a social secretary, Richard Gully, who was "teddibly" British and whose responsibility it was to project a classy image for Jack. Mr. Warner wasn't about to project a classy image for himself; any conversation with him bristled with four-letter words, and he let you know instantly where you stood with him. Richard is just the opposite; he strikes you more as a member of British royalty than as a PR man.

He called to deliver my invitation. "Hello, old chap, the Colonel (Mr. Warner's preferred nickname) would like you for dinner this Sunday."

"On a platter?"

"Now, Merv, old boy, you musn't make jokes. You'll be among royalty on Sunday."

"Movie stars?"

He coughed, "I mean *royalty*, a gathering of titled people who are visiting the area. You'll fare much better if you can bring a date who is titled. But I don't suppose you know . . ."

"Sure I do. We'll be there."

"Splendid. Tell your date black or white gowns, formal, of course."

A girl, Lorraine Manville, whom I'd dated a few times, had once been married to a Count. I called and asked if she would mind dragging her title out for an evening.

I'd been to plenty of Hollywood parties, but never one like this. First of all, Jack Warner's house—house isn't the word, *mansion*—looked like it belonged at 1600 Pennsylvania Avenue. The gardens and trees leading to the front door were so perfectly trimmed I thought they might be out of the prop department. A butler extended a silver tray for my calling card while another took Lorraine's—excuse me the Countess'—wrap. We were told our host was in the bar. Some bar. It was the size of a convention hall and jammed with the most lavishly dressed crowd I've ever seen—precious stones by the pound. Waiters wearing black tie and tails weaved throughout the room carrying trays of champagne and caviar; a string quartet serenaded us with Mozart.

A strong hand grabbed my shoulder and I recognized the voice behind it. "Griff? Jack Warner."

He was a stocky, solidly built man who emitted an aura of power like expensive cologne.

"Mr. Warner, how nice to meet you."

"Yeah, good, kid, glad you made it."

"I'm delighted to be here. May I present my date, Countess Lorraine Dumanceaux?"

"Hiya, Countess, how are ya, sweetheart?"

"Fine, thank you."

"I hate to tell you this, sweetie, but you're a little outranked tonight. For instance—" he reached out and grabbed the arm of a woman I instantly recognized—"I want you to meet the *Princess* Aly Khan. I get to call her Rita Hayworth, though. Princess, this is the Countess." The women nodded at each other, while Warner whispered to me, "Do you want to meet some more of 'em, Griff? It's like the wax museum around here." He pointed around the room, "There's the Queen Mother Nawzli, Princess Fawzia, I got a coupla duchesses and plenty of countesses. How do you like those titles?" The way his voice carried made me nervous, and when Richard Gully announced dinner I was relieved.

I don't think "dinner' is an adequate word for what we experienced. At my place setting alone there was more silverware than I owned; gold-trimmed china reflected Steuben glassware and silver candelabra. A butler stood stiffly behind *each* couple at the table and served the food as kitchen assistants wheeled in carts of delicacies. At the head of the table Jack Warner orchestrated the dinner, barking orders to the butlers and telling stories to the guests around him.

After dessert, Mr. Warner rose, as I learned was his custom, to recite an impromptu poem about the evening. All 189 the titled guests paid rapt attention to their host, as if he were delivering a State of the Union address. But it was a crazy poem:

> Oh what a night, none could be wittier
> Filled with jokes, and girls much prettier.
> We certainly dined in royal company,
> Please someone pay the bill for me. . . .

And he went on and on, until what seemed like the end, where he snagged on a rhyme. I will never know why, but I ad-libbed the last line of the poem, and the table roared. Mr. Warner's dark eyes flashed at me; no one, least of all a young contract actor, dared intrude on a Warner recitation. I think the guests were laughing at my brashness as much as my line. Warner's stern gaze turned quizzical, as if he were inspecting an odd bird who had just landed on his table. Somewhere in that gaze I saw approval. But the great man was not about to be upstaged. "Well, I hope you all enjoyed the food", he said to thunderous applause. "And now, all the men are going to have our cigars, and that will give you ladies a chance to go and piss."

What can you say to that? The ladies went—and went.

I think what Jack Warner recognized and liked in me is a quality I've always had, for better or worse; I'm not cowed by important or famous people. I'm fascinated by people, but never intimidated. Mr. Warner began including me in his regular Sunday social gatherings. There was tennis in the afternoons—sometimes I think he ran his studio to get tennis games rather than make films—and then an elegant meal. He had the same group around each Sunday: Elizabeth Taylor, Michael Wilding, Ursula Thiess, Robert Taylor, Vera-Ellen, Bill and Joy Orr, Barbara Warner and me. And I can say without a doubt I loved those Sundays at the Warner mansion, which is more than I can say about the Mondays-through-Fridays at Mr. Warner's studio. Talking with the renowned people at Jack Warner's gatherings was far better than any script that came my way.

Some of my early practice as a talk-show host came out of those Sundays sitting around the table, talking about show business and issues of the day.

After dinner, on a signal from Mr. Warner, the butler would push open massive wooden doors and the bar filled with more guests, stars who'd come just to entertain Jack Warner. On various nights it was Judy Garland, Rock Hudson, Doris Day, and many more, all waiting to perform. Mr. Warner always took the same seat, his throne, while the dinner guests scattered around the room to watch the show. And I'll tell you something else: if Jack didn't like the entertainment he didn't keep it to himself. One night, Mimi Benzell, a star from the New York Metropolitan Opera, did twelve songs one after the other, none of which Jack liked, and she gave every indication we were going to get twelve more.

Warner tapped me on the shoulder and instructed, "Griff, get her off."

"How?"

"You're an entertainer, you figure it out for chrissakes."

Mimi completed her thirteenth number and asked, "Is there anything in particular you would like to hear?"

I promptly suggested in an innocent voice, "Do you know 'Tippy Tippy Tin'?"

The whole room laughed, and we all started getting up from our seats and milling around. The concert was over.

Whenever I visited the Warner estate it was purely social. Mr. Warner never mentioned my movies, perhaps out of courtesy, and I certainly never brought the subject up; after all, there wasn't too much to talk about. I knew I was no great actor and films weren't going to be my life, so I didn't get too worked up on the subject. However, the studio publicity office continued to insist I keep my face in the public's eye by attending premieres and doing interviews. And to show you how silly the publicity mill could get, they wanted me to go to the opening of *Charge at Feather River*, the movie in which I did the voice of a man dying on the battlefield, as one of its "stars." How about that one? And they told me who I'd be going with—a "star-let" by the name of Dolores Dorn-Heft, who was every bit as big a movie star as I.

A limousine deposited us at the foot of a long red carpet leading into Grauman's Chinese Theater, and on either side of us hundreds of fans filled portable stands. They didn't look too thrilled when Dolores and I took the walk down the carpet. I heard, "Oh there's what's his name and he's with that girl, you know, she was in *something*. . . ." A press agent herded us to the broadcaster's stand where a radio personality was talking wildly into his microphone: "Wait a minute, folks, yes . . . *yes* . . . it's *Merv Griffin* pushing through the crowd, and the fans are going *wild*. He'll be lucky if his suit is in one piece after this. I think, I hope . . . yes, I think we can get a word with him. . . ." I'm standing right next to the guy while he's blabbering on like this. "Merv," he screamed into my ear, "what do you hear about *Charge at Feather River?*"

"Oh, I hear it's one of Warner Brothers' best films ever."

"How terrific! Thanks for stopping by. Oh, and now I see. . . "

The press agent sent us off to the lobby, where we bid each other goodnight, snuck out the side door and went to meet our real dates for an evening on the town. That was the first and last I heard of Dolores Dorn-Heft.

A few weeks later I thought I might *really* have a story for the publicity department. Jerry Lewis was throwing a big costume party, and my friends Tony Curtis and Janet Leigh called to see if I wanted to double with them. My date, Marilyn Erskine, and I decided to go as characters from *Come Back, Little Sheba*, with the switch that I would go as the Shirley Booth character, wearing a torn house-coat and stringy wig, and Marilyn as Doc, in a frumpy suit and long bow tie. Our costumes were funny, but Janet and Tony were hilarious. They had studio makeup men come to their house and do them over as each other. Tony went as Janet, and Janet as Tony. They looked like a pair of high-class transvestites.

So we roared off to Jerry's party in Tony's car, and I mean *roared*. Sure enough, a cop pulled us over on Wilshire Boulevard. He took one look in the window at us and pushed the tip of his cap back. He said, "Jesus, Mary and Joseph—what the hell are you folks up to?"

Tony said, "We're on our way to a party."

Tony's deep voice caught the officer off guard. "Just who are you?"

"Tony Curtis."

"Yes," Janet said, underneath her crewcut wig, "he is, and I'm Janet Leigh."

"Holy God. . ."

"It's very easy to explain, officer," Tony said.

"Oh, really?"

He took a peek in the back seat. The four of us must have looked like the worst bus stop in Greenwich Village.

"Do you have some identification?"

I saw Tony's shoulders sink, and my heart went with them. "A . . . no . . . officer. . ."

I started picturing myself down at the police station calling Jack Warner for a character reference.

Tony called upon all his skills as an actor to finally convince the cop to let us go on our way.

Despite my penchant for distressing press agents, Warners sent Kathryn Grayson and me on a promotional tour for *So This Is Love*. First stop was Knoxville, Tennessee, Grace Moore's home town. Our party, consisting of Kathryn, myself and five studio reps, was greeted at the airport by hundreds of fans and the official welcoming committee led by Grace Moore's brothers. These guys were huge, and each one insisted on slapping me on the back. By the time I met the whole family I'd been knocked halfway through the terminal.

Kathryn and I were taken immediately to a theater to rehearse a few musical numbers for the evening's premiere. Kathryn was the big star, so she rehearsed four numbers with the Knoxville Symphony, and I one. Then we were off for an afternoon of one official function after another, including a much publicized parade that drew thousands of onlookers. When the motorcade reached the theater our driver took a wrong turn and delivered us to the side entrance. Of course this threw the press agents into a frenzy, and they restaged our entrance so we'd arrive in front of the news cameras. Governor Frank Clement of Tennessee greeted us at the door and proceeded to make a fiery speech to the press on behalf of Grace Moore, Kathryn, myself and the movie. As Kathryn and I walked down the aisle to the stage, she whispered, "I'm tired, Merv, I'm only going to do one song. You do the show."

I looked at her in disbelief.

"You're an entertainer, Merv. You entertain these people."

I hoped she was kidding as we took our seats and the ceremonies commenced. First there were three or four speeches by Chamber of Commerce people, and then the big moment came when Kathryn was introduced. She did her song, bowed to the wild applause, then sat down. The master of ceremonies broke out in a sweat and threw me a pleading glance. I nodded to him and he brought me to the microphone. "Ladies and gentlemen," I said, "your national anthem." Governor Clement jumped to his feet, and the crowd followed. I sat down at the concert grand piano, turned to the crowd and sang "Tennessee Waltz." *Well*, the place came down.

Put me at a piano and I can do a show any time night or day, and I did a show that night in Knoxville. Kathryn sat calmly applauding as I did one number after another until it was time to roll the film.

"You could have given me a little more warning." I said to Kathryn.

"You were fine, Merv, really good."

I have to admit, I *loved* being back in front of an audience.

The Governor insisted I accompany him to a post-premiere party at the home of some wealthy constituents. It was a hell of a party, and by two in the morning we were all pretty smashed, especially the Governor, who slapped me on the back—they do a lot of that in Knoxville—and said, "This is really a big occasion in your life, son, isn't it?"

"Oh, it sure is, Governor."

"Have you called your mother?"

"I beg your pardon?"

"Did you call your dear mother back home on such an auspicious occasion?"

"Well, no, I haven't."

"Boy, call your mother. I'll talk to her."

"It's kind of late . . ."

"*Certainly* it's late, but it's never too late to call your mother."

I shrugged and dialed the number. The Governor grabbed the phone. When my mother answered, he said, "Miz Griffin? This is Governor Frank Clement of the great state of Tennessee."

I heard my mother's reply: "Now, Joe Darcy, stop that. Are you and my husband out drinking again?" Mervyn, Sr., and friends were famous for their practical jokes.

"A . . . Miz Griffin, this *is* the Governor of Tennessee here . . ."

"Sure, and I'm the Mayor of New York. Where is Mervyn?"

"Merv is right here with me in Tennessee, ma'am, and I want to say what a fine young man . . ."

"Joe, cut this out and put my husband on the phone. I want to talk with Mervyn."

"You just don't understand, Miz Griffin, Mervyn your *son* is standing right here with me in this lovely home in Tennessee . . ."

"Joe Darcy, you . . ."

He handed me the phone. "Boy, talk to your mother."

To this day my mother refuses to believe it was the Governor of Tennessee she talked to.

After Knoxville, Kathryn and I split off to promote the picture in different parts of the country.

My next stop was Boston. Skimming through the paper 195

I saw Freddy Martin's orchestra was in town so I called them up. "I've got the presidential suite at the Statler. Get the whole gang over here after the show."

The entire band showed up that night and I had room service cater a buffet and bar for them. We ate and drank all night, and I sent the married guys into the bedroom to use my phone to call their wives. When I checked out, the bill came to three thousand dollars, charged to Warner Brothers. I knew I would have a lot of explaining to do, but these were old friends from all those one-night stands; I had reached some degree of star status and wanted to spread it around. It gave me a great feeling, and I know they had a good time.

When the publicity tour hit Denver I was in for another parade. Miss Denver and I rode in a convertible through the city, but there weren't many people looking at us. Embarrassing as it was, we waved and smiled for the photographers, so next morning when the picture hit the front page it looked like the Rose Bowl Parade.

Warners hosted a reception for the press in my suite at the Brown Palace, and I did my best to be charming and act suave like a Hollywood star. Everything went smoothly until midnight when the doorbell rang and an uninvited but, at least on my part, welcome guest turned up. I was standing with a studio publicist when I saw the woman in the doorway and exclaimed, "My God, it's *Peaches* Browning," and I stepped forward to give her a hug. The publicist staggered a moment as though he was having a heart attack, then whirled and formed a human wall between the photographers, Peaches and me. And now let me explain why.

A few of you, I'm sure, remember Peaches as being involved in a scandalous divorce trial during the twenties. From 1925 to 1927 you could hardly pick up a paper without seeing an article about Edward "Daddy" Browning and his little "Peaches." Here's what happened. Daddy was a wealthy Manhattan realtor who decided to "adopt" a young 196 orphan girl as a playmate for his previously adopted daughter, Sunshine. He placed an ad in *The New York Times* announcing his search for a protégée who would be taken care of in luxury for the rest of her life. Eight thousand girls lined up outside his office the next day, and as you might guess, the search for the lucky girl was a three-ring circus. The first girl selected turned out to be a fraud; she was a twenty-one-year-old trying to pass herself off for fifteen to get some quick money. That was good for a few hundred column inches. Next came Peaches. Much to the shock of all decent people, a few months after the "adoption" Daddy married his little Peaches, with the consent of Peaches' mother. Six months after the marriage came the divorce trial, covered in mass by the gossip-hungry media. There were bizarre allegations by Peaches regarding Daddy's sexual behavior; apparently he liked to imitate a "honking goose" in the bedroom, and often rose in the middle of the night to "sand his shoe trees for hours." Daddy died before the two were ever legally divorced, and Peaches pursued a career as a vaudevillian. Eventually she moved to the San Francisco area in search of a new life and married Joe Civelli, who ran the San Francisco Emporium. This is where I come into the picture. It's World War Two and I'm singing and playing piano to sell war bonds, and Peaches hitches up with the Red Cross to help her standing as a society matron. I met her at a fundraising function, and she took a liking to me and my music. We ran into each other socially several times after that.

So there she was showing up out of the blue in Denver at the Brown Palace, and the last thing the Warner Brothers publicity people wanted was for me to be pictured with a woman whose name was synonomous with scandal. But the photographers backed off. Peaches and I renewed our acquaintance, and she turned out to be the life of the party, as always.

And the tour for *So This Is Love* continued. Unfortunately, however, the day after our premiere, CinemaScope was introduced to moviegoers. Compared to the wide screen, our film looked like a postage stamp.

By the end of 1954 here's where my film career stood: *Cattle Town* (1952), I had twelfth billing and even less of a role; *By the Light of the Silvery Moon* (1953), the megaphone upstaged me; *So This Is Love* (1953), my best role; *Three Sailors and a Girl*, a chance to hear Jack E. Leonard's ad libs on the set; *The Boy from Oklahoma* (1954), the boy from San Mateo is no cowboy (just ask Michael Curtiz); and my last Warner film, *Phantom of the Rue Morgue* (1954), made in 3-D just as the 3-D vogue died, along with the picture.

Putting together all my performances I had a half hour of film. With this in mind, I returned from my tour for *So This Is Love* knowing I had to make a move. The scripts coming my way had fifty thousand fingerprints on them, and I was infinitely more excited about performing onstage in Knoxville for *So This Is Love* than I had been making the movie. All my friends—Bullets Durgom, Tony Curtis, Janet Leigh, Jeff Donnell and Bill Orr—said I looked much happier at home at my piano than I ever did on the Warner lot.

Any Sunday I didn't spend at Jack Warner's home I spent at my own, hosting a barbecue and sing-along like the ones the Griffins of San Mateo used to have.

Janet and Tony were frequent guests, along with Jeff Donnell, Aldo Ray, Peter Lawford, and their various dates, and Bill and Joy Orr.

One Sunday I was awakened by that familiar Jack Warner ring, like a bucket of cold water dumped on my head.

"That you, Griff?"

"Yes, good morning, Mr. Warner."

"You having a party today?"

"A few friends are coming by . . ."

"Griff, you've been to my house twenty times, how come I never get invited to yours?"

"Well, I didn't think . . ."

"Don't think. What time is the party?"

"Brunch is at one."

"I'll see you at twelve-thirty."

That woke me in a hurry. What could I do to entertain Jack Warner? I called Uncle Elmer and asked if he'd come by and talk tennis with him.

What really made me nervous was I hadn't made any secret of my dislike of film work. I'd told my friends, my girl, my manager, just about anyone who would listen. Jack Warner always kept an ear to the ground, and this could make the afternoon uncomfortable.

Not only did Jack Warner arrive early for the party, he *was* the party.

"Hello, Griff, nice of you to have me. Start playing the piano."

"What would you like to hear?"

"Start playing, I know everything."

And he did. He sang, whistled and, to the strains of "Tea for Two," tap-danced on my kitchen floor. The rest of us looked on in disbelief as the king-mogul of Hollywood carried on like a vaudevillian. I don't think anyone ever had a better time at a party than Jack Warner did that day.

Uncle Elmer sat and watched Warner with the rest of us, and while the food was being served Mr. Warner asked, "What does your fat uncle do for a living, Merv?"

"He's in real estate—and he plays tennis."

"Him? Tennis? He's too fat."

An idea popped into my head. "Colonel, my uncle can beat anybody who ever comes to your court. He's quite good."

Warner balked at the suggestion. "OK, Griff. Next Sunday. Bill Orr and your fat uncle will play Solly Biano and me."

Elmer accepted, and the match was set.

Mr. Warner chose his partner well. Like Bill Orr, Solly Biano ran the casting department, but played tennis at the tournament level and was not about to let Jack Warner lose a match, particularly to my "fat uncle." At the studio Solly handled touchy situations all the time. But all his finesse availed him nothing the day he brought Humphrey Bogart to the set of *East of Eden* to meet James Dean. Bogart, one 199 of the original rebels of the film business, wanted to meet this interesting new actor. Solly made the introduction, but Dean never looked at Bogart. He said hello and stared at the floor. For a minute and a half Bogart tried carrying on a gentleman's conversation; he paid Dean a great compliment by saying he admired the young man's technique. Dean said, "Yeah? That's OK by me." Suddenly Bogey grabbed Dean by the lapels, nearly yanking him off the ground. "You little *punk*, when I talk to you, you look in my eyes, you understand? Who the hell do you think you are, you two-bit nothing?" Then Bogey shoved the stunned actor away and stormed off the set.

A tennis match would be simpler duty for Solly.

On the way over to Warner's mansion, Elmer asked me, "You want me to win this match, Merv? If I do, it will mean trouble for you."

"I know that, Elmer. Can you win it?"

"Of course."

"Solly Biano is tough."

"Don't give it a second thought. But why?"

"I want out of my contract. This will make it easier."

"We won't want the match to last too long."

When we walked on the court Jack Warner was already warming up with Solly and Bill Orr. A gallery of twenty looked on from the shade of umbrellas. Judy Garland was there looking bored, Doris Day was there looking gorgeous (and interested), and the rest of the gallery sipped iced tea and cheered each time the Colonel made a good shot. They didn't have much to cheer, though.

Elmer controlled the match from first point to last, and as the outcome became inevitable Jack's temper grew shorter and shorter. He threw his racquet, questioned line calls, and barked a stream of words America thought Doris Day had never heard.

The final score was 6–1, 6–2, and Elmer and I got the hell out of there in a hurry.

The match came at the same time that the studio was 200 slashing away at its budget; I hastened what was coming.

In a couple of months my option was due on the contract, and Bullets called me to talk about it. "Merv, they are willing to let you out of the contract if you don't work for another studio for at least two years."

"I probably wouldn't work at *this* studio for another two years, Bullets."

"That could be true."

"I want out, a clean break. Just put me back on a stage."

When I put the receiver down on its cradle, my career at Warner Brothers was over. I couldn't get out of Hollywood fast enough.

13

My first stop was Las Vegas, where I'd been booked at the Sands Hotel to open for the great Tallulah Bankhead. She remembered me from an appearance I had made on her NBC radio program "The Big Show" in 1951.

At the time she was suing her former housekeeper for embezzling money from her checking account, but the trial turned into a circus, with Tallulah's personal life as the main event. The housekeeper claimed Tallulah "was never sober or rarely so." That she "spent a fortune, enough for you to send your kids to college . . . on cocaine, marijuana, booze and scotch and champagne." The housekeeper also maintained that Tallulah made her learn how to roll joints for Tallulah to smoke. This was big news all over America, and hundreds of fans stood outside the courthouse every day just to hear the latest dirt. While the housekeeper was on the witness stand Tallulah kept having coughing fits, which sent the spectators into hysterics.

I happened to be booked on "The Big Show" a few days after the trial ended, along with Phil Silvers, Loretta Young, Ethel Merman and Sarah Vaughan. We were sitting around backstage waiting for Tallulah to arrive for the script conference, and of course the number one topic of conversation was the trial. Ethel Merman waved away the newspaper stories: "Anyone who'd call Bankhead a pot fiend is a stupid son-of-a-bitch who . . ."

In swept Bankhead. Everyone clammed up so we could
202 determine how seriously she'd taken the trial. She walked

right past us and out to the stage, where the huge NBC orchestra was sitting, and yelled, "Has anybody got a reefer?"

That answered that question.

Tallalah took a liking to me. As I stood in the wings waiting to be introduced for my song she walked over to me and said, "Darling, I want to wish you a lot of luck, you're just *wonderful*," and she spit on my cheek. I jumped back in horror. "What the hell was *that* for?"

"Why, darling, that's a French theater custom."

Three years later we were reunited at the Sands in Las Vegas. I stopped by her dressing room on the first day of rehearsal. "Tallulah? It's Merv."

"Oh, my *darling* Merv . . . come in . . . we're going to have a wonderful time together."

I walked in.

"Where are you?"

"I'm in *here*. Do come in."

I walked through another doorway and there was Tallulah, sitting stark naked on the toilet. I made a hasty retreat.

"What's the matter, darling, are you chicken or something? I always have my conferences in here."

"I'll wait, if you don't mind."

"Oh, come here, I've just had one of those breast lifts and I *must* show someone."

"Some other time."

Our show sold out every night. Guests at the hotel offered me hundred-dollar bills to sneak them into the showroom. Tallulah told stories, did a few musical numbers and tossed out lines which had the audience in a continuous roar.

I loved every minute of the engagement. Every night after the show I was out on the town with a girl from the Sands' chorus line. Hotel policy forbade entertainers from dating the girls in the chorus, but Jack Entratter, the entertainment director, chose to overlook my little indiscretion. The relationship took a ninety-degree turn when the Las 203

Vegas police showed up in my dressing room one night and dropped the news I'd be needing protection because I was dating a girl who a very prominent mobster used to date. "As long as this guy is in town," they told me, "we're going to have to have two men escort you wherever you go." I told the police to forget the guards, I wouldn't see the girl. But plainclothesmen followed me anyway. I pulled up to the Flamingo one evening and the cops stopped me. "He's in there, you can't go in—he might get angry if he sees you." "Let's get this thing settled right now," I said. "Point him out to me." I marched up to the mobster, who was having drinks, and said, "Look, I don't know you, but you are causing *me* a lot of trouble. I don't know anything about your girlfriends and don't want anything to do with them so just leave me alone." I don't know if I was being stupid or brave, but I didn't hear any more about it from either the gangster or the police after that.

Tallulah adored the story; she was mad for gangsters. On closing night she threw a party and invited a lot of guys who wore their hats indoors and had names like "Wingy," "Lefty" and "Cincinnati."

She grabbed me the second I walked into the suite. "*Darling*, Merv, there's a new punch I've just heard about and we're going to have it . . . it's called Zombie."

"That stuff will put us right on the floor."

"Don't be silly, darling. Waiter! Two Zombies."

We toasted the successful engagement and downed the drinks.

"Why there's nothing to this drink," she complained. "It's only fruit punch . . . waiter . . . two more please. . . . "

Down they went.

She stopped the waiter. "Those Zombies are *boring*. Bring my darling Merv and me frozen daiquiris."

I figured, what the hell, it was my last night in town, why not? . . . We started in on the daiquiris.

The Zombies hit us about fifteen minutes later and transformed us into stumbling drunks.

"God," Tallulah shouted, "I've got to gamble. I feel *lucky*."

I think I was the only person in the room drunk enough to decipher her ravings.

The hotel had a strict rule then against the entertainers gambling during an engagement.

"We can't, Tallulah, Jack Entratter will be furious."

"Then we'll buy him a Zombie. Come on, darling, we're going to win some money."

We wobbled our way to the casino and sat down at a blackjack table. Tallulah had two thousand in her purse, and I had a thousand plus my paycheck from the Sands. There was no stopping us; we bet like crazy persons, throwing money all over the table. We were too drunk to know a good bet from a bad one, but someone up above was watching over us because we started winning like mad. I mean *winning*. A crowd formed around the table and watched in awe as Tallulah and I raked in armfuls of chips. By six in the morning I was fifteen thousand dollars ahead and there was no telling how much Tallulah had won. We were so tired and drunk we could barely stand up, but we kept placing bets. Then Jack Entratter showed up. He took each of us by an arm and said, "Bedtime." As Jack dragged us up the sweeping staircase that led from the casino to the rooms, the crowd followed us; everyone in the casino knew the great Bankhead wouldn't leave without an exit line. At the top of the stairway Tallulah stopped rocking on her heels and looked down at the gathering crowd. "Well," she yelled, "isn't anyone going to lay me?"

I staggered to my room and found a message from a friend of mine in the orchestra who had promised to give me a lift back to L.A. It read: "Leaving from front of hotel at seven A.M." That was in fifteen minutes. I stuffed my belongings in the suitcase and, still in my tuxedo, staggered out front where my friend, Howard, was loading the car. He didn't look in much better shape than me, but I was too tired to care. I climbed in the back of the car, kicked my shoes off and passed out.

A few hours later I woke up with a bell-ringing, bomb-blasting headache. My mouth was dry and it tasted like an ashtray after a party. When I moved the slightest bit my head pounded from ear to ear; the reek of rum and to-bacco from my clothing nauseated me. Then I realized the car wasn't moving. I heard a buzz-saw whining off in the distance, and the occasional whish of another car going by. The last thing I remembered was drinking the second Zombie, ordering a daiquiri and heading for the casino. I felt in my pocket for my paycheck and cash. Neither was there. That woke me in a hurry. Adrenaline shot through my system and I jumped up and banged my head on the roof of the car.

Howard was asleep in the front seat.

I took him violently. "Howard, where *are* we?"

"Huh . . . somewhere . . . near Barstow I think. I was tired of driving."

I could hardly hear him through all the noise in my head. "What happened last night?"

"You gambled all night with Tallulah."

"Oh, no—I gambled?"

"All night."

"I don't remember it. Did I win or lose?"

"You lost."

"Oh, no—lost?"

"Lost. Big."

"My paycheck. . . "

"You lost that, too."

"How can I be so *stupid*? How can I be such an idiot?"

I was on the verge of tears, but my head and body hurt too much to let me cry.

"I'm going to walk over to the diner and get some cof-fee." I tried pulling on my shoes but they wouldn't fit. I thought my feet were swollen. I stuck my hand in one of the shoes and pulled out a wad of money. Both shoes were stuffed with cash.

I looked at Howard. He was smiling.

"You had hundred-dollar bills spilling out of your pock-ets this morning so I stuffed it all in our shoes so it wouldn't blow out the window. It's all there. And the check. You won fifteen thousand dollars."

It's amazing what finding fifteen thousand dollars in your shoe will do for a hangover. My headache left immediately and my mouth wasn't dry anymore. I started laughing, laughing out loud until tears fell down my face; I sang at the top of my lungs the rest of the way back to Los Angeles.

With my winnings, I bought a new car and headed for New York.

In her last years Tallulah made several appearances on my show, and I remember her final ad lib.

She was on the show with Margaret Truman, who at one point started discussing the reluctance of American women to reveal their age. "I don't think we should make such a big thing about it," she said, "I'm quite willing to say that I'm forty-three years old."

Tallulah gasped, "Oh, *please,* dahling," and pointed to the camera. "People are *eating.*"

14

When I moved back to New York to wipe the Hollywood slate clean and start over as an entertainer, I sublet an apartment through one of the agents at MCA who represented me—Jay Kantor, the man who married Judy Balaban. He was primarily involved with film work, and his clients included Marlon Brando, Monty Clift and Paul Newman. When I asked him if he knew of a place, I received a call a few days later from Celia Meredith, Brando's secretary, telling me that Marlon was going to Europe and I could take his apartment if I wanted. I took it sight unseen.

It was a roomy, comfortable one-bedroom apartment that retained remnants of Brando's idiosyncrasies. For one thing, there was a hole in the wall by the door where the intercom was supposed to be; Marlon hated buzzers and bells so he ripped the box out of the wall. He'd kept a pet raccoon in the apartment—doesn't everyone?—and every time I moved a chair I found another pile of hardened droppings. Celia asked if I'd leave one closet locked where Marlon and his roommate Wally Cox could leave a few of his things; I looked in there only once and found most of the closet crammed with a miniature-train set.

The oddest thing about Marlon's apartment, however, was the doorman out front of the building; he could have been Brando's talking double; and his speech pattern was a duplicate of Brando's in *On the Waterfront*. One day, after two months of seeing this guy, I finally had to ask him why he spent his life mimicking Marlon Brando. "Are you kiddin', buddy? That Brando stole his whole act from me. *I'm* Marlon Brando but he's the one what's gettin' the money. He useta sit down here right where you're standin' and talk to me half an hour every day. Then I go to his movie and there *I* am except he's sayin' the words and he's gettin' the money. What you talkin' about, impersonatin' Marlon Brando? Geez . . . Marlon Brando . . ." Actors Studio could have used him.

The first two weeks I lived in Brando's apartment the phone rang constantly with reporters calling and banging on the door to ask Marlon about his latest love affair; they were sure I was Brando disguising my voice. Once one of the gents from the Fourth Estate asked, "Marlon, is it true you shower in your underwear to save money on laundry bills?" That gave me some understanding of Marlon's mercurial relationship with the press.

One year later I found out about a nicer apartment on Fifty-seventh Street that was coming up for rent, and I asked Jay Kantor if he had another client who might want Marlon's place. A day later he called back and asked if he could bring someone by tomorrow morning. "Sure, just bang on the door because the bell doesn't work."

I went out on the town that night and didn't get home until about four in the morning, and by then I was in no condition to even remember the appointment with Jay's client. At nine o'clock there was a loud knock on my door, which sounded like an explosion in my head. I dragged myself out of bed, pulled on a robe and stumbled to the entry hall. I'm sure I looked like hell but at the time I didn't care; I only wanted to go back to bed. When I opened the door and saw who was standing there I thought I was hallucinating. She was wearing a gray raincoat but there was no mistaking the face. I just stood and stared and tried to wake myself.

"I'm Marilyn Monroe," she said.

For all I know it might have been five minutes before I answered her. "What d'ya want?" I ad-libbed.

209

"Can I see the apartment?"

"You're here to look at the apartment?"

"It is Marlon Brando's isn't it?"

"Yes."

"Then I'm at the right place."

Jay Kantor popped his head into the doorway and started laughing so hard he started Marilyn and me laughing, too.

I put some water on for coffee, and got myself dressed while Marilyn and Jay poked around the apartment. She was, indeed, looking for an apartment because she was planning to spend some time in town working with Lee Strasberg. Brando was her idol, and this visit was a pilgrimage. She was like a child in a toy shop as she wandered through the apartment, peeking into closets and touching the furniture. When she reached the locked storage closet she asked me about it.

"Marlon left some things in there. He asked me to keep it locked."

She gave me a pleading look that weakened my knees. "Can't I just have a look?"

"I promised him . . ."

Then she walked over to the piano, ran her hand over the keys and asked if it was mine or Marlon's.

"It's his."

"Really? Will you play something for me?"

"Sure, if you'll sing."

"We'll all sing."

And we did, the three of us, for over an hour, running through all my sheet music of show tunes.

Marilyn left, and she never sublet the apartment, but I'm sure that wasn't her purpose from the start. I went back to bed and decided I wouldn't even *bother* telling my friends that Marilyn had come by to visit.

When I moved out of the apartment I asked Celia Meredith if Marlon wanted the piano, and she told me if I took over the payments it was mine. I came up with four hundred bucks, bought the piano outright, and it sits today in my farm in Califon, New Jersey.

Shortly after I moved back to New York, Monty Clift called to invite me to a dinner party; I sensed a purpose beyond being social in his voice but he wouldn't reveal anything to me over the phone.

A few of Monty's friends were already there when I arrived. Kevin McCarthy was there with his wife, Augusta Dabney, and three or four other people. Monty was playing a recording of Dylan Thomas reading Dylan Thomas poems, and the volume was turned up so high the windowpanes rattled every time Thomas' booming baritone voice recited a line. We were shouting, trying to carry on a conversation. Finally I suggested to Monty he turn down the volumn. Instead, he put on another record, this one of baritone John Charles Thomas; Monty stared at the speakers as if he expected to see the singer in them, and I was at a total loss to figure out what was going on. I looked at Kevin for a clue but he just shrugged.

After several drinks Monty said to me, "You know, I've been taking singing lessons."

"I didn't know that."

"Yes, and I'm going to sing for you tonight, and I'd like you to play the piano for me."

I rolled my eyes skyward at the thought of Monty's voice, which was too intimate and held in the mask of his face— not the kind of voice for a singer.

He took the needle off the record and announced, "Merv's going to play piano and I'm going to sing a song for everyone."

I played and Monty sang. He had the beginning of a voice, I mean, he wasn't desperately out of tune, but he lacked control and wandered over the notes without fluidity or strength. I tried covering the imperfections of his voice with piano embellishments, but everyone in the room had been around show business enough to know a good voice from a bad one. When Monty finished, he turned his challenging and vulnerable eyes toward me. "What do you think, Merv?"

"You're off to a good start, Monty. It's a beginning   211

and I'm amazed you've done this well in such a short time."

His eyes fired up. "You're cloaking what you mean with a lot of shit."

"Singing is like acting, Monty. It's a lot of work learning to control the voice and project; it doesn't all happen at once. You've made a start, and if I were you I'd stay with it."

"Stay with it? Fuck! I'm going to do a Broadway musical."

"You're not ready. They wouldn't hear you past the fourth row."

He was both hurt and angry, so I said, "Monty, here's my other choice: 'You're the most brilliant singer I've ever heard and you should open on Broadway tomorrow." Now do you want that or do you want the truth?"

Fortunately the maid announced dinner.

As soon as he sat down Monty launched into a confused monologue about great singers and ended up by saying, "Pearl Bailey is the greatest entertainer show business has ever known." Then he looked at each person at the table, one by one, and asked if they didn't agree. I ignored him.

Monty glared at me. "From the look on your face I suppose you don't agree with me, Mr. Griffin?"

The moment Monty said "Mr. Griffin" I knew I was in for a problem. His obsessive opinions weren't anything new to me. One night at dinner in Los Angeles we'd gotten into a row about the music in *From Here to Eternity*. I casually mentioned that the theme sounded like the song "Picnic." Monty wouldn't let the subject drop. Finally he had insisted upon leaving dinner half eaten, driving to a music store, and comparing the sheet music of the two songs note for note.

"I think Pearl Bailey is a wonderful performer, Monty, but not the greatest singer in the history of show business. If it's your opinion, though, that's fine. Stick with it."

"A lot of people *do* agree with me."

212   I shrugged.

"Oh," he said, "you mean Pearl Bailey *isn't* the greatest entertainer in show business?"

I wouldn't even look at him.

He lifted the huge roast beef off its platter and threw it at me.

I caught it against my chest. Onions and carrots attached, not to mention *au jus*.

I put it back on the platter and I saw Monty retreating to some place deep within himself. There was no conversing with him in that mood. The evening was subdued and uneventful after that.

What happened may seem strange, but this was business as usual with Monty. His friends stood by him as long as they could.

When the newspapers headlined the story of Monty's automobile accident in May 1956, I was filled with sorrow but not surprised. He had the aura of a man headed for disaster, and he barely escaped death in the crash. His nose and jaw were crushed, and he spent nine weeks recuperating.

The finely chiseled, even pretty, features of his face were gone. Though he recovered with remarkably few scars, he looked like a different man.

A few months after the accident he arrived unannounced in New York, carrying a list of home addresses of several old friends. The bell of my apartment rang late on a Wednesday night, and since the intercom wasn't working properly I took my dog and went downstairs to see who it was. I opened the door a crack and saw an unfamiliar man who wore an overcoat and wide-brimmed hat. He was standing perfectly still, the hat covering his eyes.

"What can I do for you?"

The man didn't say a word.

"What do you want?"

My heart started to pound and I was about to slam the door when the man whispered, "You don't know me, do you, Merv?"

I knew the voice instantly. "Monty . . . I couldn't tell it was you, it's so dark out here."

He turned and walked quickly away. I called after him but he kept walking.

Kevin McCarthy later told me Monty had made a number of stops that night, and very few people had passed the test.

I moved to the apartment on Fifty-seventh Street, and continued pushing my television career, trying to make the transition from someone who sang songs on variety shows, which I did on Arthur Murray's "Dance Party" and "The Robert Q. Lewis Show," to someone who gets a chance to *talk* and show his personality—which I began to do as host of a religious program, "Look Up and Live" and on the radio program "Network Time."

Living across the street from me on Fifty-seventh was a young songwriter named Burt Bacharach, who was trying to make the transition from being a conductor for other performers, like Marlene Dietrich and Vic Damone, to becoming recognized as a composer of pop songs. We became friends through mutual acquaintances in the music business and used to chum around on double dates to nightclubs around town.

One summer he and I and Rose Tobias, a casting director Burt was dating at the time, pooled our money to rent a weekend place at Ocean Beach. This was trouble from the start. We each had a dog and they fought constantly. Then Burt and Rose got into an awful row and I jumped in trying to be a peacemaker and they *both* became angry with me. The topper was a party where we had too much to drink and I started doing a wild dance on the fence and fell off, narrowly missing a boulder but landing in a patch of poison ivy that kept me scratching for weeks.

There was, though, a good side to that summer. Burt got a job playing piano in a tiny fishermen's bar at Ocean Beach. The show-business and literary crowd from New York had been frequenting another bar nearby, until word started getting around about Burt, and gradually the crowds picked up. This being a resort area, some of the patrons tended to get a little wild and lend their talent to Burt's act. He is an absolute perfectionist who likes to work alone. I spent half my evenings trying to talk some guy out of punching Burt because he'd insulted his girl's voice. Burt came up with a solution to the problem. One day he shows up at the bar with a pile of wood and some tools and has me help him build a small fence around the piano so no one can get to him. Now, *that* is a perfectionist.

A critic from *Variety* turned up in the bar one night and wrote a fabulous review of Burt; and he was on his way toward the career he desperately wanted.

Fifteen years later I was the neighbor of another song-writer, Jerry Leiber. With his partner, Mike Stoller, Jerry was responsible for writing songs such as "Hound Dog," "On Broadway," "Poison Ivy," "Kansas City," "I'm a Woman," "Jailhouse Rock"—and I could go on listing their hits for pages. Jerry used to run up to my apartment now and then and play his latest compositions. One day he arrived with a song he said he wanted me to record. Naturally I was interested. He sat down and played the song, but it was a talking song rather than a singer's song. "I can't do a song like that, Jerry, it wouldn't work for me. I honestly don't see how it could ever be a hit. Where's the melody?" So he took the song called "Is That All There Is?" to his friend Peggy Lee, who recorded it and sold so many millions of copies I get a headache thinking about it.

Twelve years after I lived in Marlon Brando's apartment he called me at the office and asked to come by and discuss the Martin Luther King Foundation, which he was raising money for. We talked business first, then reminisced for a couple of hours, until it came time to do my show. "Just for fun," I said, "let's take a walk through the production office and I'll introduce you as a new writer on the show."

We walked into Bob Shanks's office and before Bob had a chance to react I said, "Bob, this young man, Mark Johnson, is going to be writing for us. And please don't tell him he looks like Marlon Brando because everyone tells him that." Then we popped in on a few secretaries and watched the color drain from their faces while I introduced "Mark Johnson." Brando was beginning to like the game, and since he was in a good mood I asked if he'd walk out for a moment at the top of the show. He agreed and stayed for a forty-five-minute interview. We talked about the Martin Luther King project and his involvement with various causes; we discussed some of his work in films and the work of others he admired.

After the show we went next door to Sardi's for dinner. Brando didn't hang out in show-business restaurants often, so it was like being with Liz Taylor in Lindy's all over again. The jaded Sardi's clientele watched every gesture of the great actor.

Later we walked around the corner to Broadway to catch a cab, just as the theaters started letting out. Brando and I were spotted at once, and a large crowd formed around us. We pushed our way out to the middle of the street, and the crowd lined the sidewalks, pointing and shouting excitedly. Finally a cab stopped and picked us up but we were caught in traffic and people ran out into the street and pushed up against the window of the cab. I'd never seen this kind of gawking hysteria Brando generated. He slid down his seat and closed his eyes until the driver found an opening and we sped away. I was stunned by the experience, but Brando seemed to drift into a meditative state. I could see by his face his thoughts were a million miles away from the interview he'd just done and the crush of fans on Broadway. He was off to that place in the actor's mind I never found.

PART FIVE

Starting Over

1957-1972

15

MY YEARS as a contract player with Warner Brothers seemed so long ago to me on an afternoon in 1969 when I sat in the living room of my apartment on Central Park West and told Julann about the commitment I'd just made to CBS. I was taking myself out of the relative security of syndication with Westinghouse and diving into direct competition with two other talk shows in the eleven-thirty time period. When I left Hollywood for New York at the end of my Warner Brothers contract, I didn't make the move with the intention of becoming a talk-show host. The thought of hosting a talk show didn't much cross my mind until 1957 when I became a faithful viewer, along with the rest of America, of Jack Paar and his nightly ritual known as "The Tonight Show." I knew I didn't want to be a singer on a variety show, but it was Paar who put in my mind the idea of what I *did* want to do. What appealed to me about Jack and "The Tonight Show" was the spontaneity; you never knew what was going to happen next, and I didn't dare miss the show because if I did, that would be the one everyone was talking about next morning.

During those early days in New York I told Julann, Irving Mansfield, Burt Bacharach, Jaye P. Morgan, and just about everyone else I knew around New York that someday Jack Paar would give me a chance to host "The Tonight Show," even though I had no reason to believe it might happen. In fact, belief was my *only* reason. Somewhere, somebody was listening, because I did get my 219 chance at "The Tonight Show," and that one night hooked me on the format for life.

As should be obvious by now, however, once I did get my own talk show it wasn't smooth sailing. I put in six months on NBC, felt the ax of cancellation, then found a comfortable home two years later in a show syndicated by Westinghouse. Then CBS came along waving a dollar-laden contract, and I couldn't look away. I might have, though, if I'd have known what I was in store for, professionally and personally.

Opening night on CBS was a debacle, but our shows improved considerably as the weeks rolled on. We overtook ABC and "The Joey Bishop Show" in rating points immediately, and on certain nights showed strongly against Johnny and "The Tonight Show." But the cumulative strength of "Tonight" asserted itself, and it became obvious we weren't going to move them off the map. The CBS corporate structure started getting nervous; if "The Merv Griffin Show" failed, it would be a whopping multimillion-dollar disaster; certain people at the network would be held responsible; and no one in a network's executive structure wants to be tainted by a loser. CBS President Robert Wood stayed firmly in my corner, encouraging me to develop the show and find our audience, but we didn't deal on a daily basis with Bob Wood—we dealt with a dizzying maze of executives whose titles and faces melt together in my mind. Robert Blake has a term for them: "the suits." I'll tell you how the suits work. They try to wear you down by persistence, with telephone calls, letters and memos, jabbing away with ideas meant to present the corporation's opinion. They'll make a comment about a guest's "revealing" attire, an off-color line, a song you did, or the importance of guests you booked, nitpicking until you want to cave in from fatigue. At NBC I wasn't on the air long enough to meet the suits, at Westinghouse there weren't any. But at CBS I started meeting them after the first two weeks of shows.

220

I didn't want to think about how much decolletage Eva Gabor was showing, or if Joan Baez made too pungent a remark about President Nixon; I had bigger problems to worry about. For one, the number of stations in our network.

NBC carried the clout of two hundred twelve stations for "The Tonight Show"; we challenged them with one hundred fifty. This meant a zero rating in the fifty markets we weren't in. So even though we showed strongly in Los Angeles, San Francisco and a few other key markets, the cumulative ratings of "Tonight" were beyond our reach. Television can be a maddening game of "who's hot and who's not," and the moment we showed a negative trend in our ratings, the suits got very nervous. Imagine how disconcerting it is for a performer to put his heart and soul into a show every night, trying anything he can to keep the show bright and entertaining, then to come in to work the next morning and have his performance judged by a set of rating points dumped on his desk by a young executive who doesn't know if the name is Griffith or Griffin. That is the reality of television, and you have to expect it with those big contracts, but it makes for roller-coaster emotional rides. Certain stations in the CBS network, once it became clear we weren't going to overtake "Tonight," defected and chose to run old movies instead of my show. This sort of news travels fast in show business, and we were scratching and clawing for life two weeks after our first show.

Ratings are always the bottom line, but they weren't our only problem. Booking the show became a battle to challenge master strategists. Four national talk shows—"Tonight," "Merv Griffin," "David Frost" and "Dick Cavett," who replaced Joey Bishop—taped five days a week in New York; Mike Douglas taped just ninety miles away in Philadelphia. Start multiplying five guests per show, five days a week, and *then* try and find one hundred twenty-five unusually interesting people per week, and you'll have some idea of what I'm talking about. Imagine the bloody war 221 whoops sounding all over town when a really great guest, like Peter Ustinov, popped into Manhattan long enough to do one or two shows. Some days it seemed like we were pulling people out of phone booths to see if they had an interesting five-minute story to tell.

To illustrate what was going on during these talk-show wars, there's a story behind the visit by Hubert Humphrey I mentioned earlier. We landed him the same day as David Frost, the deal being he'd do twenty minutes with Frost, who taped at the same time we did, then make a quick trip to our studio. Talent coordinator Jean Meegan was standing by in Frost's studio to make sure everything went according to schedule. She started getting very nervous as Frost's interview with the Senator rolled past the twenty-minute mark and it looked like it might go right on for the rest of the show. Well, Jean had booked Senator Humphrey for me and wasn't about to lose him, so at the next commercial she marched out on Frost's stage, informed the Senator he was due at the Griffin Show, and hustled him right out to the door to a waiting limousine.

The classic talk-show shuffle was performed by the agile Jerry Lewis, who set a record by making Johnny, Merv and Dick on the *same night*, without informing any of us of his plan. Listen, when I tuned in the tube that night and saw Jerry all over the place, I knew New York was getting too crowded.

In response to the booking problem, we took the show to Hollywood and to Las Vegas a week at a time, and this move pumped up our ratings temporarily, but a little better wasn't good enough.

I felt the pressure in every bone of my body.

When I'm paid to do a job, especially the millions CBS was forking over, I expect to deliver, not only on behalf of the people who are paying me but also for the people *I'm* paying. I don't like a constant turnover of people around me; I work better with people who can sense what I want in a show. It takes years to build a solid staff, and I had several people who'd been there from the beginning: Bob Shanks, who started out as low man on the totem pole at

"Tonight" and in six years became the highest-salaried talk-show producer in show business; Bob Murphy, my childhood friend who started out in 1963 with my game-show company and was now high on the masthead of my show (eventually my producer); Tony Garofalo, who started in 1962 as a page and moved up as interviewer and writer; Murray Schwartz, with the William Morris Agency, who worked with me on a daily basis and would soon become president of my company. I knew these people as employees and friends, and I knew their wives and children. They'd been through good times and bad with me, and I didn't want to lose them.

During this time—the end of 1969 through all of 1970—I gained thirty pounds and increased my smoking from one pack of cigarettes a day to three. In fact, I was smoking up such a storm, on the air and off, that my mother called from California one morning to tell me she could hardly see the faces of my guests through the cloud of smoke I was creating.

These professional problems were placing a strain on my personal life, too. When I signed the CBS contract Julann was happy for me because it represented such an important step in my career. But I think she had an instinctive wariness of a deal that would require even more of my time than was already spent at work. By the spring of 1970 the show was suffering in the ratings and I was headed for an emotional crisis. All my life when I've had problems I've always tried working them out myself. I just never have been one to burden others with my woes. So it did not surprise Julann when I told her one morning I had to get away to make some decisions. In recent months our marriage had cooled but we both suspected it was because of business pressures, and hoped time would correct the situation. We were having breakfast when I said, "Julann, I really have to get away for a bit. We have to make changes in the show, and I've got some decisions to make."

"Then I think you should do it. And do it without wasting any time."

That afternoon I boarded a flight for Los Angeles. From 223

the airport I called Bob Shanks and told him I was getting away for a few days; that's all I told him because that's all I knew. I felt an uncentered anxiety that had to be uprooted and met head-on. I flew to my home state and spent the night at the Beverly Hills Hotel. In the morning I rented a car and drove to the beach. Many of my most peaceful, reflective moments as a child were near the ocean, when my family spent weekends on the Monterey peninsula. And I had no other thought when I reached California than to head straight for the ocean. I stopped at a real-estate office and watched the receptionist do a double take.

"Is that *you?*"

"I hope so."

"They said on your show last night you were home with a virus. What the heck are you doing way out here?"

I mumbled something about needing fresh air, and asked if she had any beach-front homes available for rental. I took the first house she showed me, leasing it for a month at a cost of eight hundred dollars. Now, I can't tell you why I did that; I could have taken the house for a week, or even a weekend. I *knew* I had to be back in New York in just a few days, but I wanted that house for a month, and wrote out a check for the full amount. Then it was time to buy groceries. No matter how much heavy thinking I have to do I always remember to keep some food around. I spent one hundred dollars on groceries, which in 1970 meant I had a very full cart. I went about it like I was settling in for the summer, buying jars of mayonnaise, mustard, ketchup, packages of butter, bottles of olive oil and vinegar, canisters of salt, pepper and spices. I bought two roasts of beef and a dozen steaks for the freezer. It was like I'd won a contest where you see how much food you can stuff in a shopping cart in fifteen minutes.

When I reached the house I carefully went about setting up housekeeping. I filled the freezer with meat and two cartons of ice cream, I stocked the shelves with milk, eggs, 224 cheese, fresh vegetables and fruit, the cupboards I loaded with crackers and condiments and spices and breakfast cereal, and on a lower shelf I stored a few bottles of wine. Then I brought my bags to the bedroom and unpacked, placing my clothes in the drawers and the closet. At the store I'd also bought soap, shampoo, toothpaste, shaving cream, deodorant, aspirin, vitamins and moisturizing cream. I stocked the medicine cabinet. In the living room there was a desk, and I emptied the contents of my briefcase on it, sorting out some memos and notes I'd been meaning to read. I sat down at the desk and tried to work. But I just stared at the papers; the words meant nothing to me. The sun was setting in soft washes of gold and red over the ocean, and I walked out to the deck to watch it. I sat in one of those canvas-and-wood director's chairs and stared out to sea. I must have been out there a long time, because when I decided to go inside the sky was totally dark, the air wet and chilly. All I heard was the rhythmic rushing of the sea, and an occasional car zooming along the road above the house.

The next morning I awoke unrested, read the paper on the porch, and decided to spend the day reading some business proposals I'd brought from New York. Then just as suddenly as I made that decision, I made another. It may sound crazy, but I decided to leave the house. I had an urge to get into the car and drive up the coast, toward northern California.

Not wanting to leave the house and food to waste, I called Ray Sneath and Jim Bradley, both of whom worked for me when we came west for our Hollywood shows. Ray, my stage manager, is a quiet, thoughtful young man who was obviously surprised to hear from me.

"I heard you were sick—in New York."

"No, I'm fine, I'm out here. I've rented a house in Malibu for a month and it's filled with food and everything you need, and I'm not going to use it. Why don't you and Jim take it? I'm driving up north to see my family. I'll leave the keys under the doormat."

I rolled down the top of my rented convertible, and 225

started up the coast highway. The ride was as solitary an experience as I've ever had. Just south of Santa Barbara I drove past fields of mustard that I hadn't seen since childhood; I remembered their smell vividly. I slowed the car and felt tears falling from my eyes. Maybe the tears were from memories of rides down the coast with my family, when my sister and I sat in the back seat, playing word games and watching the California landscape rush by. There was a security in those family journeys, and I felt no part of that security in my life now. The sadness stayed even as the scent of mustard faded. I drove past Solvang, San Luis Obispo, all the way to Monterey by early afternoon. I stopped there to walk and have a bite to eat; again, my mind turned back to earlier days and family trips to Monterey. The years had gone by so fast, yet the simple happiness I associated with my visits to the Monterey Peninsula eluded me that afternoon. I walked the streets of Carmel without noticing the people passing me, and they didn't seem to notice me, either. I was there to absorb something I couldn't name, but felt too restless to stay for long.

In the afternoon I drove to the San Francisco peninsula, where most of my relatives live. I went to the University of Santa Clara to see if my nephew Michael was practicing football. Of my sister's four children he is the eldest boy, and we'd been close ever since he could speak. Michael has always been a straight "A" student, and an outstanding athlete; he is a person with a clear head and a healthy attitude, and I responded to his youthful, optimistic outlook toward life. He was shocked to see me come walking out to the football field of his campus. "Unc, what the . . . ?"

"I wanted to get out of New York for awhile, Mike. It's nothing but problems with the show right now. I thought I'd come see the family and clear my head. Maybe we can take a ride over to Santa Cruz after you finish practice."

He showered and changed and we left.

I suppose I just had ocean on my mind. We went to Santa Cruz, with its wharf dotted with seafood restaurants, and its boardwalk where I used to perform at weekend dances when I worked at KFRC in San Francisco. Michael and I had a late lunch, then wandered through the many craft shops in Santa Cruz and its neighboring villages of Capitola and Aptos. Michael filled me in on all the latest news of the family and we talked about his plans after college. Finally he said, "You're having some problems with the show?"

So I started to unburden myself.

"I've really got myself in a thick situation with CBS. This is the first time they've tried to put programming on that late at night, and it's a big financial risk for them."

"I read the cover story about it in *Newsweek*."

"Right. And if it was all a mistake, it's going to be a very *big* mistake, an awfully big one for me to recover from. If the ratings don't pick up the show will eventually be canceled and it'll really be a mess. There are millions of dollars at stake, and a lot of jobs; the thought of letting a whole staff go . . . Christ, that's an awful thought and I don't have another deal to run to if this doesn't work out."

"You've bounced back before from shows that haven't worked out. . . ."

"The other networks will probably be afraid of me if this one doesn't work out with CBS. In television you can be the hottest thing in the business one week and the next week you can't get arrested."

"So what are you going to do to save the show?"

"That's what I'm out here trying to figure out. New York's getting to be a madhouse with all the shows chasing after the same ten guests. It just doesn't seem to make sense any more."

"Do you have time to save it?"

"CBS has too much money invested in the show for me *not* to have time. It's the 'how' that's bugging me."

During the afternoon of talks with Michael a plan started shaping in my mind. I came to the realization that New York was too crowded, with its four talk shows; that I had to look outside of New York for my answer.   227

"That's enough talking about me," I said. "Tell me what is going on in your life."

He told me he was saving up to buy a car.

I nodded and pulled off the road at a car lot and picked out a Volkswagen for Michael. I felt as though he'd earned it, but to see the pleasure on Michael's face was the bright spot of my day. He drove his new car back to school, and I went to visit my mother.

First of all, I should say that my mom is not a traditional Irish mother who hovers over her son. She isn't one of those "how come you haven't called?" mothers. She loves her family more than anything, loves having them around, but is never clinging or demanding, and it is always easy to go to her with troubles because she never says, "You wouldn't have this problem if you listened to me in the first place."

When I arrived at her house she knew instinctively there was a crisis in my life, but she didn't press me for information. Over the next couple days we had lots of family gatherings, but after the second day my mom said to me that something seemed strange at the gatherings, something wasn't right. She asked about Julann and Tony, asked if I'd been ill at all lately, and if I'd been enjoying my weekends at the farm. From my answers to these simple questions she saw I was troubled.

I sat up nights, quietly playing piano in the darkened living room. It was Aunt Claudia's piano, the one she'd taught me on. I played songs from my youth, the ones she and I had learned together and the ones all my family liked to sing. Those were the only moments I did not spend worrying about my show and the direction in which my life was headed.

When I left for San Francisco airport I knew a major change had to occur in my show, but I resisted naming the change in my mind. My head swirled with emotions evoked by driving up the coast, talking with Michael and being around my family. Even though my problems weren't

solved, there had been a security in being with my family

in northern California; suddenly I didn't want to leave all this behind. When the stewardess sealed the fuselage door, I jumped up from my seat, wanting to get off the plane.

The man in the seat next to mine tapped my arm. "Why don't you sit down, Merv? You're going to be fine. You don't have to get off the plane."

I whirled and looked at the man.

"I'm a doctor," he said. "An analyst. You're having a nervous reaction is all, don't let it throw you. Why don't you sit down and we'll talk."

The reassuring look on his face calmed me, and I sat down.

"You look like you could use a good rest," he said.

"That's what I was supposed to be getting out here the last four days."

"Yes, I heard on your show you weren't feeling well."

"It's a bit more than that."

"I see that. Maybe it would be good for you to talk it out."

The only time in my life I had unraveled my thoughts to a stranger was in the confessional. And the priests who heard confession, at least those I knew growing up, were not trained to guide you through your psyche; you told them what was bothering you and they told you to say five Hail Marys and four Our Fathers and that was that. On my show I'd interviewed analysts from every school of therapy; Freudian, Jungian, Gestalt, and all the touchy-feely fad doctors. But those were always professional interviews. I never sat down with them and asked how to handle a specific problem in my life. On the plane I started talking with this man and we went for four and a half straight hours. I told him what I'd done the past few days, and he suggested my anxiety might be coming from the realization that if I had to move my show out of New York, I would be uprooting my family, tearing them away from the farm we'd all grown to love, possibly even uprooting the marriage. He suggested that my coming out west like this had been a test, to see if I could live out here again. Setting up 229 housekeeping on the beach was saying I could take care of myself if I had to, reestablish my own identity away from the show, away even from my family. The doctor I was talking to wasn't giving me answers to questions; rather, he was guiding me through my own mind, allowing me to explore my own thoughts. He didn't give me Hail Marys and Our Fathers; this intrigued me and opened the door to my seeking professional help two years later when my life again faced a crisis. I told the doctor on the plane about my fears of failure at CBS, of how failure would affect the friends who worked for me and my family as well; he led me more and more to talk about my marriage. He won my confidence by discussing my professional life, then steered the conversation toward Julann and Tony, and suggested that the heart of my anxieties came from concerns about them. And my mind turned toward the girl I'd met sixteen years ago, when I was struggling to start a career in television.

16

JULANN WRIGHT grew up wanting to be an actress, and you can be sure acting is not the usual calling for a citizen of Ironwood, Michigan. When Julann was growing up in Ironwood it was a town of about six thousand, if you scraped together the miners living in the woods. Because it snows as many as seven months out of the year in Ironwood—it has even snowed there on the Fourth of July—kids have to be inventive with their indoor time, and Julann was fond of organizing carnivals and shows, just like another kid growing up across the country on Eldorado Street in San Mateo, California. What appealed to her about acting was that one day she could be a fairy princess, the next a scrubwoman. As an actress she would never be locked into one job, like so many people in Ironwood were for their entire lives.

So at age seventeen she bravely set out from Ironwood to make her way in the world of theater. New York was the obvious destination, but the city's size and pace overwhelmed her; she heard about a good acting school in Roanoke, Virginia, and that sounded hospitable to her. She put in several months there, where she met another young acting student by the name of Gene Wilder, then ventured farther north. But instead of making it to the Great White Way, she settled temporarily in Philadelphia. To support herself she took a series of odd jobs, which included running a hot-dog stand and one notably successful cottage industry which she created. That one deserves 231 explaining. She needed quick cash one afternoon to make a rent payment, so she set up a stand in a children's park and hung out a sign reading "Noses Painted Green, Ten Cents." Who could resist that? Children lined up all day to have Julann paint their noses; they thought it was the most marvelous thing to happen in their lives. They rushed home to show their friends, wash their noses, and go stand in line again.

Her job at a local department store didn't go as well as the nose painting; in fact, that job lasted one day. The department-store manager felt sorry for Julann after she told him the whole story about being a struggling young actress who needed a job to pay for a place to live. She called in sick the first day, however, because she heard of an audition at a local television studio. Portfolio in tow, Julann found the studio and wandered inside, past the receptionist who was talking on the phone. She opened a door that said "Studio A" and walked into a makeshift kitchen where a woman was taking a turkey out of the oven and talking to two assistants. Because of the bright lights surrounding the studio-kitchen, Julann couldn't see the cameramen a few yards away. "Do you know where they are having the auditions?" Julann asked. The cook looked totally surprised. "Well, on the second floor, I suppose." And Julann turned around and walked out of the studio. Not only didn't she win the audition, but when she reported to work the next day, the manager said he happened to be standing in the television section of the store just as a cooking show came on, and he saw Julann's surprise appearance. End of department-store job.

I think what finally got her out of Philadelphia and on to New York were the antique shops. Julann loved crystal chandeliers, and used to go into all the antique shops and ask the salesmen how much their chandeliers cost. When told the price, she said she had to ask her fiancé about it. The salesmen offered to put the chandeliers on hold, and Julann was always too embarrassed to say no, but gave them a phony name. She was too nervous ever to walk by the store again, so whenever she came to an antique shop holding a chandelier for her, she crawled by beneath the window. When it got to the point where she was crawling all over Philadelphia, she headed for New York.

She made it to New York in 1954 and found secretarial work to pay the bills while she auditioned for every show, off Broadway and on, that put out a call. Her first lead came in a nonunion, off-Broadway cast of *Annie Oakley,* and wouldn't you know she won the part because she was the only girl around who whistled through her fingers. *Annie Oakley* played briefly in Manhattan, then embarked on a tour of small towns. My future wife not only starred in the play but also drove the truck, changed flat tires, and supervised setting up the tent before a performance. As you might guess, the manager of the company was paying the players next to nothing, and the players poured what money they did make right back into the show. When the beleaguered troupe finally made it back to Manhattan, Julann was still behind the wheel of the ailing truck. What happened next belongs in a movie. The troupe's truck broke down, for what must have been the two hundred and thirty-seventh time, when it reached Times Square. Julann grabbed her bag, gave a last glance at the crippled truck and the tired actors, and ran down Broadway in tears, all the way to her apartment.

Annie Oakley was enough to motivate Julann to search for steady work, which she found as secretary to television and radio personality Robert Q. Lewis. He did his TV variety show during the week, and on Saturday a live radio program. Saturday, Julann's only duty was to bring Robert Q. his coffee, but she had to do it quietly because he was on the air. One Saturday he spoke to her—just a simple "What's new, Julann?"

For two months he'd hardly said a word to her and now he was talking to her on the air. She said the first thing that popped into her head.

"I'm trying to lose weight."

"A special diet?"

"No. I read in a magazine you have to burn energy to lose weight. So I thought if your body gets cold, then it burns energy to warm up, and you'd be losing weight as it did. Last night I left my window open and slept in the nude and the cold air made me burn lots of energy. So I'm losing weight. However, I did catch a bad cold."

From then on Julann was Robert Q. Lewis' secretary *and* part of his show.

This is where I came into the picture. I was hired to sing on the Lewis show in 1956 and that's when I first laid eyes on Julann. She had fiery red hair down to her waist, and a gangly walk; I could tell she was a funny girl by her eyes, which always indicated that something was about to go wrong, and something usually did. She took a liking to me because I was the best audience for her jokes.

You wouldn't call Robert Q. Lewis a natural matchmaker. In fact, he couldn't stand me. The main reason for my lack of popularity with Lewis came from my being brought to the show by producer Irving Mansfield. Mansfield, whom you may know as the husband of the late Jacqueline Susann, was brought to the Lewis show by CBS when the show was in trouble. Lewis preferred being his own producer and didn't like taking orders from anybody.

My friend Jaye P. Morgan had worked on the Lewis show and she was full of warnings about Robert Q.: "You have no idea what kind of bear trap you're walking into, Merv. Lewis will scream at you in rehearsal, he will throw things. He just goes into fits and there's hell to pay. You'll know he's about to blow when his face gets red and his nostrils flare and his eyebrows go up to his hairline—that's when to duck. And you especially have to watch out because he knows Mansfield is bringing you in, and he doesn't like the fact that CBS is forcing Mansfield down his throat. He'll be out to get you from the opening whistle."

After that speech I was prepared for anything. During my first two days at the show, Lewis never spoke to me. But he had a lot to say to everyone else. Ray Block, the orchestra leader, was working out an arrangement, and

Lewis didn't like one note of it. Finally, Robert Q. turned beet-red, picked up a chair and threw it at Block, who had to do a fancy sidestep to escape it. Then he went after Tommy Donovan, the director, who was in the process of "blocking" a singer. A director blocks a singer after listening to a song and deciding what camera angles and techniques will best fit the character of both song and performer; the performer is given "marks" on stage, spots were he must be at a certain moment in the song, so the cameras will have access to angles the director wants. Well, Robert Q. didn't like the way Tommy was blocking this musical number and his shouting brought rehearsal to a dead stop. I was sitting in the wings looking over the lyrics to a song when I heard the commotion. I poked my head around the curtain in time to see Robert Q. facing the director's booth and screaming, "MR. DONOVAN, COME OUT HERE."

There were two dozen people scattered around the audience seats, some of whom were familiar with Lewis' moods, and some not. I was part of the "some nots" so I was horrified.

Tommy walked out of the booth. He was a shy, intellectual young man, who wouldn't think of having a public confrontation if there was any possible way to avoid it. He went downstage to meet Lewis, but Lewis started in before Tommy got there.

"MR. DONOVAN, HOW DID YOU START AT CBS?"

He whispered back, "I started in the mailroom, Bob."

"YOU ARE GOING BACK TO THE MAILROOM!"

Robert Q. folded his arms and turned his back on Donovan.

Tommy returned to the booth and rehearsal continued.

Then it was my turn.

We were doing a show every day and I had to learn two new songs for each show; it was a full-time job for me to learn the lyrics. I was having problems with a particular song during one rehearsal, and Lewis had positioned the TelePrompTers (a rolling version of cue card) at floor 235 level, so the singers looked foolish if they relied on them too often. When I blew the song for the third time, Lewis threw up his hands to stop rehearsal. By then I was tired of him bullying everybody, and I flashed an impatient look in his direction.

"MR. GRIFFIN. WE ARE NEW ON THE SHOW, AREN'T WE?"

"Yes."

"AND WE HAVEN'T LEARNED OUR WORDS, HAVE WE?"

"No, we haven't."

"AND WHAT, MR. GRIFFIN, ARE WE GOING TO DO ABOUT IT?"

"*We* are going to stop bugging me."

I've never seen a face turn red so quickly as his; his nostrils flared and his eyebrows shot up his forehead. He whirled, charged offstage and slammed his dressing-room door so hard we thought the roof was coming down. I looked sheepishly around the studio and shrugged; I didn't want to make everyone's job that much harder by steaming Lewis, but by then I had learned it pays off professionally to assert yourself when you know what's best for yourself as a performer.

Hence, Robert Q.'s moods became a form of recreation to me. I used to tell friends to stop by rehearsal for the best show in town, and I didn't mean the one we were doing on stage. Chairs flew, mirrors shattered and props came crashing to the ground around Robert Q. But his wildness did have one enlightening side effect; it proved to me that Julann, this wonderfully funny girl I was growing fond of, *had* to have a great sense of humor to remain old Robert Q.'s secretary.

As I heard her stories about painting noses green and crawling in front of antique stores in Philadelphia I began to realize that this was the girl for me. Every time we caught five minutes backstage for a cup of coffee Julann had me in hysterics.

The only problem with Julann's humor was, it had to be spontaneous. Her wit was so natural and original that if she repeated herself it fell flat. But she *did* get a shot on

"The Tonight Show" long before I did. It came about when talent coordinator Paul Keyes heard a story about Julann and decided she should tell it on "Tonight." The story he heard happened to be true. When Julann first came to New York, she was walking down Fifth Avenue one afternoon, wearing a rumpled raincoat, and she paused in front of Van Cleef and Arpels. In the center window glittered the famous diamond tiara once owned by a Russian empress.

Julann wanted to try it on.

Looking like a lost waif, she wandered into the store, which was patroled by a dozen salesmen, attired in crisply pressed morning coats, waiting on fashionably dressed patrons. A salesman quickly ushered Julann to an inconspicuous corner of the store where chauffeurs stood chatting about horse races.

"What may I do for you, miss?"

"I would like to try on that tiara in the window."

She might as well have said she wanted to waltz with Fred Astaire.

"It's not for sale, miss. I'm sorry."

"I couldn't possibly buy it, anyway. I would just like to try it on."

By then the manager was listening; the salesman turned to him and shrugged. He smiled patiently. "I'm sorry, miss, the problem, you see, is the tiara may only be placed on the heads of visiting royalty. That's our policy. So, really we . . ."

"*I'm* royalty."

The men looked at one another.

"Oh?"

"Yes."

"Royalty, miss?"

"I'm a fairy princess."

The salesman rubbed his forehead, but the manager found a total lack of pretension in Julann's voice and he was touched by her. Snapping his fingers, he summoned two clerks, who in turn produced a velvet-covered chair for Julann. With great ceremony the manager unlocked 237 the display case, cautiously removed the tiara, and gently placed it on Julann's head. Her neck grew long and regal, trumpets seemed to blare around her. The store's patrons looked bewildered as Van Cleef and Arpels' manager bowed respectfully to the girl in the raincoat.

When Paul Keyes heard the story he brought Julann to "The Tonight Show" and tried recreating the incident on air as a surprise. Of course, it fell flat. It was not Julann's nature to be instantly funny when a red light flashed atop a television camera; her imagination couldn't be locked into the boundaries of a script.

But Julann was a joy to be with, and after a few weeks of brief conversations and lots of glances going back and forth, I asked her out for our first date. Two things still stick in my mind from that night as I walked into her apartment. She had a large window box, but instead of growing geraniums or something simple like that, Julann grew sunflowers. The stems of the sunflowers were so thick and tall they looked like prison bars, but the people on the next floor had blossoms in their window. I went to use the bathroom and I noticed a sign on the shower curtain, "Do not touch." A sign like that is the last thing a future talk-show host will pay any attention to, and I stuck my head right in there. I was knocked backward by a yeasty smell: the bathtub was full of brown liquid. My date was a bootlegger! She insisted I sample some beer further along in the brewing process, and the way it hit me I thought for a moment I was losing my sight.

During the first months of our friendship we both dated other people. I think it may have annoyed Julann just a little to see me in the columns with Jaye P. Morgan. But as the weeks rolled on Julann and I found we enjoyed each other's company more and more. What started out as laughs developed into real love.

Finally Robert Q.'s television show was dropped from CBS and he was down to doing his Saturday radio program. At the same time I was signed to host ABC's weekly

religious show called "Look Up and Live," and also a daily

radio show. This made things ice-cold backstage between Robert Q. and me. Here he was only on a Saturday radio show, and his boy singer was on national television. He glared at me, but never said a word. One day I had had enough; I quit his show. What really steamed Robert Q., however, was the fact that I signed Julann to work with me on *my* radio program. She did her usual free-form comedy, read crazy poems, even sang a little; she also did on-air commercials with me. The first week she received two paychecks from ABC, two hundred fifty dollars of salary and eight hundred dollars for the commercials. That evening I answered a frantic knocking on my door, and there stood my friend and business associate, Julann Wright, wearing an overcoat with her pajamas on underneath.

"Just what are you proposing, Julann?"

She tiptoed by me as if she were being followed by the FBI.

"What's the matter?"

"They've made an awful mistake, Merv," she said, taking out her two paychecks. "ABC has paid me twice. They gave me an extra check for eight hundred dollars."

"That's not an extra check. The eight hundred dollars is for doing commercials all week; it's sponsor money."

"It's not a mistake?"

"No."

"You're sure?"

"It's all yours, Julann."

Suddenly I was looking at the happiest girl I'd ever seen, who said, "There's a cuckoo clock I've had my eye on for months, and I'm going out to buy it."

And within the hour, she did, pajamas and all.

That's when I stopped calling her Julann Wright and renamed her Julann Wrong.

Soon Julann and I began dating each other exclusively. It wasn't as though we decided to "go steady" or anything as official as that; it was just we realized we had more fun when we were together. We loved taking weekend rides 239 and sharing stories about our pasts, and believe me, we laughed. I bought a new car just to make the rides even better.

I spotted the car one afternoon when I finished rehearsing with the Arthur Murray dancers for an upcoming show. Wearing old rehearsal clothes, I was walking down Fifty-seventh Street when I stopped at a rounded glass showroom that jutted into the sidewalk. Sitting in that display window was a new Cadillac convertible, beige with brown leather seats. I stood there looking at it with my mouth open. That was my car, that car needed me. Mesmerized, I walked into the showroom and circled the car, touching the smooth finish and feeling the rich leather of the seats. I opened a door and the sound was so *solid*. When I climbed in behind the wheel a salesman in striped pants and black jacket hurried over.

"Read the signs, kid," he said. "The signs say 'Don't touch.'"

I barely paid him any attention as I walked circles around the car.

The salesman looked at his partner and winked, then said to me, "Do you like it, kid?"

"It's the most beautiful car I've ever seen."

"Bet you wished you owned it, huh?"

"Yeah. I'll take it."

He chuckled.

"Oh." He winked at his partner again. "And how will we pay for it? Charge or cash?"

"I'll write you a check."

"I suppose you have references?"

"You could call the bank and my lawyer."

He called my attorney without taking his eyes from me.

Roy Blakeman came on the line, and the salesman asked me, "What's your name?"

"Griffin."

Roy told him my check would certainly be good, to call the Bank of Commerce to clear it. He did, and they did.

240   The salesman stared at me.

"May I have the keys?" I said.

I raced over to Julann's apartment and we went for a ride with the top down, singing and laughing through the streets of Manhattan.

During the courtship she put vanilla behind her ears instead of perfume, and for months, whenever she was around, I smelled cookies; she had my number from the word go.

On a balmy evening in April 1959 we were driving in Manhattan through Yorkville. The convertible top was lowered and warm air rich with scents of schnitzel and beer blew in our faces; we heard singing coming from the beer halls. Above us the moon was large and bright and I was getting more romantic by the minute. "You know, Julann, we've got our separate apartments but we're just about living together and we're happiest when we're together. We're crazy about each other, in fact. So let's get married."

By the next cross street we were engaged.

"But that doesn't mean," I said, "that you're going to be making beer in my bathtub, does it?"

"Well, I've got to make it somewhere."

"Oh."

"Maybe I can make wine, that's not as messy."

"All right, we'll make wine."

"And you won't mind my cuckoo clock. It's kind of noisy in the middle of the night."

"I forgot about the cuckoo clock."

"And I have that crystal chandelier."

"I don't think that's going to fit in my apartment."

"We'll have to find a place for it."

"O.K., we'll find a place for your chandelier."

"Do you think your dog Poochie is going to like this?"

"She'll get used to it."

"Is your window box big enough to hold my sunflowers?"

"Let's get married, Julann, and we'll think about the sunflowers some other time."

"When do you want to get married?"

241

"Soon."

"Let's go tomorrow."

"Tomorrow? All right, tomorrow."

We flew to Norfolk, Virginia, where we could get the license, blood test and ceremony all in one day. Our first hurdle was the blood test. Julann cannot stand the sight of blood, particularly when it is flowing from her arm. While the doctor inserted the needle in her vein I sang, tap-danced and told jokes; I did an entire vaudeville sideshow just to distract her. While we were waiting for the results of the blood test and the processing of the license, we went for coffee and grabbed a newspaper. Walter Winchell's column carried a big scoop: "Merv Griffin and singer Jaye P. Morgan are shopping for furniture—can wedding bells be far away?"

So with all New York reading this, Julann Wright and I went off to the chapel to become Mr. and Mrs. Merv Griffin.

We both had to be at work in the morning so we flew to New York after the ceremony and went to my apartment. I climbed right into bed and when Julann tried joining me, my dog Poochie jumped between us and started growling. We were facing territorial war.

"Now, Poochie," Julann said, "we're friends, aren't we? We're all going to be living here now . . ."

Grrrrrrrrrrrrr . . .

"Merv, aren't you going to do something about this?"

I was having too much fun watching the scene to get involved. "You'd better work it out, Julann. We're all going to be together a long time."

Resourceful girl that Julann is, she found a box of dog yummies in the kitchen, and we were one big happy family after that.

In the morning she called Robert Q. Lewis, for whom she was working again, to tell him the good news and ask if she could be late for work.

"You married Griffin? You're doing this just to *get* me!"

Our marriage and our careers were off and running,

and we didn't stop running for an entire year. I was doing "Network Time," a radio show for NBC, and Julann remained a regular on the Lewis radio program. Both of our jobs required a lot of ad-libbing, so to stay current with everything in New York, we accepted every cocktail party, movie, show, gallery and concert opening we heard about. We went on a subway party to Coney Island, to a party on the *Ile de France,* book-publication parties at Doubleday's; we were all over town. It never stopped. In the mornings we scoured the *Times,* the *Mirror* and the *Daily News,* rushed to our studios and rushed home to make whatever social engagements we were covering that evening.

Maybe it's a good thing we didn't spend too much time in my apartment; it wasn't that big. I had a small living room, a tiny kitchen, and enough room in my bedroom for the bed and a dresser. Julann and I were always bumping into each other. To make the party merrier, I had a cleaning lady and a cook, who had been with me for several years, come in early every morning. Four thirty-two East Fifty-second Street was like a bus station.

By the end of that hectic first year of marriage Julann and I realized we hadn't taken time to know each other any better than we did the day we married. Two major events in our lives changed all that.

One we named Anthony Patrick Griffin. Julann and I knew we wanted to have a child; exactly when was a matter under discussion, but thanks to that good old Catholic rhythm, Tony decided on his own when to enter the picture. You never saw a more nervous father than Merv Griffin; I walked circles around the father's waiting room and puffed through two packs of cigarettes. My first view of Tony was through the glass of the nursery. I don't think I can describe the feeling when I saw him; it may have been the single greatest moment of my life. There before me was a brand-new person called Tony, and a new way of life for us. What I didn't realize, gazing at our son, was while I stood there dangling a cigarette from my mouth, the nurse was smoking from the ears. You've never heard 243 such a dressing-down in your life. If I wasn't already in enough of a daze from contemplating our little carbon copy in the bassinet, the nurse sent me into a total spin.

I rushed to see Julann. Based on all the pictures I'd ever seen in women's magazines, I visualized her propped on billowly satin pillows, her auburn hair brushed over the shoulders of a silk robe, a beatific, fatigued smile barely parting her lips. Life, I found, isn't like the women's magazines of the 1950s. The birth hadn't been an easy one, and Julann's head was still spinning from anesthesia. Her hair was knotted and her eyes glazed. When I kissed her I was nearly knocked out by the smell of ether. But even through Julann's glaze and my daze, we were able to look at each other and smile and know our lives were changing, and that the lad in the nursery would be the focus of our new life.

Tony was a joyous baby. I don't remember any problems with him at all. Since we traveled frequently, our friends always warned us, 'Don't take the child, kids can't take changes in water and climate and time zone." We took Tony everywhere. He traveled around America, to the Caribbean and all over Europe; he loved it.

He also loved the other major change in our lives, which came in the form of a farm.

During our courtship and the first year of our marriage, Julann and I retreated to the countryside of New Jersey whenever we could steal a weekend. We visited my radio show producer, Bunny Caughlin, at his Califon farm, spending afternoons at the antique auctions and the evenings at a square dance or sitting on the front porch listening to crickets and watching lightning bugs. Throwing the top down on our Cadillac and cruising the country roads was our idea of relaxing, though while she was pregnant Julann kept warning me to take it easy over the bumpy roads or I'd be delivering my own baby. We had our eye on a particular farmhouse in Califon—an early American clapboard farm with lots of acreage, a stream, waterfall, pond and mill barn. Sunday nights, driving back to the city from Bunny Caughlin's, we fantasized about some day owning that storybook farm. We told friends we had made in Califon to let us know if the farm, called Teetertown, ever came up for sale.

On a day in 1960 a call came through to me in New York from Leonard Rambo, owner of Califon's general store.

"Hello, Merv? Rambo here. Teetertown Farm is for sale. Good price, too. Thought I'd let you know. Bye."

That's all he said, and it was enough. Even though Julann and I didn't have the money, we scraped up the down payment with a loan here and a promise there, and bought our farm.

From that day forward all our weekends were spent in the country, which was the way I always hoped it would be. All my life I've loved country and small town living. Today San Mateo is a booming suburb, but when I grew up there it was surrounded by fields of heather, with ranches where I fed horses carrots through the fence. Maybe my need to live away from the metropolis comes from a feeling of my wanting to be an "audience" like anyone who watches my show. My pleasure is going to movies, sitting around a dinner table with friends and relatives, shopping in neighborhood stores. I don't like going to big parties, premieres or keeping the pace of a glittering celebrity life. A few nights a year a big event with tuxedos, klieg lights and champagne is fun, but if I accepted one tenth the invitations generously extended to me, I'd be checking into a nuthouse six months later. Instead, I retreat from the centers of my work; buying Teetertown Farm was my first tangible investment in recognition of this need.

Julann dove head first into our new rural life. Pots full of jams and jellies boiled constantly on the stove; Julann, my favorite moonshiner, made wine out of any fermentable substance. I used to warn our house guests not to leave their socks lying around or my wife might make wine out of them. When a New Jersey newspaper wrote up her recipe for crabgrass wine—it tasted better than it sounds—I was so proud I talked about it on my show, and the 245 next day Treasury Department agents arrived at our New York apartment. Julann called me in a panic. "Merv, they're going to haul me away for making wine without a license."

"Well, my little moonshiner—did you just explain to them you only made a couple of gallons?"

So that's what she did and the T-men closed the case.

Julann tended the grape vines at the farm as if they belonged to Château Latour, despite the fact that our vineyard was five feet by ten feet. Aphids outnumbered the grapes a hundred to one. The "solution" to this Julann found in a country magazine that advertised "sweet ladybugs, eaters of aphids." Julann ordered forty thousand ladybugs; they were shipped to her in a box with instructions to refrigerate them until used. I didn't know a thing about any of this until I came home from New York on a Friday night and opened the refrigerator for a snack. A hundred thousand tiny legs were waving at me.

"Julann! What the hell is in the refrigerator?"

"Those are my ladybugs. I put a tablespoon of ladybugs in the vineyards each day—and they will kill the aphids who are killing the grapes. And then we'll have wonderful wine."

The next morning I was in the kitchen munching on a chicken leg when I heard screams from the vineyard and rushed out to find Julann holding an empty tablespoon; bugs were crawling all through her waist-length hair.

I started laughing and Julann yelled, "Well, it said a tablespoon, so I *used* a tablespoon."

A few days later we discovered a hornet's nest outside our bedroom window, and I was elected to roust them out. I dressed in three overcoats, fishing waders, ski gloves, fencing mask and two wool caps. Julann and Tony fixed themselves cold drinks and watched from an upstairs window, while I marched to battle with the hornets. Julann told me the hornets died of fright long before I reached the nest.

246   The next domestic crisis came when Teetertown Farm

somehow became the cat capital of New Jersey. People who watch my show evidently think I look like the kind of person who wouldn't kill a stray cat, so our farm became a dropping-off place for every stray in the county. I'm not kidding you; we'd be sitting at dinner around the pool, hear a car approach, stop, then roar away, and five minutes later four cats would come walking through the hedge toward our table. Pretty soon we had fifty cats roaming our farm. One night Tony and I rounded up all the cats, loaded them into a truck and drove to a farm ten miles away where we knew dozens of cats already lived. In the morning Julann scraped the name "Griffin" from our mail box and painted in R. J. KATKILLER.

If our life at Teetertown is beginning to sound like a Rube Goldberg cartoon, then you've got the idea. But it was a paradise for Tony and for our many visitors from New York, and a wonderful safety valve for us. I think my favorite frequent guest at Teetertown was Arthur Treacher. Arthur and his wife, Virginia, visited us often during the middle sixties, and we enjoyed them so much, and they us, that I built a cottage for them on the property. We called it "Treacher's Corner" (that's what Arthur called his position on the show). I designed the house myself and received an estimate of seven thousand dollars to build it. But when I finished turning it into an English country cottage the cost was thirty-nine thousand dollars. Each morning Arthur arose, gazed for a bit out at the green acres of lawns and ponds, then took his *Times* to the swimming pool, where he chatted with Tony. Tony adored him. While Arthur sipped his coffee and read the paper, Tony would say, "Watch this, Mr. Treacher" and do a dive from the board, then, "Watch *this* one, Mr. Treacher" and do a somersault. Finally Arthur would playfully say, "Here's a silver dollar, Tony, for no more 'watch this, Mr. Treacher.' " And then Tony would sit and tell Arthur about school. "I hate that little Tommy kid."

"No, Tony," Arthur corrected him. "We *never* hate. We dislike intensely." 247

We mixed together groups of our friends from New York with our neighbors in Califon. The Rosses, Bests, Ambiellis, Hintzes and the Friars were always over for a square dance and barbecue, (after which everyone ended up jumping in the pool). Afternoons we all went to antique auctions to buy beautiful early American furniture at bargain prices. The people of Califon had a nice attitude toward me; they watched the show and were curious about "stars" but not particularly impressed by them. When I went into Rambo's General Store and sat around the cracker barrel, Leonard Rambo might say, "Saw that Zsa Zsa on the show. Fun to talk to?"

"Sure."

"Mrs. Griffin ever get upset about those dresses she wears on your show?"

"Nope."

"Hmmmmmmmmmmmm."

The favorite local joke was a reality—a nudist colony tucked away in the nearby hills. People always pulled up in front of my pasture when I was out tending the horses and asked me for directions to the "Sun and Fun" club; I'd shout back, "Oh, you mean the *nudist* colony. Yeah, they're just down the road.

Each year they put on an all-nude play at the colony; I was constantly invited to see their production, and I always declined. However, one year a reporter from *Variety* raved about their production "Barely Possible." So a bunch of us decided it might be fun to see it. I made the director of the camp promise not to let anyone know I'd be in the audience. As soon as my party arrived I was besieged for autographs. The director of the camp stood onstage watching my entrance, and when she saw the commotion, took a microphone and announced, "Will you all please leave *Merv Griffin* alone." I sank in my chair. The play was about a girl from a family of sun-worshipers who brings a boy home to meet them without telling him of their particular lifestyle. The boy and girl are standing in the living room 248 when suddenly her brother comes leaping through a doorway, totally naked, and says, "Tennis anyone?" Everyone in the audience gasped at his entrance (this was 1965), but after a while we got used to the stage being jammed with naked performers. Julann nudged me and said, "After about ten minutes of seeing everybody nude you realize what bad actors they really are."

Though we had a lovely apartment at 135 Central Park West in Manhattan, we considered Teetertown our home. For Tony, a private world of ponds, fish, geese and ponies; for Julann, a family center, a gathering place where she could catch fireflies and put them in her hair to make children think she was magic; for me, a retreat from work. In New York I interviewed the front page movers and shakers of America, and it was important for me to be curious about them just as much as my audience was. Teetertown Farm put sufficient distance between me and the people who appeared on my show. If I had lived year round in Manhattan my entire career might have gone differently. During the Westinghouse years, Teetertown gave me the peace and perspective I needed to come up with new ideas, ideas that kept my production company busy.

Here let me explain more fully the reasons I wanted a production company of my own. Networks budget a certain amount of money for a show and then contract with a production company to deliver that show. The production company hires a staff and profits from the moneys left after all expenses, including salaries, are met. And, more importantly, as producer you control the content of the show, make the creative decisions. My talk show is produced by my own company. This differs, for example, from "The Tonight Show"; its entire staff, including Johnny Carson, are employees of NBC. On my show the staff is employed by Merv Griffin. The bottom line is I am paid as the star, and my company makes a profit as producer of the show. I also write all the theme music to my shows, and keep those royalties in the family as well. But the key phrase is "creative control."

When NBC offered me the game show "Word for 249

Word" in 1963 I took the opportunity to start my own company. It was a family operation right from the start.

A game show starts with a good idea, then is developed by lots of trial and error. The concept for "Word for Word" was to take a master word, like "streamline," and see how many smaller words contestants could make out of it. That was just the start around which an entire game had to be constructed. To create the game we conduct "run-throughs," dry runs used to test various forms of a game's structure. We used the dining room of my New York apartment as our run-through room and conscripted friends and relatives to be trial contestants. My best game player was always Sally Latchford, one of Julann's three sisters. We'd invite Sally and her husband for dinner, then rope them into testing my latest game show.

As I mentioned earlier, the show that put Merv Griffin Productions on the map was "Jeopardy!"

Julann and I were flying home from a visit to Ironwood one weekend. I was scribbling on a new game idea and bemoaning the absence of good quiz shows since the quiz scandals of the fifties. My wife, as a joke, said, "Why don't you do a show where you *give* the contestants the answers?"

"Sure, and I'll end up in the slammer."

Then she said, "Five thousand two hundred eighty feet."

I answered, "How many feet in a mile?"

"Right. Seventy-nine Wistful Vista."

I *questioned*, "What was Fibber McGee and Molly's address?"

Bells went off in my head, and the moment we touched down in New York I rushed to a phone, called the office and told everyone to be standing by for a meeting. There had been a hundred question-answer shows on the air, but never the reverse, an answer-question game. It took Julann Wrong to come up with the idea.

We went to work, and it was hard work. The premise was simple, but to build an exciting game took months of trial and error. When the game was ready to show to NBC I knew it was a winner. NBC agreed. But never, *never* do you get a show on the air without battles. I insisted the answers-and-questions on "Jeopardy!" be a real challenge; we wanted a show true game-players could lock horns with. To find contestants we tested and screened five hundred people a week, out of which we found twenty qualified for the game. NBC complained that some of our contestants looked like Marxist radicals, but we weren't running a beauty contest, I explained, we wanted game-players.

The show was a resounding success. And what most people don't know about game shows and daytime television is *that's* where the money is. Audiences are huge for a successful game show. A popular prime-time show like "Bonanza" or "All in the Family" gets all the publicity, but the stars of those shows sometimes get paid more per show than it costs to produce an entire week of game shows. The profit margin for a successful game-show company is attractive, to say the least.

With "Jeopardy!" a runaway hit, Merv Griffin Productions was in business in a big way.

The games were fun and profitable, but going back on the air in 1965 with a talk show meant more to me, personally. With the solid backing of Chet Collier at Westinghouse, we turned the syndicated "Merv Griffin Show" into an established success. And that's why I said earlier my pride was hurt when Westinghouse dragged its feet in renegotiating my contract in 1968. Along came CBS, offering a salary that knocked the wind out of me, and I found myself back in network television.

Before I ever had a chance to enjoy the big salary, I was kicking and clawing for ratings points; by spring of 1970 I was on that lonely plane ride from New York to Los Angeles, where I rented the beach house, left it to drive up the coast, talk with my nephew and visit my family. The psychiatrist sitting next to me on the return flight heard the story of my plight with CBS, and a whole lot more. By the time we landed in New York I knew the show *had* to move to Hollywood, and the doctor helped me realize that 251 the underlying cause of my anxiety was knowing the move had to be made, but realizing Julann wouldn't like the decision.

She mistrusted Los Angeles; to her California was a big resort, not a place where serious people lived. When we did our location shows from Hollywood Julann brought along floppy summer hats and suntan oil and treated the trips like a vacation in Jamaica. She knew about show-business marriages that faltered after a move to the free-and-easy life of California.

But it was clear to me and it became clear to Julann that if we stayed in New York the show would sink and disappear; moving west at least gave it a fighting chance. We both understood this, but I sensed an unspoken uneasiness in her because of it.

CBS flat out didn't like the idea of moving the show. I had not arrived at the decision rashly, but once I made it I didn't want it to be watered down. I took my case directly to Bob Wood.

"We *know* the ratings aren't making it, Bob. I can't operate from New York anymore. The show has to go permanently to Los Angeles; it's the only way to save it. The whole business is moving out there, and we're sitting here with four talk shows in New York, beating each other's brains out for the same ten guests. It's gotten so I can't tell if I've interviewed them or just heard them on another show."

"You can't move, Merv. The company won't accept it after putting all that money into the theater."

It was easier for CBS to keep the show in New York and let it die a natural death than to wage an all-out fight to save it and look like a loser if the show went down. But it was *my* career and *my* staff at stake, not a network's prestige.

"The company will have to accept it, Bob."

"What are we supposed to do with this two-million-dollar theater?"

252   "I told you from the start I could have done the theater

for half the money. Anyway, you'll find another show for it. My show has to go west."

I knew CBS wouldn't give in easily. They weren't happy with the production values of the show; they felt we needed a new look, and new blood to provide it.

The weekend following my talk with Bob Wood I flew to England to meet with Ernie Chambers and Saul Illson. They had been the producers of "The Smothers Brothers Show" and were in England doing a Carol Channing special. Over lunch I explained my problems with CBS and asked if they had any ideas for revitalizing my show. Prime-time variety shows were their field, and they didn't indicate much interest in talk shows. We met again a few days later, but still they resisted on the grounds there wouldn't be enough money in it. I offered them two hundred fifty thousand dollars a year, and they started rewriting the show right there in the restaurant.

CBS was delighted with Illson and Chambers. But I explained that Illson and Chambers were California-based and wouldn't work in New York City. CBS gave in, but not without another demand—one which devastated me.

CBS did not like Arthur Treacher—not for professional reasons, but because he was old. Illson and Chambers had been brought in to give the show a younger, more vital look, and Arthur didn't fit into the network's conception of young *or* vital. In 1970 every third word uttered by network executives was the term "demographics"—How old is your audience? What is their spending power? Arthur Treacher was almost eighty. Networks were not interested in eighty-year-old people. Eighty-year-old people are bad demographics. I again explained to the suits that Arthur's biggest fans were young people, college students; they liked his honesty and wit. But, damn it all, he was eighty.

Arthur let the suits know how he felt about them. One afternoon we were rehearsing during a location visit to Hollywood, and a high-level CBS executive arrived on the set accompanied by five assistants.

"Merv, how good to see you!"

It couldn't have been *that* good because my show was doing lousy in the ratings.

He shook my hand and then greeted Arthur.

"Arthur, I've noticed from watching the show at home, you should wear makeup on your hands. Your hands are going very white on camera."

Arthur stared with disdain at the executive and dryly replied, "Did you jet all the way from New York with that great corporate decision?"

The band and the crew broke up laughing, but the executive and his entourage weren't amused.

After that, the calls came with increasing frequency.

"You know, Merv, Arthur is really holding the show back. He just doesn't work anymore." "Merv, Arthur is *sinking* your demographics." "Our tests prove it, Arthur is a tune-out on the show."

And, finally, they played their ace. They would allow the show to move west, if Arthur did not go with it.

Confronted with this, I reflected on the times Arthur had sat by the pool at my farm and said to me, "You know, you dear little man, I've played butlers and character roles all my life in movies, and then you gave me the opportunity to be myself, to say what was on my mind. And people liked me. Do you know what that has meant to me, to be liked for being myself? I only wish it had come earlier in life, that is my only regret."

Demographics. Damn them.

Luckily, I never had to tell Arthur about demographics. When I told him I must move to California, he said, "You go along without me. Virginia and I won't leave New York. We'll visit you, but I won't live, at my age, in a State that shakes."

I moved west ahead of Julann and Tony to oversee the setting up of the show's offices and find a home for us. It took me a couple of weeks driving around Beverly Hills and Bel-Air to find a house I liked. I signed the lease and called Julann and Tony. "It has a guest house, tennis court, and, listen to this, Tony, two swimming pools. . . ."

254

"*Two* swimming pools . . . wow!"

"We'll all get lots of exercise and be thin and tan."

The furnished home was at 730 North Bedford in Beverly Hills; Tony and Julann seemed pleased with my choice. But when you're renting someone else's house, surrounded by their furniture and living in a new city, it's hard to feel at home. We all felt a bit like we were house-sitting for a wealthy owner who was away on safari.

Beverly Hills schools are among the best in America, so we had no worries about Tony's education. But I've always felt strongly about a "neighborhood" upbringing for a child, and you won't find that in Beverly Hills. On Eldorado Street in San Mateo I could wander from house to house—one of the moms always looked out for the kids; friendships you made were special and durable. You can drive the streets of Beverly Hills all day and never see anyone around the yards except gardeners and delivery men. You won't see kids tossing a football out front, or dads hitting chip shots on the lawn. The first time Tony went out front with the Steve Lawrences' sons at our new house to play catch, neighbors peeked through their curtains wondering who the hayseeds were across the street.

Tony's growing up amidst the opulence of Beverly Hills certainly was a concern of ours; I don't think the name "Gucci" should be in a ten-year-old's vocabulary. In New York, even when you live in a nice neighborhood, as we did, you are surrounded by the give-and-take of city life; a stroll through Central Park is worth three years of sociology lessons. If a child in Beverly Hills walks from home to school and home again, he can easily grow up thinking wealth is a natural condition of mankind, expected rather than earned. We tried avoiding that situation with Tony by taking him with us whenever we traveled; instead of packing him off with a nursemaid, he was all over the world with us, and due to that he didn't have to become annoying simply to get our attention. I always smile thinking about the time Tony and I were flying down to Mexico with Dustin Hoffman and a few other friends. Tony and Dustin got into a long conversation about their hobbies and interests, 255 and at the end of it Dusty said to Tony, "Hey, it's amazing, you're not one of those fucked-up Beverly Hills kids, are you?"

We hardly had our bags unpacked in Beverly Hills when tour buses started stopping out front. The tinted windows slid open and out poked fifty Instamatics. I was flattered to become a stop on the Beverly Hills celebrity house tour so quickly. When they caught me standing out front I wondered if I should stand there and wave, or if that simply wasn't done.

A month after moving to California we threw our first party. One of my guests was Hollywood columnist James Bacon. When I greeted him at the door he said, "My God, Merv, I'm delighted you decided to move the show out here. And you know I haven't been in this house since the famous night . . ."

"What famous night?"

He was surprised. "Since the night Lana Turner's daughter stabbed Johnny Stompanato. Come on, I'll show you the spot where she did it."

"No, don't . . ."

Jim Bacon's story sent a chill up my spine; it reminded me of the macabre history of Teetertown Farm. The Teeter family built the farm and willed it to their daughter, who married a minister new to the area. Shortly after her marriage she fell ill and was confined to her bedroom. Each day the minister brought her an apple fresh from Teetertown's orchard, and each day his wife grew increasingly ill. Six months later she appeared unexpectedly one Sunday in church. No one was more surprised than her husband, who was in the midst of his sermon. Five minutes after arriving the Teeter girl sighed quietly, then fell over dead. The minister coolly walked down the aisle to his wife, touched her forehead and said, "From dust thou art, to dust thou shalt return." The coldness of his attitude stuck with the parishioners, and when he started dating other Califon girls a month after his wife's death, suspicion 256 swirled through the community. A county official sought and secured a court order to exhume the woman's body. Her corpse was found to be full of arsenic. The minister was brought to trial and convicted of poisoning his wife with arsenic-laced apples. He was the last man publicly hanged in New Jersey.

When I realized the Beverly Hills tour buses were stopping in front of our house and hearing the story about Lana Turner's daughter stabbing Johnny Stompanato, I thought it was time to move. We rented the old Firestone house from inventor Bill Lear. This one had thirty rooms and required more people to staff and maintain than I had in my family.

A friend of ours from New York was visiting the house one afternoon and remarked, "By God, Merv, this is Lenny Firestone's old house."

"Yes, it was."

"Sure, now I remember it. I remember the whole story."

"What story?"

He pointed to a spot near a stairway. "Right there is where they shot the kidnapper."

"Kidnapper?"

"Yeah, someone tried kidnapping Firestone and the security people shot him, killed him I think."

A poisoning, a hanging, a stabbing and a shooting. I thought it was time to buy a house without a history.

In a sense we'd been rootless since moving to the West Coast. The farm was our last real "home" and we had never quite adjusted to renting. Now it was time to find a place of our own again. We did. It was in this house, our first since the farm, that Julann and I were divorced.

17

WHEN A MARRIAGE ENDS, everybody asks you what went wrong. I think it is more useful, and less damaging, to consider what changed.

Julann came to feel she was living in my shadow. The ballyhoo accompanying my move to CBS, and the partner of that move, pressure, pushed me away from, rather than toward, Julann. It was a pivotal time in my career, one of uncertainty and constant doubt. So much attention was being focused on *me* that my marriage felt the strain. When Tony was born Julann turned her energies into being a homemaker and mother, and a good one, but in later years I don't think that role could contain all her abilities. While I was down at the office running around trying to build my company and save the show, she was becoming increasingly interested in helping establish a women's bank in Los Angeles, and pursuing a longtime interest in psychic phenomena and parapsychology. Obviously, she was searching for new directions. There was a coolness around the house which made me realize the marriage was in serious trouble.

I thought of Tony. Beverly Hills children are the most aware in the world in terms of relationships between their parents. Right down to first- and second-graders, they are steeped in the knowledge of broken homes; they learn from one another how to manipulate their parents, how to get what they want from this parent and what they want from that one. I was well aware that most of the kids in Tony's class were from homes of divorced parents. And he

258

was at the crucial age, almost a teenager, when a boy moves from the years of being closer to the mother and turns to the father to learn more about manhood. When the father isn't home, look out. If there are lots of brothers and other male relatives, fine. But with Tony there would just be him and his mother; if there was a separation, there would be no male influence in the home at all. When I realized the marriage was in trouble, I knew enough to turn to professional help. Five years earlier I might have kept it all inside and tried to work it out; but after my talk with the analyst on the plane returning from my desperate trip to the West Coast, I knew enough to seek someone of experience.

I had read a book called *Beyond Laughter* by Freudian analyst Dr. Martin Grotjahn, in which he discusses what makes people laugh, and how we reveal ourselves by our humor. It was a book of profound insight, and I knew about his lofty reputation among Freudians. I called him for an appointment. When I first read the book I had invited him to appear on the show, but he turned us down. So when I arrived at his office he thought I was going to make a personal appeal for a TV interview.

He made a statement as soon as I sat down. "Mr. Griffin, you must first realize that it is not appropriate for me to appear on television because if I make a remark that is misinterpreted, it could damage the confidence of my patients. I work mostly these days with groups of younger analysts, and I have very few private patients. Most of what I have to talk about would not be of general interest. However, I must tell you I watch your show and I advise my students to watch it also because, like an analyst, you misdirect the guest in conversation and gradually work toward the subject you are truly interested in."

"Doctor, thank you, but I'm here as a patient. I feel my marriage may be at an end and I need to understand how to help my son through what may be a difficult part of his life."

"I see."

So in November of 1972 I started my sessions with Dr. 259

Grotjahn, a most exceptional man of the mind. In our talks he was particularly interested in significant events happening right then in my life, rather than dragging me back to childhood memories. We talked at length about my buying a plane, because it was a purchase Julann was dead set against. She felt I was buying the plane as an escape. I wanted to get over my awful fear of flying. I knew the only way I'd get rid of my fear of planes was to know how they worked and be able to fly one. If there was ever a contest for the best taxier of small planes, I would be the front runner, because that's all I did for my first three months of flying lessons. My teacher would ask, "Do you want to go up today?" and I'd just shake my head and say, "Nope I'll let you know when." The guys in the control tower got used to the eccentric Mr. Griffin who liked to come out to the airport and drive planes around on the ground all day. They put me to work parking planes after a while. I never went up until I moved to California. The only thing that made me do it then was buying an expensive plane; that way I forced myself to fly. Julann didn't want me to buy that plane. It meant something other than just transportation to her.

The other major event during those months with Dr. Grotjahn was my purchase of a condominium at Pebble Beach. Julann and I spent occasional weekends at Pebble Beach Lodge, and she encouraged me to buy the condominium since I liked the area so much. I don't think Julann was interested in having the place for the two of us.

Early in January of 1973 I described to the doctor an increasing coolness between us and we talked more about the plane and the prospective purchase in Pebble Beach. He stopped me in the middle of a sentence and said, "How old is Julann?"

I told him.

"When is her next birthday?"

"In three weeks."

He nodded then said, "You will be served with divorce papers in exactly two weeks."

I was stunned. "Doctor, I would not be so specific if I were you because if it doesn't happen I'm not going to trust you or your ideas. Julann and I haven't talked about divorce."

"This is a crucial birthday for her, in light of what's been going on. She will file for divorce one week before the birthday."

I left the appointment in a daze.

By some stroke of prescience my mother came to visit a few days later. She learned of my divorce before I did. Julann and my mom were always close, and Julann sat her down in our living room and told her. While she was saying it, Rona Barrett came on the television with her celebrity news and reported: "A famous Hollywood television host is soon to get his walking papers from his wife." Driving home from work that evening, I heard the same report on the radio. That was the first I'd heard about it; and the next day I was served with the legal papers.

Telling Tony was the awful duty awaiting us.

That was the single worst moment in my life.

Dr. Grotjahn instructed me carefully about how to explain it to Tony, and Julann and I discussed the doctor's recommendations.

We took Tony outside and sat down by the pool.

"We love you very, very much, Tony, and we want you to know, it's *important* you know, that *you* are in no way responsible for the change coming in our lives."

He looked quizzically at me, wondering what I was trying to say.

"But, Tony, it's possible for two people not to want to live together anymore."

He said, "Who?"

"Your mother and I are getting a divorce."

The tears didn't roll down his cheeks, they shot out of his eyes.

"Oh, don't do that to me," he said.

The three of us sat there by the pool and just cried.

Because Tony is an only child, the doctor explained, it   261 would be hard for him not to feel he was in some way responsible for the divorce. I stayed in constant touch with Dr. Grotjahn, and even brought Tony in with me one day so we could talk with the doctor together.

Once we told Tony, I knew it would be agony for me to continue living there; I moved out that same afternoon.

I called a real estate agent and asked her to find me a house. She told me about a house available in Bel-Air that belonged to Fred Ebb, the songwriter who wrote "Cabaret."

I took it.

"Don't you want to know the price?"

"No."

"Or the furnishings?"

"No. As long as there is a housekeeper I'll take it sight unseen for a year." Three hours later I moved in with a few clothes and shaving kit.

When I took the home in Bel-Air I assumed I would feel like a new man on the town, footloose and fancy free. I thought I'd be kicking up my heels and having a hell of a good time; I could come and go when I pleased, take off for a trip on a whim, you name it. But it didn't work out that way. Separating from Julann was a lonely, terrible process. It is like a whole person inside you ripped out and pushed off to some dark distance. Friends start dividing you up, deciding who was right and who was wrong; memories of the happy times follow you around like ghosts. No, I wasn't a carefree bachelor dancing up and down the streets of Beverly Hills. I was lonely and I was depressed.

Then the lawyers started in. Julann's first attorney had leaked the story to the press, and she dismissed him. But the settlement took three years to untangle. I had been sued for seventeen million dollars in community property, and as the legal machinations dragged on I realized her attorneys were hounding me to try and force me into throwing up my hands and saying, "Take it all." I thought seriously about quitting my show; I hadn't worked my entire life at building a career so I could sit back and watch lawyers divide up my talents and accomplishments like it was a garage sale. Never in my life have I come that close to just walking away from show business and saying, I've had enough. Many evenings I sat down with Murray Schwartz and Bob Murphy and Roy Blakeman and told them I wanted out, but I stayed with the show, and am glad I did.

The public's reaction to my divorce completely surprised me. People who watched the show over the years often heard me talk of Tony and Julann and tell stories of the farm and our travels. They'd seen Tony growing up when he made his occasional on-camera visits. My viewers reacted with shock. I thought everyone was so used to reading about divorces in Hollywood they would just nod and say "There goes another one." Instead, it was "I can't believe it." People stopped me in airports to ask "Is it really true?" On the day the story hit the news wires, a friend of mine was flying to New York, and he later told me the pilot had come on the speaker and said, "The weather in New York is cloudy and cool, and you might be interested to know that Mr. and Mrs. Merv Griffin have filed for divorce." My friend reported a good third of the people on the plane gasped, "No!"

My first big step after the divorce was to buy a home in Pebble Beach. It was an English Tudor mansion with the most breathtaking view of Carmel Bay I've ever seen. I decorated and furnished it myself and I didn't care if the rooms were ever going to be photographed for *Architectural Digest*; I wanted every room and every piece of furniture to frame my new life.

18

My original contract with CBS called for two years firm, then renewal at six-month intervals. Moving to California pumped up our ratings enough to get us through the first renewal period. But the problem persisted. I never adjusted to having fifty different executives filtering down advice from the corporate tower to me. I'll give you an example of the kind of battle that was going on all the time.

When I was preparing to leave for my Christmas vacation, I submitted a list of guest hosts to the network for approval. We put a lot of thought into that list, looking for hosts who could handle the show *and* help our demographics (my least favorite word in the English language). I received an immediate call regarding two of the choices.

"Merv, we don't think Desi Arnaz, Jr., is right for the show."

"Why?"

"Not the right image."

"What do you mean?"

"Merv, do you realize Desi is only eighteen years old?"

"I realize that, yes."

"You can't have an eighteen-year-old kid hosting."

"First you tell me Treacher is too old, now Desi Arnaz is too *young*. He's eighteen, and because of his age he'd be great publicity for the show; an eighteen-year-old has never hosted a talk show. Anyway, he's eighteen going on forty; he's charming and will handle the show fine."

264   "We just don't think it's a good idea."

"Do me a favor then. Call his mother and explain to her why you don't want her son on my show."

Lucille Ball was CBS's top star. The call was never made. Desi, Jr., hosted my show and did a fine job.

CBS then objected to my choice of Sonny and Cher.

"You're not going to have that old rock-and-roll couple host the show? They are out of show business. Why the hell would you want *them* anyway?"

"They're funny."

"They're singers and they're not funny."

"They have a funny attitude together. It'll work great in our format."

"No, Merv, you don't get this one. We'll let you have Desi but Mr. Silverman says no on Sonny and Cher."

"It's my show, my neck, and they are hosting. Goodbye."

Sonny and Cher hosted my show and were signed within days by CBS to do their own variety show. In a few months they were television's hottest act.

Now, for the coup d'état.

We decided to salute the cast of a new CBS show called "All in the Family." It wasn't doing much in the ratings yet, but it was innovative and lively, and the stars were good talkers. Carroll O'Connor, Jean Stapleton, Rob Reiner and Sally Struthers were my guests. Next day the call came. "Why are you putting *them* on? The show probably won't last the season."

It was a CBS show, and *still* we drew fire from the network.

It was during this time my life was really in a mess. My marriage was failing, the show's ratings were sinking, I was putting on weight, and I was going to an analyst; it was war on every front. Out of this tangle came a phone call that changed my life. It was from Al Krivin, and believe me it was good to hear from an old friend. I knew Al from 1965, when he had bought my Westinghouse show for the Metromedia station in New York, the station where it broke loose and started the emergence of "The Merv Griffin Show." He is one of the greatest administrators I've 265 ever known, and I'll tell you why: he *allows* you to discover ideas. When I started on Westinghouse our show was in black and white, while most other shows were in color. Going color would be an expensive conversion, but the stations buying our show were clamoring for it. Al Krivin was our biggest buyer; Metromedia by then had our show on their stations in both New York and Los Angeles, the number one and two markets. So Al sent me little pictures of color-television sets from magazine ads. But he knew those pictures would stir my business sense enough to get after Westinghouse to make the conversion to color. And his plan worked. I lit a fire under Westinghouse until they made the switch. That's the way Al works, quietly and effectively.

When I made the move from Westinghouse to CBS Al said to me, "Merv, you'll hate it there. I know all the money you're going to make, but they will judge your show on a night-to-night basis, not for the long haul. CBS is not used to being in the talk-show business. You and I are used to talk shows, and we know it takes a long time to get one off the ground, a show has to slowly define itself. You can't keep changing the format each night, based on the ratings of the previous day. And that's the way CBS is used to working. They'll be after you day to day, and I know you, you can't work that way. You'll fold under that kind of pressure and the show won't be your best. They won't know *how* to get the best out of Merv Griffin."

But with all that CBS cash dangling in front of me, I don't think I heard Al's warning. Two and a half years later the words came back to me loud and clear.

Al called me in the fall of 1971 and made a date for lunch. He didn't see a happy man sitting across from him. Al is not a person who would say "Didn't I warn you?" He had something better than that to say to me.

"I've been watching the ratings of your show on CBS, Merv, and following the reaction of the affiliate stations. I can tell you from experience it won't be much longer before all of your stations start defecting because they're losing too much local advertising money; they'll want to put in their own programming. When that happens CBS is going to make a move. And I want you to know, for your own security, that if you leave the network you can start any day you want with Metromedia, and we'll match what CBS is paying. I can't say exactly what kind of deal we'd make, but I want you to know you always have a place to go."

Al's words carried the weight of five Metromedia-owned stations, including New York and Los Angeles, which guaranteed other stations around the country coming in behind the strength of the major markets.

I called Roy Blakeman immediately after the luncheon to tell him the good news. He told me not to mention it to another soul, because even though it might be to my advantage to leave CBS and go to Metromedia, I had a clause in my CBS contract that required a two hundred fifty thousand dollar payment to me if the network canceled me. If *I* pulled out of the contract I didn't get another penny.

We were closing in on the date for the network to notify us if they were going to renew the show for another six months. As that day neared I saw the nervous faces around my office. The staff knew we were in trouble. I looked at Bob Murphy, Tony Garofolo, Paul Solomon and others who'd been with me for years, and couldn't say a word to cheer them up. Items appeared in the papers about death rattles at the Merv Griffin show, but I had to keep my mouth closed.

Roy Blakeman quietly met with Al Krivin and Metromedia Board Chairman John Klugie in New York, while in California I anxiously waited for the call from Bob Wood at CBS. Friday, December 2, 1971, the call came. While Bob and I talked, Roy Blakeman waited by his phone and Al Krivin by his.

Bob was apologetic which, come cancellation time, is not always the tactics of a network executive.

"Merv, I want you to know we think you're an outstanding talent, but we are not in a ratings position to pick up your option."

"You're canceling me?"

267

"I'm afraid so."

"I understand the problem, Bob. You, if anybody, have supported me all along, and I appreciate it."

"I know you'll move on to bigger and better things, Merv."

I had Roy waiting on another line, and I grabbed his call the second Bob Wood hung up.

"We've been canceled, Roy!"

The news was worth two hundred fifty thousand dollars.

Roy alerted Metromedia but advised me to sit tight until Monday, when the cancellation became official. Of course, the cancellation was general knowledge at CBS by that Friday afternoon, so my staff had to be told that as of February 15 we would be off the air. I looked around the room at Murphy, Garofolo, Solomon, Murray Schwartz, Donnis Gold, Don Kane, Betty Bitterman, all people who'd been through the wars with me, and I just couldn't be as noncommittal as Roy wanted me to be. I said, "I'm sorry to tell you we'll be off CBS in a month and a half, but we've been through tough times over the years and have somehow come up with something when we had to, so you never know, by Monday maybe things will have turned around." The people who'd been with me the longest flashed glances at each other and guessed I had a card or two I wasn't showing.

Over the weekend the cancellation hit the papers around the country, and there was a good deal of speculation about whether Griffin would decide to retire from performing and concentrate on producing game shows. On Sunday I called the *Hollywood Reporter*, one of Hollywood's trade papers, and told them I had a major announcement to make. They hustled a writer over, ready to take my tearful retirement interview. Instead, I dropped the Metromedia deal on them, and Tuesday's *Reporter* exclusively headlined:

MERV MOVES TO METROMEDIA

Merv Griffin has secured his release from his contract at CBS and signed a five-year contract with Metromedia calling for no less than 39 weeks of show nor more than 48. He is out of his CBS contract as of Feb. 15.

"Although I can't give you the exact figure for the Metromedia deal [Merv said], let me say that the end result will be much more money than the CBS deal. The basic amount up front is almost the same, but the percentage is much more and there are no restrictions like I had with CBS and no booking problems. . . ."

By Tuesday afternoon the offices of "The Merv Griffin Show" had gone from Friday's gloom to jubilation.

CBS was not as thrilled with the Metromedia news as my staff. In fact, because of the two hundred fifty thousand dollar penalty they were forced to pay, I became a "nonperson" in CBS history. When the network did their fiftieth anniversary special in 1977, a lavish production bringing together every major living star who had worked for the network (even many who caused CBS executives to sweat blood during contract negotiations), my telephone never rang. Also, to reuse the tape stock, they erased every one of our shows, even irreplaceable moments like the reunion of Bob Hope, Bing Crosby and Dorothy Lamour for their only time together on a talk show.

"The Merv Griffin Show" was dropped from the CBS history book.

PART SIX

Coda

1972-1980

19

MOVING FROM late-night network television on CBS back to syndication with Metromedia pumped new life into "The Merv Griffin Show." Stations across America and Canada again were able to buy our show and place it in whatever time slots best suited their market. On the Metromedia-owned stations in New York, Los Angeles and Washington, D.C., our show was placed in prime time, giving us the distinction of being the only talk show able to make that claim. Ratings climb higher each year; now we renew our contract with Metromedia for five-year periods.

We've plowed our profits over the years into new projects and companies involved in the communications industry. Let me tell you about some of them.

"Wheel of Fortune" is our current game show on NBC, with several more in pre-production. "Dance Fever," a disco show we produce in association with 20th Century-Fox, is a success in syndication. We have several other shows in development. And we're about to jump into the movie business.

"The Merv Griffin Show" and "Dance Fever" are taped in studios owned by Trans-American Video (TAV), another of our companies. Production offices for all our shows are housed in the TAV buildings, covering a half-block area of Hollywood near Sunset and Vine. Along with its two television studios, TAV operates complete video-tape editing, dubbing and tape-transfer facilities, a distribution department (which sends tapes of syndicated shows   273 to TV stations all over the country), and a fleet of specially equipped "mobile units," television recording and control booths on wheels, which we lease out to production companies and networks for use at sporting events and TV specials. (If you watched the Muhammad Ali-Leon Spinks fight from New Orleans, our cameras were bringing you the pictures.) TAV has branches in Las Vegas and Hawaii, as well as Hollywood.

Teleview Racing Patrol, Inc., is our Florida-based company that supplies closed-circuit cameras and projection screens for horse- and dog-racing tracks in both North and South America.

We operate three radio stations on the East Coast: WBAX in Wilkes-Barre, Pennsylvania; WPOP and WIOF in Hartford.

The daily operation of these companies is handled by my capable team of executives and administrators. Still, my phone rings constantly with a problem here and a decision to be made there. That's why some of the most peaceful moments of my life come when I'm onstage doing my show. Once tape starts rolling, the phone calls and questions stop, and I'm again in control of my life.

The luxuries I've afforded myself from the money I've made in television are reasonably simple. A home near my office in Los Angeles, with a tennis court for exercise, and a mountaintop retreat in Carmel Valley for rest and recuperation. I own a Mitsubishi M-2 turbojet to take me between the two. You know what my biggest luxury is? Being able to use time as I see fit. At this point in my life I am able to pursue and develop ideas and projects that interest me without having to dilute my energies on the more mundane tasks of living. That is the luxury I treasure most.

At the height of my success in New York, after signing the CBS contract, I taped a television special in which I did a song on the deck of the *Ile de France* as it left New York's harbor. We wanted to catch the excitement of the boat leaving for Europe; I had to lip-synch my song, then leap onto a tugboat to take me to shore. The song was "Softly as I Leave You." Because of the lip-synch I was acutely conscious of the song's words. Looking at the receding Manhattan skyline, listening to the words of the song, suddenly I was very sad. By the end of the song I had tears in my eyes. I suppose deep in my mind I knew my marriage was collapsing and that I would have to leave New York, where I'd come to fame, in order to save my show; the two were tied together, somehow. The moment reminded me of my eighteenth birthday, when I went walking on the railroad tracks in San Mateo and had the vision of my life changing drastically in the near future.

I feel that way now, as though my life is about to undergo major changes. We're doing six weeks of shows a year back in New York, and I have to admit I'm tempted to move back there permanently, back into the excitement of Manhattan. I have so many ideas for new shows, maybe I'll head more in the direction of producing. But as long as I wake up in the morning anxious to come to work and do my show, then that's what I'll do.

So where do I go from here?

In 1970 two high-ranking NBC executives requested a private meeting with me. I agreed to the meeting, despite the fact I was under a talent contract with CBS; because I did game-show business with NBC I wanted to keep our relations cordial. The meeting was held clandestinely in a private dining room of NBC's New York headquarters.

"Merv, let's preface our conversation by saying no matter how hard you fight, you're not going to be able to beat 'The Tonight Show.' CBS hasn't got the stations for your show to do it on a network basis. We know you won't agree with us on that, but those are the facts as we see them. CBS will ultimately end up in a cancellation situation with your show, and that's why we've asked you here. We'd like to offer you a *life*time of security with NBC."

"Meaning what?"

"We want you to host the "Today" show. At least, we 275

want you to consider the offer. It's a respected, powerful show. We know you'd handle it perfectly. The network is willing to give you a contract for life, meaning there will be all the money there is with CBS in the long run, but with more security. Merv, a lifetime of security—think about it."

I did. And turned it down. I won't sign a contract for a lifetime of *anything*. Changing, and a desire to outdo myself, is what keeps me going. If I signed a lifetime contract, no matter how much security it promised, it would rob me of one asset I do have—the capacity to dream. When I was an overweight, rudderless teenager in San Mateo, dreaming of stages in Hollywood and New York kept me going. When the dream of those stages came true a few years later, other dreams took its place.

I'm still dreaming, and working at making these new dreams come true. Here's what they are. I have an idea for a movie, a children's fantasy musical, that I'm working on; I'm outlining the story and have already written several songs for it. I would also like to produce a Broadway musical. The Billy Rose of Eldorado Street can't check out without bringing at least one musical to Broadway. And there is one more dream in the works as I write this.

I want to go back to my beginnings, to the days when I was producer and star of back-porch shows, and put together a stage show that will knock you all out of your chairs. The talk-show format is comfortable to me now; I love my show, but it's too easy to call for commercial if I'm stuck for an idea or if the guest I'm interviewing is boring. It's time to stick my neck out in front of large showroom audiences and give them a show that's fresh and fast, happy and sad . . . entertaining. As a boy I worked with bedsheets, milk crates, broken lamps and record players that skipped. Now I've got the money and time—hopefully the talent and imagination, too—to do the kind of glittering stage show I dreamed about doing as a kid.

I can't wait to get started.

Index

281